PRISONER OF CONSCIENCE

PRISONER OF CONSCIENCE

A Memoir

To Francis and Lance
a sister and brother in
the struggle,
Ken Kennon

Kenneth Kennon

Author's Photo: Sterling Vinson
Cover Art: "Silence" by Raymond K. Kennon

Library of Congress Number:		2001118185
ISBN #:	Hardcover	1-4010-2517-X
	Softcover	1-4010-2516-1

This book was printed in the United States of America.

To order additional copies of this book, contact:
Xlibris Corporation
1-888-7-XLIBRIS
www.Xlibris.com
Orders@Xlibris.com

CONTENTS

:ENN

to Mary Ellen

our children and grandchildren

It is not enough to be compassionate.
You must act.

—His Holiness, Tenzin Gyatso,
Fourteenth Dalai Lama, 1992

To us all, to every nation
comes the moment to decide,
in the strife of truth with falsehood,
for the good or evil side;
some great cause, God's new endeavor,
offering each the bloom or blight,
and the choice goes by forever
'twixt that darkness and that light.

—James Russell Lowell, 1845
adapt. W. Garrett Horder, alt.

QUICK REFERENCE

Who's Who

Family Members (Cited more than once)

Amanda, granddaughter
Amber, granddaughter
Bruce, son
Cora, niece
Daryl, son-in-law
Jeannie, daughter-in-law
John, son
Julie, daughter
Katie, granddaughter
Linda, former daughter-in-law
Lynn, sister
Mark, son
Marvin, brother
Mary Ellen, wife
Paul, son

Friends & Acquaintances (Cited more than once)

Aaron, El Paso, seminary student
Amy, Tucson colleague
Barbara, NH correspondent
Bernie Muller, Tucson
Bill [Walker], My Tucson attorney during incarceration
Bill Johnson, Community Christian Church of Arizona City
Bob Allen, ministerial colleague

Carol, CA correspondent
Charles Muller, Tucson
Cliff Pine, Silver City NM
David [Perkins], one of our Tucson business volunteers
Denny, [Rev. Dennis Williams], Regional Minister, The Christian Church (Disciples of Christ) in Arizona
Elna Otter, one of our Tucson business volunteers
Esther, OR correspondent
Frankie Oliver, ministerial colleague
Gary MacEoin, San Antonio, long-time writer friend
Jane [Warner], one of our Tucson business volunteers
Jesus Cruz, Government covert informant and principal prosecution witness in the Sanctuary trial, 1985-86
Jean Miller, Sister of Charity, Sunland Park NM
Jim Kolbe, My U.S. congressman
Joan Brown, Sister of St. Francis, Sunland Park NM
Kathleen Rumpf, NY, SOA prisoner of conscience
Keith Watkins, AZ colleague
Lil Corrigan, Wife of a SOA 13 prisoner of conscience
Louis Freund, Long-time artist friend of the family
Louise Rauseo, El Paso
Marianne, Tucson colleague
Mark Holdaway, one of our Tucson business volunteers
Mary, Tucson
Nick Rauseo, El Paso
Nona Johnson, Community Christian Church of Arizona City
Punch Woods, Tucson
Richard Hamm, General Minister and President, The Christian Church (Disciples of Christ) in the U.S. and Canada
Rosemary Lynch, Tucson
Paula, Randy Serraglio's significant other
Sharon, Secretary of Tucson attorney Bill Walker
SOA, U.S. Army School of the Americas, training center for Latin American militaries, headquartered in Panama 1948-1983, and at Fort Benning, Georgia since 1984

SOA 13, Thirteen prisoners of conscience who served sentences in 1995 for protesting against the SOA
Stig, Community Christian Church of Arizona City
Suzanne, Community Christian Church of Arizona City
Yvonne, Acting co-director of national SOA Watch during the incarceration of the SOA 25

Prison Inmates & Officers (Pseudonyms, cited more than once)
Adam Finley, inmate
Bill Murphy, inmate
Carl Gooding, inmate
Carlos Gonzalez, inmate
Doc, inmate
Dylan Roberts, inmate
Fred, inmate
Gordon Harris, inmate
Hector Cortez, inmate
Jack Sutton, inmate
Jay, inmate
Jim Bob Elder, inmate
Jose, inmate
Kevin, inmate
Leo Blanco, inmate
Lloyd, inmate
Lt. Solis, officer
Lt. Towers, officer
Lt. Wilson, officer
Luis, inmate
Matt Rogers, inmate
Mr. Butler, camp administrator
Mr. Green, inmate
Officer Grijalva, officer
Oscar, inmate
Pablo Garcia, inmate
Popeye, inmate

Ralph, inmate
Rich, inmate
Robby Wright, inmate
Ted, inmate

SOA 25—Prisoners of Conscience

Fr. Bill Bichsel, SJ, Tacoma WA, Jesuit Priest, former Dean of Students Gonzaga University, Catholic Worker

Fr. Roy Bourgeois, MM, Columbus GA, Maryknoll Priest, Founder of SOA Watch, Vietnam Veteran, Missionary

Rev. Dr. Nicholas Cardell, Syracuse NY, Minister Emeritus the Unitarian-Universalist Church, retired, WWII Veteran & POW

Mary Earley, N. Palm Beach FL, Special Education Teacher works with terminally ill children

Sr. Marge Eilerman, OSF, Booneville KY, Sister of St. Francis, Teacher, Missionary, Pastoral Associate

Sr. Mary Kay Flanigan, OSF, Chicago IL, Sister of St. Francis, Co-coordinator 8th Day Center for Justice

Anne Herman, Binghampton NY, Christian Peacemaker Team member

Paddy Inman, Mead WA, Teacher, Farmer, Past Chairman of Spokane Catholic Services

Christopher Jones, Portland OR, Doctoral Candidate in Cultural Anthropology and Mayan Studies

Rev. Ken Kennon, Tucson AZ, Pastor Community Christian Church of Arizona City

Ed Kinane, Syracuse NY, Anthropologist, Editor, Teacher, Peace Brigades International

Dwight Lawton, St. Petersburg FL, Corporate Executive, retired, National Farm Worker Ministry, Korea Veteran

Rita Lucey, Orlando FL, AT&T Supervisor, retired

Bill McNulty, Setauket NY, Teacher, Contractor, Veteran

Sr. Megan Rice, Manlius NY, Sister of Holy Child, Missionary in Africa, Inner City Ministry

Rev. Carol Richardson, Washington DC, United Methodist clergy, Co-Director of SOA Watch

Dan Sage, Ph.D, Syracuse NY, Professor Emeritus Syracuse University, Department of Education

Doris Sage, Syracuse NY, Special Education Teacher, Storyteller

Randy Serraglio, Tucson AZ, Community organizer regarding environmental and Latin American issues

Sr. Rita Steinhagen, CSJ, Minneapolis MN, Sister of St. Joseph, Medical Technologist, Works with homeless and victims of torture

Richard Streb, Ph.D, Roanoke VA, History Professor, WWII Veteran

Ann Tiffany, Syracuse NY, Mental health nurse and supervisor

Mary Trotochaud, Atlanta GA, Potter

Judith Williams, Waukesha WI, Professor of Music Therapy, Executive Director of Waukesha Catholic Worker

Ruthy Woodring, Chicago IL, Student at the University of Illinois, Catholic Worker

GLOSSARY

A10, U.S. military aircraft

ACLU, American Civil Liberties Union

A&O, Administration and Orientation; a bureaucratic work designation given new federal prisoners

ASAP, As soon as possible

BOP, U.S. Bureau of Prisons

C130, U.S. military cargo plane

C1-C6, Cervical vertebrae 1 through 6

Callout, A posted list of inmate work assignment changes and institutional appointments, e.g., education and medical appointments that inmates must obey or they will be disciplined

CCA, Corrections Corporation of America

CD, Civil disobedience

CIA, U.S. Central Intelligence Agency

Chiapas, State in southern Mexico

Contras, The counter-insurgency force, trained and backed by the U.S., fighting to overthrow the Sandinista government of Nicaragua in the 1980's

DC, Washington, District of Columbia

DEA, U.S. Drug Enforcement Agency

DPF, Disciples Peace Fellowship, The Christian Church (Disciples of Christ) in the U.S. and Canada

FCI, Federal Correctional Institution

FDR, Franklin Delano Roosevelt

FPC, Federal Prison Camp

GED, General equivalency diploma

HR611, 1998 U.S. House Resolution 611 to deny funds to the SOA

IFCO, Interreligious Foundation for Community Organization
INS, Immigration & Naturalization Service, U.S. Department of Justice
ISM, Institutional Systems Management office, BOP
Lectionary, A list of assigned Bible readings for days of divine service used by Christian churches
Manzo, Manzo Area Council, a community social service agency in Tucson, AZ
Mark manuscript, A manuscript by Marvin L. Kennon
MP, Military Police
MS, Multiple sclerosis
NAFTA, North America Free Trade Agreement
NCAA, National Collegiate Athletic Association
NKJV, New King James Version of the Holy Bible
NRSV, New Revised Standard Version of the Holy Bible
Our Place, Business name of Mary Ellen's assisting living homes
PA, Physician's assistant
Q&A, Question and answer
R&D, Receiving and Departure office, BOP
SB980, 1998 U.S. Senate Bill 980, companion to HR611 to deny funds to the SOA
Self-surrender, Some sentenced persons are released by the Court on their promise to surrender to U.S. Marshals or at an assigned prison on a date and by a time demanded by the U.S. Bureau of Prisons
SIS, Special Investigations Service, BOP
SOA, School of the Americas, U.S. Army, headquarters at Fort Benning, GA
SOA Watch, An independent grassroots organization that seeks to close the SOA, with national offices in Columbus, GA and Washington, D.C.
StarNet, Website of *The Arizona Daily Star*, Tucson AZ
TCU, Texas Christian University
TEC, Tucson Ecumenical Council

UCA, University of Central America, San Salvador, El Salvador

UFO, Unidentified flying object

UPS, United Parcel Service

U.S., United States of America

USAF, United States Air Force

v.v., Verses

WASP, White Anglo-Saxon Protestant

WHISC, Western Hemisphere Institute for Security Cooperation; the clone of the SOA "opened" January 2001, with the same mission and in the same location

Yellow Dog Democrat, A person who will vote a straight democrat ticket, even if the candidate is a yellow dog

PREFACE

Compassion Is Not Enough

This is the story of a WASP's struggle to be true to his conscience in the habitually ambiguous world of America. It arises out of both pain and hope.

My journey as a prisoner of conscience is by no means unique. I am only one of scores of Americans whose conscience, and commitment to non-violent direct action, has led to imprisonment in recent years.

There are prisoners whose stories are more compelling than mine. There are women and men who have paid a higher price for their commitment to conscience. Yet mine is one story among the many. The particularities of my life give me a singular perspective.

When I wrote my journal, while serving a six-month sentence in a U.S. federal prison, I had no thought of a book. Rather, writing was a way for self-preservation and expression in a very repressive environment where few such positive opportunities exist.

When I got back home I stuffed this journal, along with other prison writings and letters to family members, in a storage box and set it on a shelf for two years.

It was only after attending the trial of ten more people of conscience, in which they also received prison sentences and fines, that I decided to write this book. It is important that stories of commitment to the welfare of others be told in the midst of the dominant "me-first" culture of self-indulgence.

I want my children and grandchildren, and the other children of America, to know something of why prisoners of conscience do what they do and why it is necessary. I dream of a nation that gives more than lip-service to its highest values. I hope for generations of American citizens committed to more than self-interest. I want to encourage all Americans to celebrate real community in our diversity and to love their neighbors. I long to leave a better world for our children than I've found.

I stick by what I told the judge at the time he sentenced me: "I hope, Your Honor, that by my life and my witness, by my faithfulness to what I believe, I can teach my grandchildren what my mother taught me: the greatest law of all is to love God with all your heart and with all your being and your neighbor as yourself."

The motivations of prisoners of conscience, as well as their life experiences, come in great variety. However, there are some common touch-points. One seems to be personal deep experience with pain and suffering. I've never known one of us who ended up incarcerated because of embarking on some ideological lark.

The introduction is a fast-forward through my life story meant to reveal what it was in me that led to a prison cell.

Chapters 1 through 7 are directly from my prison journal and letters to family members. All the names of prison officers and inmates have been changed. I have withheld or altered some information to protect the privacy of these individuals. I have tried to accurately reflect my experience as an inmate in a low-security federal prison camp.

The epilogue offers some brief closing words about what has transpired since my incarceration.

A quick reference of who's who and a glossary of what's what is provided at the front for rapid reference to identify persons and terms.

Be forewarned. Prison life is not what you may imagine. It is much more day after day dehumanizing routine than one is exposed to in movie and television dramas. It is monotonous and frustrating. My problems were with officers, not inmates. In America today incarceration is not, by any stretch of the imagination, about rehabilitation. It's all about punishment.

If my daily entries during incarceration are a little gray, that's just a reflection of how I was feeling at the time. A prisoner's primary focus is on matters pertaining to survival and sanity by necessity.

Over the years I have studied corrections as a sociologist and visited inmates as a clergyman. It is a very different experience being a prisoner.

INTRODUCTION

Moment to Decide

By the time I was born in the Missouri Ozarks during the Great Depression my Dad had left a steady job to follow his dream of becoming an artist. He took the risky step that led us into a life of poverty. I came to resent his choice by the time I was a teenager. I nursed this bitterness for decades.

It wasn't until I was 45 that I learned, almost by accident, that Dad had talked this life-changing move over with Mom beforehand and told her if she didn't want him to take this step, he wouldn't. She encouraged him to do it.

"Why on earth did you do that?" I asked her.

"Because I believe everyone should be encouraged to follow their dream," she replied.

Dad had warned her that once he put his foot on this artistic path he would never turn back. He never did. His dream and her encouragement changed our family forever.

This revelation of Mother's complicity, and her reason for it, somehow ameliorated my long-standing attitude and dissipated my anger over the material consequences of Dad's fierce commitment to his dream.

There were benefits that flowed from his outrageous decision. By parental example, I was taught from birth that there are more important things in life than the almighty dollar. My father valued creativity, beauty, and the unity of all Creation. Mother added empathy, community, and religious faith.

My parents always maintained a lively interest in world affairs and promoted the quality of community life. Politically-speaking they were conservative Republicans who were committed to the best aspirations and myths of the American people. They firmly believed such positive national values should be lived out in our daily lives.

They were such staunch Republicans, as a family story goes, that when Mother was in labor with my impending birth she held on until after midnight so I wouldn't be born on FDR's birthday.

My life-partner Mary Ellen and I met in kindergarten. That is a fact that we didn't realize until after we were married.

Sorting through some old photos one day I said, "Oh, look. It's my kindergarten class picture."

"No," said Mary Ellen, "It's my kindergarten picture."

"But there I am," I said pointing.

"And there I am," Mary Ellen pointed out.

We started dating in our sophomore year of high school, were engaged before our senior year, graduated together, and got married three days later in my mother's rose garden.

I had lived in the same little house on Clay Street all my life up to that time but, with the encouragement of my new father-in-law, we moved from Springfield, Missouri, to Denver so I could take advantage of a scholarship I had been awarded. We didn't know a soul there, but we secured employment quickly and by the time the fall term started I had landed a new job working as the graveyard shift security clerk in the Denver Field Office of the Federal Bureau of Investigation.

Changing life direction toward ministry, after the birth of our second son we moved to Fort Worth so I could finish a degree in sociology and get a seminary education at Texas Christian University.

I served several student and one full-time pastorate and worked at several other jobs, including a major defense contractor, making our way through school during the next twelve years. By the time I graduated seminary in 1968 and moved on to a pastorate in Michigan we had five children.

In the four years at Dowagiac I got involved in the community.

The congregation had told me that was expected. It was only after I was deeply into ministry with migrant farm workers, and a community project to produce much-needed low-cost housing for the poor and the elderly, that I learned what they really meant was I should join the Lions Club, period.

After that pastorate, and more than five years of service as the associate regional minister for the Michigan Region of the Christian Church (Disciples of Christ), we moved to a pastorate in Tucson, Arizona.

My very measured goal, as I came to Tucson's Broadway congregation, was to build it to a membership of 700-800, remain for the next twenty years or so and retire as their beloved and institutionally-successful pastor. This was not to be.

Looking back I now realize that I made a fateful choice soon after moving to Tucson that would have more radical implications than I ever imagined. I accepted George Tolman's invitation to participate in a weekly ecumenical ministers' brown-bag lunch to study selected Bible passages in preparation for preaching.

I had never used the common lectionary in my practice of ministry before. I thought it might prove to be a good discipline for me. It was.

This fellowship introduced me to many of my ecumenical colleagues. Beyond mutual support, these weekly gatherings became an opportunity to wrestle with important community issues that came along. The bonds of friendship that developed became a powerful personal and community resource. What unexpectedly flowed from my participation proved to be amazing.

Less than two years later I received news that shifted the whole earth beneath my feet.

When our friend phoned from Michigan he asked, "Are you sitting down?"

I wasn't but I should have been.

"Mark is in intensive care on life support," he said.

Immediately it was hard for me to breathe let alone stand up.

It was January 1980. Our 23-year-old son, Mark, was living in Lansing with his wife Linda and 9-month-old daughter Amber.

"What's the matter, Ken?" my wife Mary Ellen asked. When she took one look at me, she knew it was bad news.

"This morning Mark went to work as usual," our friend said. "He left the job after telling his boss that his family needed him. When he got home he was very agitated and told Linda that he had to protect her and their baby against some imagined enemy. He got out his gun and fearfully peered out the windows. Linda called 911.

"When the paramedics got Mark strapped onto a gurney, and were moving him into the ambulance, he went into cardiac arrest. They brought him back. He's now at the hospital on a ventilator because he cannot breathe on his own. The doctors don't yet know what's causing this."

In less than three hours Mary Ellen and I were on a plane heading toward Michigan.

Mark never regained consciousness. We learned only after an autopsy that he had a toxic reaction to a prescription medication he was taking for pain. Unbeknownst to him this FDA-approved drug was known to cause such extreme reactions in a small number of persons. Mark was one of that small number.

His death was absolutely devastating to me. Despite the fact that I had known other losses in my life, and indeed for years I had ministered to many in the midst of their grief, this loss was like no other.

When we buried his body, I was unable to control myself. As his pallbearers arrived at his grave, and set his coffin on the apparatus over the mouth of it, I completely lost it. To the discomfort of all the other mourning family members and friends, and very much to my own surprise, I wailed uncontrollably like a waif. I was utterly inconsolable.

It expressed itself in guttural groaning. I felt as though I was being turned inside out. I had never personally experienced anything like it before. It erupted like a gusher from subterranean depths. My unbridled cries went on so long that the minister started the service, attempting to speak above my abiding bellow long before I could hush.

Soon after returning to Tucson I suffered a back injury and ended up in the hospital. It was a double whammy. I've been in and out of the hospital with this back injury ever since. It is irritatingly restrictive and constant, but usually manageable. It's a painful condition that continues to be a daily reality in my life. Because the two events are so closely associated my miserable back is a regular reminder of my tragic loss.

After the assassination of Archbishop Oscar Romero in March 1980, more and more Salvadoran refugees crossed the Mexican border into Southern Arizona seeking a safe haven. That sizzling summer a large group were discovered in the desert. More than half were already dead from exposure to the extreme heat and thirst. Some were rescued by the Border Patrol and brought to Tucson. The community opened its arms to receive these survivors and advocate for their asylum.

I started getting personally acquainted with some of the rescued desert survivors. Their harrowing stories of pain and the loss of loved ones in death squad actions hit the raw nerve of my own recent grief. I thought to myself, "If the death of my son by accident brings me such relentless misery, how can these people remain sane and go on living?" It boggled my mind. I came to have great admiration for the faith and courage of many refugees in the face of hell on earth.

My involvement in Central American issues at this point was minimal at best. I was still licking my own wounds. My personal goal and focus was elsewhere. My pastoral leadership of the Broadway Christian congregation was bearing fruit. We had moved off dead center and were beginning to experience a measure of institutional success. While others in Tucson pioneered in a community response to the refugees, who arrived in greater and greater numbers, I was continuing on my safe and acceptable career path, leery of being sidetracked by attention to other and more problematic objectives.

One otherwise typical Monday morning I received a phone call at my office from a stranger. The young man was doing volunteer work for a new group in the Tucson Ecumenical Council (TEC).

He told me the TEC was seeking volunteers to provide legal representation to Salvadoran refugees in a California Immigration and Naturalization Service (INS) detention camp.

I cut him off. I told him that, despite the merit of his concern, "I don't need one more commitment; not one more meeting. I have more than I can say grace over now."

"I understand that you are a very busy man, Pastor," my caller said. "However, you may have some people in your congregation who would have the interest and the time to help if they just knew the need. Do you have just thirty minutes in your busy schedule that you would be willing to give me to explain the situation?"

He got around my defenses.

"Sure. I'll give you thirty minutes," I said reluctantly. "Can you come to my office right now?"

"I'll be there in ten minutes," he said and rang off.

When he got there he told me Manzo Area Council (a community organization who had been working with immigrants for years) had discovered refugees were being routinely picked up in Arizona, transported to a Southern California detention camp, and deported directly back to face God-knows-what in El Salvador.

"My God, we sent Jews back to the Holocaust. Are we're doing it again?" I wondered as he talked. Fifty years before Jews fleeing persecution in Europe were turned away from the United States and returned to Nazi control to face the Holocaust.

Manzo was willing to supply legal representation to the Salvadorans in the El Centro INS Detention Camp in Southern California. They requested the TEC to recruit volunteer interviewers and typists, find typewriters that could be borrowed, and money for expenses for a long weekend of work there.

Thinking it over I decided I wanted to go and see for myself.

With my conservative Missouri upbringing, it was hard for me to imagine my government and its agents forcing refugees back into the agony from which they had so recently escaped.

I found the situation at El Centro was not only all I had been told but even more troubling. Of the more than 200 Salvadoran men in detention at that time, we were able to give legal representation to more than 100 that long weekend. Their stories of persecution were taken down in Spanish, translated into English, and then typed onto government forms. As I typed the detainees' asylum applications, I was stunned by their stories of systematic state terrorism, imprisonment, torture, and the death of family members and neighbors at the hands of the Salvadoran military and death squads. The blinders were stripped from my eyes. The stench of human savagery was in the air.

The soul-wrenching recital of survivor stories was to be repeated over and over and over again, in never-ending nightmarish tales of cold-blooded brutality, in the years that lay ahead. Men, women and children suffered persecution (imprisonment, rape, torture, death and dismemberment) all in accord with government policy.

How is it that any human being can sit back silently and do nothing in the face of such atrocity? The Golden Rule seemed to apply here. Not the one that says, "Whoever has the gold rules." Rather, the one that says, "In everything do to others as you would have them do to you."

When we returned home we created the Tucson Ecumenical Council's Task Force for Central America to respond to these horrors.

Over months—by phone, letter, and personal face-to-face meeting, we contacted every government official we could think of, and got nowhere. Our concerns were met by a spewing of paternalistic poppycock or simply directly dismissed. Even our friends didn't think we could do anything about it.

It very quickly became clear, from our own experience, just how the Holocaust proceeded without serious disruption and why people, in close proximity to what was happening, would claim they didn't know what was going on.

I starting reading everything I could get my hands on about the Holocaust. My wife thought it was morbid, but I was trying to understand the present horror we were experiencing in America. Evil is not a thing of the past.

After months of struggling to provide basic human services to arriving refugees we decided that a different tack had to be taken. The numbers were escalating and included not only Salvadorans, but Guatemalans, Hondurans, and others. The Contra War in Nicaragua and the civil wars in three other Central American nations were in full tilt.

On the second anniversary of the assassination of Archbishop Romero, we launched what came to be known as the Sanctuary Movement. After giving written notice of their intentions to both the local U.S. Attorney and the Attorney General of the United States, congregations in five U.S. cities publicly declared themselves sanctuaries of safe haven for Central American refugees.

The history of the Sanctuary Movement, that became national in scope, is well-documented. Beyond safe haven, the movement provided advocacy for their asylum and a way for citizens to work together toward changing U.S. government policy.

We had been changed by hearing first-hand heartbreaking stories of persecution, so we made opportunities for refugees to share their experiences with the American public.

This witness by refugees in sanctuary was the most powerful tool for changing our national policy. Nevertheless, to continually ask sufferers to repeat accounts of their excruciating losses over and over and over again could become, in effect, an exquisite form of torture.

We developed a civil initiative to uphold our obligations as citizens under both U.S. and international refugee law. In every public forum possible, we insisted that established refugee law be fairly and fully implemented by all representatives of the United States Government.

Our witness provoked a governmental attempt to repress us. It engaged in intimidation, clandestine infiltration, electronic surveillance, and finally, federal prosecution. To their chagrin, these tactics did not diminish the movement. On the contrary, they spurred us on.

In holy defiance of outrageous policies, hundreds of religious congregations across the nation publicly declared themselves sanctuaries for Central American refugees, as did colleges and universities, cities, and even states.

During all this time I continued to serve on the task force, assist refugees, host some in our home, seek redress through the offices of government, educate the public on the issues, and protest the government policy that was creating the refugee stream.

I have never thought that getting arrested was, in any way, glamorous. Being a law-abiding citizen is in my bones. Protest that risks arrest is always an act of last resort. It is a shame that any injustice should ever make such an act of conscience necessary. Nevertheless it is a personal risk that one may feel morally compelled to take after all other avenues have been exhausted. It is an exceptional step to be practiced with nonviolent discipline following the historic tradition of Gandhi and King.

While I was arrested, processed, and briefly held by the authorities a few times in my more than sixty years, as a result of peaceful protest, I never spent time in jail.

Nevertheless, hearing that their pastor was arrested in Senator DeConcini's office, and seeing me led away in handcuffs to a paddy wagon on the evening television news, rankled some church members. This was understandable. Of course, nothing I said would make some of these people happy. They wanted me to quit these involvements. Or, better yet, just leave quietly.

One afternoon I was asked to call on one of the couples of the congregation. I didn't know why I was summoned until we were casually seated in the well-appointed parlor of their posh foothills home sipping coffee. After a few polite pleasantries the man of the house disclosed the reason for the invitation.

First, he directly assured me of the fulfillment of all my ministerial career dreams. He and his friends were in the position "to see to it" that our congregation became preeminent among our denomination's sister churches, he told me.

"We can guarantee that you'll be fully supported in your ministry here. You will never want for financial resources to carry forward your best plans," he promised.

After all this fanfare the real agenda was revealed. All that was expected of me was that I abandon my "troublesome preoccupations with controversial political entanglements."

Dumbfounded by this man's directness, I hesitated. Did I hear him right? Yes, I heard him right. I was being propositioned in the biblical sense.

I tried to explain that my involvements were honest attempts to follow my conscience, to be obedient to the gospel, but he wasn't interested.

"Perhaps you want a little time to think it over," he suggested, rising to shake my hand. I took my leave.

This encounter was followed up some time later by another parish opponent. This parishioner asked to talk with me privately following worship one Sunday. When we were alone in my study he reiterated his clique's agenda and promise. I had had time to think.

"I won't turn my back on these refugees," I told him. "That would be like turning my back on Jesus Christ."

"We only seek what's best for the church," he said.

"What good is the church if it leaves the gospel behind?" I asked.

Seeing that I didn't intend to budge on this point, he informed me, "We are going to starve you out."

"I'm sorry you feel that way," I replied to his back as he got up and left, shutting the door behind him.

This little group went about its subversive work. When the mere withholding of their money didn't work they moved on to other strategies. They tried to turn as many members of the congregation against me as possible. They went to the federal immigration office and turned me in because we had a refugee living in the church's parsonage with our family. They reportedly told the local INS director that they were "concerned" that the government might confiscate church property. They put the refugee in more jeopardy than me. Nothing came of that. They approached every new visitor to the church and told them whatever they had to say to get them never to come back. They set out to undermine the congregation itself and had some ill-gotten success. They resorted to the most diabolical strategies that I've ever experienced in the church. Nothing seemed beneath them.

I am part of a denomination in which clergy serves at the pleasure of the congregation by contract. There are ways of "getting rid" of any pastor. It speaks volumes about this congregation's courage that these opponents could never force me out. While many members didn't agree with some of my actions, they did support my right to follow my conscience.

Eventually my colleague, Frankie Oliver, and I took a month off without pay to help lessen the financial impact. I was away on this unpaid leave added to my vacation, visiting family in Missouri, when the government inserted its spies into the Sanctuary Movement.

These government undercover operatives included Jesus Cruz, who earned immunity from prosecution for smuggling human cargo for profit by becoming an INS informant. Cruz infiltrated Bible study groups, worship services, and church-sponsored refugee ministries. He would be the government's principal witness in the trial of Sanctuary workers that was about to come.

For a long time I thought these agents didn't appreciate the depth of my involvement. I was out of town for the first six or eight weeks of their undercover operation. Did I miss prosecution because of a quirk of timing? That may not have been the case. It appears the prosecutor dropped some of us, and added others who lived in Maricopa County, because the government wanted to try the case in Phoenix, not Tucson.

In any case, January 1985 brought federal indictments against several of my colleagues for their protection of refugees. One of the defendants was our task force director. We had to find another fast. We were determined to keep the work going despite the prosecution.

I applied for the job of acting director. Inasmuch as I had been in on every aspect of this movement from the beginning, and had served as the first and present task force convener, I convinced the search committee I was their best choice. I resigned as pastor of the Broadway congregation and started my new work just as the trial was beginning.

We expected the trial to last three months. It went six. I had expected my position to be temporary. Our director was given probation and decided to enter seminary instead of returning. So, it lasted for almost three years.

During this time, in addition to local coordination of programs and fundraising for the Task Force, I participated in the ongoing Sanctuary work in a variety of regional and national forums, speaking tours, educational engagements, and church-related groups.

I also continued my involvement in sanctuary border work assisting refugees to arrive safely in Tucson, get legal representation, apply for asylum, and make contact with family members.

In the summer of 1987, I was stopped and arrested by the Border Patrol southeast of Douglas, Arizona—along with a rabbi, a Presbyterian elder, and a Lutheran layman—as we transported refugees. We were released and bonded the refugees out of INS detention to await their asylum hearings. Our vehicles were confiscated, but we were never charged.

The General Assembly of my denomination had requested all related agencies and institutions to divest their investments in companies doing business with the racist government of South Africa. While there were some foot-draggers, one institution flatly refused to divest. That was my alma mater. As a member of the Texas Christian University family of graduates I was perplexed and deeply saddened by their policy announcement at the Louisville Assembly in the fall of 1987.

I received what I can only describe as the call of God to go to the steps of the TCU chapel, fast and pray. Though I had prayed before, I'd never been on a fast. One has only to take one look at me to realize fasting is not my thing.

After more than two months of trying to evade this "assignment" because I didn't want to do it—it seemed foolish, costly, and impotent—I finally had to decide to do it or forget it. I even tried to get my doctor to tell me it would be bad for my health. That guy was absolutely no help. He said, "It will probably do you good." I couldn't shake this no matter how hard I tried. Damn!

I moved out into the incredible vulnerability of the unknown. On the seventh day I wrote in my journal: "Fasting is a leap into darkness in search of light."

The personal impact of doing even this very small thing in obedience to a persistent inner voice was overwhelming, spiritually-speaking. On Day 31 I wrote: "It's like being in touch with the Heartbeat of the Universe—not because I have to be, but because I choose to be." Now I had a whole new insight into what Jesus meant when he said, "Blessed are those who hunger and thirst for righteousness, for they will be filled." The experience has had a lasting influence on me.

I started this water-only fast on my birthday, January 31, and continued it unbroken until the afternoon of March 3, the twentieth anniversary of my ordination in TCU chapel.

Pastors for Peace, a program of the Interreligious Foundation for Community Organization (IFCO), received an appeal from the churches of El Salvador to deliver an emergency shipment of basic medical supplies for civilians following a government offensive, which included the massacre of six Jesuits priests and two women on the grounds of the University of Central America (UCA).

I was arrested, processed and released, with fifteen others when we peacefully protested U.S. government involvement in this UCA massacre. Later we learned even more than we knew at the time. Nineteen of the twenty-six Salvadoran military officers involved in these murders were graduates of the U.S. Army School of the Americas in Columbus, Georgia.

The government decided to prosecute us for our protest of this massacre. By the time a trial date was set it conflicted with my participation in a second Pastors for Peace Caravan to El Salvador. I sought and received permission from the judge to miss my own trial. I had to swear to abide by the trial's outcome. As my colleagues were on trial I was in El Salvador. All of us were found guilty of a misdemeanor and served one year of supervised probation.

This was the first of three caravans to El Salvador which I was on. Two were during the war and one immediately following the signing of the peace accords.

I had never been exposed to war conditions before. That was an education in itself. Though we were not near hot military operations, and were kept out of some areas because they were deemed less safe, war was on in both Guatemala and El Salvador. It was a daily experience to hear automatic weapons fire, occasional mortar rounds, and bombs.

Each time in El Salvador, we caravanistas spent ten days distributing the goods and vehicles directly to the people. We also met with all sides to explore their perspectives—from the Salvadoran government to the guerrillas, the U.S. Embassy and non-governmental development groups, church leaders and individual citizens.

On one of my trips I told the caravan director I'd like to arrange to meet the mother of a refugee who had been living with us so long we considered him our son. His mother was in San Salvador. She had encouraged her young son to flee for his life after his uncle and several childhood friends were tortured and killed by death squads. They had been separated for years.

One afternoon in the Capital, as we were traveling in our caravan bus from one appointment to another, the director unexpectedly stopped in a residential neighborhood.

"Come, Ken," he said. "Let's meet your Salvadoran son's mother. We have to be quick about it. We don't want to call any attention to her. That could get her into trouble with the authorities."

My heart raced. What would I say?

We proceeded briskly around a corner and down a few houses. She had a tiny shop in the front of her very humble house and we bought cokes from her as a cover.

After I took a sip, I looked into her well-worn face and abruptly announced, "Your son Victor has been living with me and my family in Tucson. He's okay." My friend translated my words into Spanish.

I was so stirred in those moments that I don't remember very well what was said in our short conversation. It doesn't matter. We were just two parents, who had both lost sons, trying to hold on to our emotions.

My friend and I hurriedly finished our cokes. Victor's mother and I embraced ever so briefly. Then we Americans turned our backs as though we didn't know her and, without looking back, quickly returned to the others in our party. I broke down as we drove away.

"Could you deliver a bulletproof vest to a bishop in El Salvador?" she asked.

I have received some strange requests, but this one was surreal.

Tucsonans had quietly raised money and had it custom-made for the peril in which the bishop found himself. He was under constant death threats. They didn't want him assassinated, like his friend Archbishop Romero. Now they were looking for a way to get the protective garment to him.

The bishop and I had met during one of his visits to the U.S. when he came to Tucson. I had later visited him in El Salvador.

"Sure," I said. "I'll see he gets it." And, with a little help, I did.

Our peace caravan of vehicles, filled with basic goods, had forded the Torola River in rural northeastern El Salvador after a trip from the Capital. We were making our way up a dirt road toward a settlement of repatriated refugees. In a place not far from El Mozote, a village where more than 900 women and children had been massacred by the Salvadoran military, these people were officially naming their new community, Ciudad de Segundo Montes, in honor of one of the recently assassinated Jesuit priests.

These people had courageously returned to a war zone from years of exile in Honduran refugee camps without their government's approval and under constant military threat. All they had was what they could salvage from their camps, and bring with them on their backs, and what little remained on the land after years of bombardment. They refused to be refugees any more. They insisted on being a part of the peace process. One woman would say to us during this visit, "People like us are better able to make peace than governments."

The war was still on. For some distance, as we approached the new community of some 6000 souls, we were flanked on either side by columns of Salvadoran soldiers with ferociously-painted tiger-faces, their M-16s at the ready, and marching in the same direction.

We arrived a little late, but things were just getting under way. We were warmly welcomed and invited to make our way to the stage set up at one end of a mesa among the mountains.

The people had also invited the Commandant of the Salvadoran Army in that sector to the celebration. The Colonel arrived in his helicopter, after others had already kicked up a cloud of dry red dust circling to reconnoiter the area, as his tiger troops surrounded the gathered community. He swaggered across the mesa to the stage, through a parting crowd of civilians, intimidatingly escorted by a cadre of heavily armed troops. The people seemed to take even his thinly-veiled threats from the microphone in stride.

After the Colonel's departure, and the withdrawal of his brigade, the people got down to celebrating and danced to the music of a live Salvadoran salsa band all night.

The 1600 of Nuevo Gualcho were not so easy to find. A map was not enough. It was a good thing we had a guide. They were another group of repatriates who had returned from Honduras only eight days before our visit.

The community was on the other side of a river from where we had to park our vehicles. Thank God, it wasn't the rainy season. We scampered down the high river bank and crossed the water by walking atop a couple of felled logs.

Several old men were working by the river with their machetes and crude tools to fashion wooden plows. They already had one almost complete and had started on a second. After visiting with these men, we made our way on up the opposite bank.

At the top of the hill there stood a 250-year-old hacienda built of stone. All other shelters were tent-like make-dos, constructed of found sticks with black plastic sheeting roofs over dirt floors. A few had woven grass walls.

The community was using the hacienda as their infirmary and common kitchen. We met with village leaders there.

The incredible generosity of poor Salvadorans always put me to shame. The people of Nuevo Gualcho are a good example. After our meeting they insisted on feeding us. The women served boiled eggs in our soup when they were unable to feed their own children one egg a week. It felt like we were taking food out of the mouths of the hungry. To them it was their traditional practice of hospitality.

The second time I visited that village with Pastors for Peace, nine months later, many residents had constructed very basic beds of two-by-fours, rope, and mats woven from local grasses. A little before sunset we began to notice villagers carrying beds on their backs from their huts to the central hacienda where we were to spend the night. We had brought our sleeping bags, but they insisted we sleep on their beds while they slept on dirt floors.

Whenever I, or anyone of our number, asked what we could do to assist them the people invariably gave one answer: "Go home and change the policies of your government."

These in-country experiences scattered my lingering naivete to the four winds. I saw for myself the human toll that resulted from a public policy propelled by the greed of the very wealthy. While the United States public was mostly unaware of the realities, this son of the Show-Me State was shown.

Before my first visit in Salvador I couldn't see how the people could ever have peace without capitulation. By my second visit I was convinced otherwise.

"I don't know how," I said to others, "but these people will have peace."

I learned a profound lesson from these suffering ones. It's a wisdom that all would-be peacemakers must put into practice. If you want peace, the first thing you must do is persist. If you want peace with justice, the second thing you must do is persist. The third thing you must do, if you truly want peace, is persist.

Roy Bourgeois, native of Louisiana and decorated Vietnam veteran, became an ordained Maryknoll priest and a missionary among the poor in Latin America. I first heard of him after he had founded SOA Watch. He was serving a 14-month sentence in a federal prison for a peaceful protest at Fort Benning, the home of the School of the Americas (SOA).

I wrote a supportive letter and Fr. Roy wrote back. He had learned the worst human rights abusers of the hemisphere were graduates of this U.S. Army school that specializes in the strategy and tactics of counter-insurgency warfare. Some of its graduates had tortured and killed people Roy knew personally.

SOA Watch found a way to access damning information through the Freedom of Information Act and human rights reports. SOA graduates were linked to specific human rights abuses through the process of cross-referencing names published in reports of the United Nations and respected international human rights groups.

After an investigative piece on the SOA appeared in *Newsweek* in August of 1993, Congressman Joe Kennedy of Massachusetts offered an amendment on the floor of the House of Representatives in September attempting to strip its operating funds being allotted in the annual military operations budget. He lost that vote, but it wasn't long before he and Fr. Roy met and started working together.

Roy sent out an invitation for others to join him in a 40-day fast on the steps of the U.S. Capitol to support efforts in Congress to close the SOA down. Because of my earlier fasting experience, I immediately said to myself, "I can do that."

During those spring days we lobbied in offices on the hill. Congress itself was fallow ground for our witness. The vast majority of members had never even heard of the SOA.

We also shared information with literally thousands of visitors to the Capitol. Most of these were United States citizens, but there were many from foreign countries. I recall explaining what we were doing there, and why, to a Salvation Army delegation from Russia. All foreigners seemed to understand our point of view easily. That couldn't be said for our fellow citizens. It helped that we could distribute copies of the *Newsweek* SOA article that had been published the summer before.

There was a vote on an amendment in the House on the last day of our fast seeking to deny funds. During a closing service on the Capitol steps we learned that we had lost again. As we broke our 40-day fast, sharing tortillas prepared for us by a Guatemalan refugee, a gentle light rain began to fall. It seemed a sign of blessing to those hungry for justice in this world.

While we lost this congressional vote, we were encouraged by all the increasing awareness and support. This action ratcheted up the movement several notches and we would be back. I was beginning to see parallels to my previous experience in the Sanctuary Movement.

There were some very deep friendships born among the fasters and supporters from all across the nation in those days. I met many people for the first time who have now become dear friends, colleagues, and fellow prisoners of conscience. I renewed acquaintances with a few Central Americans whom I had not seen since brief stays in Tucson shortly after their arrival in the United States.

Though there had been annual peaceful protests at Fort Benning for many years, I had never felt compelled to go. In the first place it is expensive to participate in events in the East when one lives in Arizona. I pay my own expenses the same as all grassroots movement people do.

Rather than go to Fort Benning, I took the lead locally to establish a Tucson SOA Watch, expanding public education and lobbying efforts at home. And I continued to participate in what has become an annual national action in Washington, D.C.

Then, in November 1995, a group of thirteen did a street theater reenactment of the massacre of the six Jesuit priests and two women in El Salvador at the gate to Fort Benning, on the anniversary of that slaughter by graduates of the SOA. They were arrested and charged with trespassing on this open military reservation. These very non-violent compassionate people were tried before Federal District Judge Robert Elliott and given prison sentences of from two to six months plus fines for their peaceful misdemeanor.

When I learned this news I felt guilty about my absence. They were my friends doing the right thing. I should have been among them. Their witness was a powerful motivator. I would be at Fort Benning to peacefully protest the following November.

CHAPTER 1

March: Deer in the Headlights

March 23

It's 5:50 a.m. in Texas. I am to self-surrender to authorities at the El Paso Federal Prison Camp (FPC) on Fort Bliss no later than 2 p.m. I will serve six months in Bliss.

I'm at the home of Louise and Nick Rauseo. I just met them for the first time. They are my generous hosts. Nick picked me up at the airport yesterday afternoon when I flew in from Tucson. Louise fixed pasta and salad. Delicious. We had about a dozen folks to talk about the SOA and SOA Watch here last night. Bob Allen called. He's an old friend from a way back who is now serving as interim pastor of First Christian Church here. He had a church meeting and didn't come over. He will check on prison visitation.

I discovered this morning that I failed to put a hair brush in my bag so I will have to borrow one this morning. Since I'm not allowed to take anything into prison with me, except cash for the prison commissary, I will leave all my things with the Rauseos except the clothes on my back. According to the Bureau of Prisons' (BOP) economic plan I have to buy whatever items I need from them.

I will be entering an entirely new experience this afternoon. While I've visited prisoners in both state and federal prisons over my years as a minister I've never spent a day in jail in my 63 years. Oh, I've been arrested in peaceful protests several times. I even served a year supervised federal probation in 1990-91. But I've never been incarcerated.

I will not be alone. Two prisoners of conscience are presently serving time on this issue. Eighteen more of us enter prisons across the country today. Five await sentencing on an additional charge. Not only that spirit of human solidarity, plus the support of so many across this hemisphere, God is also present.

The spirit of all the SOA 25 is with me this morning. As we in El Paso start our vigil at the Fort Bliss gate at noon today, because of the time difference across the nation, all my colleagues in the eastern time zone will have already reported to their assigned prisons. It will be 2 p.m. there. As I start in from the gate, about 1 p.m., all those in the central time zone will have reported. Randy and I are the only ones in the mountain time zone. And after us Chris and Paddy on the west coast will complete our number.

I stopped to read over the list of 25 and recall each one in prayer. I realize that I know some more than others. The Floridians I got acquainted with just before and during the trial.

Already in: Carol Richardson and Anne Herman

Eastern: Fr. Roy Bourgeois, Dan Sage, Doris Sage, Rev. Nick Cardell, Ann Tiffany, Richard Streb, Dwight Lawton, Rita Lucey, Bill McNulty, Sr. Megan Rice, and Mary Earley

Central: Sr. Mary Kay Flanigan, Judith Williams, Sr. Rita Steinhagen, and Ruthy Woodring

Mountain: Randy Serraglio and me

Pacific: Paddy Inman and Chris Jones

Awaiting sentencing on a second charge: Fr. Bill "Bix" Bichsel, Sr. Marge Eilerman, Ed Kinane, Kathleen Rumpf, and Mary Trotochaud

"This is the day that the LORD has made. Let us rejoice and be glad in it" [Psalm 118:24]. Yesterday I awoke with this verse mysteriously and immediately on my mind. It was my first waking thought. Its ironic appropriateness is present again in the depth of these moments of reflection. It is a gift of the Spirit. It's a verse that would have never surfaced on its own in such a context.

Sunday morning with my congregation in Arizona City was full of warm and supportive love. I am so aware of how they would not accept my resignation as their pastor. And I'm still stunned by their insistence on paying my compensation while I'm in prison. They are a courageous and generous congregation. Other ministers in the region have stepped forward offering to serve them gratis while I'm gone.

My wife Mary Ellen accompanied me to Arizona City. We had brunch with the members after the nine o'clock service. The Johnsons gave us a generous gift. Nona gave me my March checks. Suzanne shared a draft of the article she is submitting to the local semi-monthly newspaper.

There was just enough time to drive the 65 miles back to the airport to catch a plane for El Paso. Some Tucsonans showed up to see me off. They included my family, a Guatemalan family, a Salvadoran family, and other wonderful friends.

It's curious the difficulty some people have with the reality of my incarceration. When I was sentenced they kept insisting I would never go to prison. They couldn't bring themselves to believe it. Some had a hard time coming to the airport because of issues with which they are still struggling. Despite the fact that we have been in Tucson for twenty years *no* clergy were present. Mary Ellen held up strongly to the last, but broke down in tears after I entered the ramp to get on the plane. When I turned back for a last look I saw her sobbing on our son John's shoulder. There's a sense in which my imprisonment is going to be harder on my family than on me. This is the most distressing dimension of this commitment.

I need to live from the depths of my soul these next six months calling on the Spirit for sustenance. So far so good. But the rubber will hit the road later today and the realities of prison life will set in. I will make it through better by living out of the deeper realities of life.

Today I join a long line of famous and nameless human beings who have walked this path of conscience before me. It's a hard path. Nevertheless, I must now walk into prison in order to live with myself and my neighbors. For me there was no other choice.

March 24

Three dozen or so El Paso Area citizens gathered for a presence at the main gate of Fort Bliss yesterday at noon. The federal prison is on the Fort Bliss U.S. Army Reservation. Some carried signs at the very peaceful vigil. I was startled to see a couple that starkly read: "Ken Kennon—Prisoner of Conscience." These people, most of whom I had never met before, were very helpful in my spiritual preparation before entering. They commissioned me to go to prison by prayer and the laying on of hands. The group included two Catholic nuns who are personal friends, in the same religious communities, of Sr. Rita and Sr. Mary Kay who were entering prison in Pekin, Illinois. Their participation provided a deep sense of connection with my colleagues.

Because of the local folks' good work we were covered by all area TV stations and, to a lesser degree, the El Paso morning paper. One result was that I was immediately recognized by many prisoners and BOP officers after entering. They had watched the vigil reported on the local evening news.

Though I was ordered to surrender by 2 p.m., because of some rather unusual circumstances, I was late in arriving and being processed through the prison in-take known as R&D [Receiving and Departure].

After the hour-long vigil, on city property in front of the main Fort Bliss gate, I hopped in a car with three local people who were to drive me the several miles into the post to prison. We stopped at the MP checkpoint.

"Were you involved in the demonstration?" the MP sentry asked.

"Yes."

"Then you can't go in. Turn around and leave."

The driver tried to explain that he was just delivering me to the prison camp and I had to report by 2 p.m.

"My orders are not to let you enter, Sir. Turn around and leave now."

As additional conversation ensued we pulled out of the traffic and parked in the median.

At first the Army personnel at the gate seemed unaware that there is a federal prison camp on the post. The officer in charge made some telephone calls. Then he told my friends that I would have to walk to prison or call a cab, but they would have to leave the premise.

Nick pulled out a twenty to hand to me but I told him, "I'll be damned if I'll pay for a cab to go to prison." He put it back in his pocket.

My new friends could do nothing but just leave me there at the guard house.

The MP in charge finally got the telephone number of the prison and called them. The prison said they would come pick me up but it would be awhile. It was. I didn't have my watch so I don't know when the three BOP officers arrived in their van.

Because prisoners can't bring anything in with them I had no identification on me. These officers questioned whether I was who I said I was. That was a surprise. The system had my fingerprints and mug shot. Weren't they expecting me? They had a folder with them. How could I prove who I am?

I offered, "I know my federal prisoner number."

"What is it?"

"88105-020."

That satisfied them. They patted me down and put me in their van. The prison was miles from the gate and I would have had a hard time finding it.

I was delivered to R&D where processing included filling out papers, getting a prison ID card, being strip-searched and given temporary prison clothing and shoes that immediately made me stand out to everyone inside as new on the block.

Housing here consists of three old two-story wooden Army barracks. I was escorted to my assigned unit and room on the second floor of Guadalupe. Rooms are crowded. Two bunk beds and four small metal lockers for personal items. Very little floor space leftover. There's only one other inmate in this room. He is known as "Popeye."

The officer proceeded to walk me to the dining hall so I could have something to eat. Supper was already underway. As we were walking the officer gave me my initial orientation to the layout and rules. I was not given a policies and procedures handbook that all prisoners are supposed to get because they "were out." Later the other inmates told me not to sweat it because in reality most of the carefully printed rules change at the whim of the officers enforcing them from day to day anyway.

The meal menu allows for some choices. I can tweak my diet within limits. The food is better than I expected. Of course, I wasn't expecting much.

After dinner I reported to the Health Services building for my initial medical processing. Despite the fact that I had had my primary physician of fifteen years send them my medical history and a list of my medical issues I was told, "We don't have it." Basically, as I told the PA [physician's assistant] who saw me, I have back, arthritis, and diabetes issues. I was given a fingerstick for a blood sugar reading and issued some diabetes medication that differs from what is normal for me on the outside. I returned again today, had another fingerstick, but nothing more.

The dorm atmosphere seems mellow. A couple of the men on my floor gave me some personal items that they said I would need: a drinking cup, a toothbrush, toothpaste. This was unforeseen generosity.

The weather here is very much like home—dry desert but more wind. The temperature is more like Phoenix. I am told that annual rainfall averages about 8 inches. We do have mountains to the west. They are not as high as those in Tucson. There's a lot of concrete and asphalt surrounding the dorm buildings. No trees except at the administration building. The heat must be magnified. It's just my luck to be here for the summer.

My initial inmate classification is A&O [Administration & Orientation]. It's a designation that all new inmates are given. It basically means that you haven't been assigned to a prison job. Everyone is expected to work. Each morning most inmates here are bussed to job assignments for the U.S. Army on Fort Bliss. They are landscapers on the golf course, orderlies in the hospital, and the like. I'll try for a job at the prison because it would be against my conscience to work as a slave for the very people who put me here. I have heard from other inmates that, "If you are not good they will send you to La Tuna." I don't know what that means.

I reported this morning with other A&O's for work assignment. Just because we haven't been assigned a job yet doesn't mean we don't work. My job today has been what is called "butt patrol." It involves picking up cigarette butts and other trash in a designated area of the grounds, sweeping sidewalks, and emptying smaller trash containers into larger trash containers for eight hours a day. There is disincentive to work efficiently even though one must appear to be busy at all times whether or not there is actually something to do.

This boring routine is interrupted on occasion with "callouts" to report to health services or administration and the like. "Callouts" are usually posted in each dorm for the following day. But they sometimes come over the public address system. Such callouts include a lot of sitting around waiting until the officer or other staff get around to you. Things appear to move at a much slower bureaucratic pace here.

There is a lot of making sure the inmates remember who's in charge and control. This is an integral part of the prison experience. It seems to be the accepted daily duty of the-powers-that-be to strip us of all vestiges of our humanity.

I got my prison clothing pretty much squared away at the warehouse today. But these shoes are too small. They cramp my feet. They don't have the right size even in a used pair. All the clothing, including my shoes, that I wore in was boxed up and will be shipped back home. It's policy.

I made some personal item purchases at the prison commissary for the first time tonight including this notebook and postage stamps. I wrote short letters to Mary Ellen and my brother Marvin.

I telephoned Mary Ellen last night and tried to reassure her that I am okay. Prisoners must phone collect. It's the only way. And it's expensive. I understand that only in very extraordinary circumstances, as allowed by the BOP, can inmates receive incoming calls.

I am going to a Tuesday evening prayer meeting in the chapel tonight. I understand it's led by inmates.

March 25

What a difference a day makes. Surprise! I was just getting settled, developing acquaintances, learning the prison ropes at FPC El Paso, and then swoosh. New scene.

At about ten this morning I was called on the intercom, by last name and number, as I was sweeping outside; dutifully doing my A&O chickenshit assignment. I reported immediately to the location demanded. The officer told me to put down my broom and go with him. As he walked me to the lieutenant's trailer I was told they were moving me to La Tuna. Well, because of what inmates had said about La Tuna, I wondered what trouble I was in now and why.

At that time I didn't know that there are two penal facilities right next to each other, about thirty miles away, called La Tuna. La Tuna Federal Correctional Institution [FCI] is higher security with razor wire, high walls, barred cells, and more restricted inmate movement. It has a solitary confinement block where both La Tuna and El Paso troublemakers go. La Tuna Federal Prison Camp [FPC] has no perimeter wire or walls nor barred cells and less restricted movement. I was headed for FPC La Tuna, but didn't know any of this until I arrived.

They had already cleaned out my locker. What I had bought at the commissary last night was in a clear plastic bag on the office floor when we arrived at the trailer.

As the duty officer was doing paperwork I decided I would venture to ask the question that was in my mind. If he thought it out of line he'd tell me so and I would be no worse off.

"Sir, may I asked why I'm being moved?"

He said, "Kennon, why are you in here?"

"For illegal reentry onto a military reservation."

"That's just the point. We are obliging a request from the Army that you be removed from Fort Bliss property."

I'm glad I asked.

The Army doesn't want further demonstrations at their front gate. It doesn't seem to be in favor of free speech even when it takes place *outside* a military reservation. They don't want the public questioning why I'm here. The powers still don't care for the light of day.

During my processing the lieutenant entered the room and asked, "Without going into details, what is the School of the Americas?" He was eager to know but didn't wish to appear *too* curious. My explanation was short and to the point.

They strip-searched me again and had me put on a jumpsuit and different shoes. The canvas shoes, like the ones previously issued, were much too small for my feet but no matter. I was handcuffed and belly chained. My ankles were shackled. This was another new experience for me. They put me in a van by myself for transport, with my personal items and records, to La Tuna. Then I was taken by one officer the thirty or so miles northwest on I-10 from Fort Bliss to FPC La Tuna near Anthony, Texas/New Mexico. It's right on the line where the two states meet.

They whisked me off the compound when almost all the inmates were away working. It's like I disappeared as far as they are concerned. No doubt there are all kinds of rumors there tonight.

It was a riveting trip in more ways than one. I was in the back. A steel and plexiglass petition separated me from the driver. There was a foot-square door between us that could be opened or closed from the officer's side. It was open.

Before we got as far as the Fort Bliss gate my escort shouted back through the opening.

"What is con-science?

"What?" I asked caught off guard.

"Con-science," he replied. "What is con-science?"

"Oh, you mean conscience."

"Ah, yes, conscience," he acknowledged.

Then there was silence again.

Like the lieutenant this young officer was curious. He must have seen the images of the our vigil at the gate on television including the signs which read "Ken Kennon—Prisoner of Conscience."

In the situation my adrenalin was pumping and my awareness heightened. Blankets of poppies were beautiful on the slopes along the inter-mountain highway we traveled on the way to I-10.

I didn't wait very long for the conversation to be initiated again. The escort said he had never heard of the SOA. He started asking questions one after another so I kept feeding him information. Shortly before we turned off the road and into the La Tuna property he asked, "Does this school have anything to do with Chiapas?" I made the connection for him.

My escort was apologetic as he deposited me at FPC La Tuna. Removing my handcuffs he realized they had been much too tight the whole time leaving deep marks on both wrists for hours. "You should have told me," he said.

In this system an inmate reports to R&D like a sack of potatoes. As I sat on a bench outside R&D a man in street clothes came up in my face and said quite gruffly, "Kennon, I want to talk with you. Report to me when you have finished processing." He abruptly turned and disappeared down a hallway. He was trying to intimidate me, but I had no idea who he was. He didn't introduce himself. I had no way of knowing he is the unit manager.

The R&D officer was decent and I was my cooperative self.

Another officer hurried me off to the dining hall just before the lunch hour ended. The food here isn't nearly as good as at El Paso. I then completed my work with R&D: filling out and signing forms, having my thumb print taken again, and creating a new picture ID card. Although I'm trying to appear so calm and confident, I must say, my mug shot looks like a deer in the headlights of an on-coming car.

I have to wait to be processed by the La Tuna medical service until tomorrow. That means I will have no medicine for at least 24 hours.

The two dormitory units each have four wings of inmate cells plus offices, TV rooms, showers and restroom facilities. They are one-story stuccoed concrete block construction and are called "camps." I was escorted to a case manager's office at Camp 1. The in-your-face unit manager was there. He asked if "my group" planned to picket La Tuna. Of course I told him the truth: "Not that I know about. That's up to them." It is truly remarkable that the system has now given me *two* prison populations and staffs whom I can educate.

I was assigned to Camp 2, G-13, bottom bunk. I will only be able to keep the bottom bunk if I can get the PA to order it tomorrow because of my back problems. I told the officer that assignment was made at FPC El Paso but I had no paper on me to prove it. I wasn't given *any* of my papers. I think my medical and other records were brought by the escort when I came. And, of course, "that was there and this is here," to all the genetically bureaucratic.

I was told to go to the camp laundry to get an issue of clothing and other basic supplies. The escort pointed the building out and cut me loose. As I walked down the sidewalk toward the laundry I met an inmate who melodramatically said as he passed by, "I have been sent by the CIA to eliminate you." He just kept walking. What a strange greeting. I didn't take it seriously but why anyone would say such a thing to a complete stranger is beyond me. A super dry and dark wit? Maybe he recognized me from the March 23 television newscasts. I don't know.

This place has some obvious pluses over FPC El Paso in my book. There is only one other man in my assigned unit room with two bunk beds. The room is a little bigger. It's not as cramped. There is a small table and slightly more floor space. The compound is more esthetically pleasing. It has grass and trees. It has a more beautiful setting, a minimum of concrete and asphalt, newer facilities, and a tighter campus-like atmosphere with a lower population. There are more mountains rising out of the desert in the distance.

No doubt all the minuses will appear soon enough. One of them is the fact they have almost no clothing to issue me. I have to wait in hope. I don't even have a belt to hold my pants up. Surely they are against indecent exposure here. The man said they have no belts to issue. Am I on a "suicide watch" for awhile? A plus is, strangely enough, an old used pair of low-cut worn-out work shoes that fit better than any prison-issued I have had so far. They are heavily scuffed and their rubber soles are worn almost smooth. The El Paso pair were too short and narrow. I lived with foot pain every day until I could get them off after dinner. I still had the canvas ones given to me at R&D, but they were tight too. These shoes aren't the best, they are too big, but thank God for them. While El Paso was short only of shoes here they are short of *everything*. Hopefully I will get some additional clothing tomorrow.

I really enjoyed talking with the inmate who helped me at the laundry with what he did have. He was truly interested in my story. He asked appropriate questions and obviously knows something about at least related issues. Tonight at supper he brought two other men over to the table where I sat alone to introduce me. He said he had been "telling them about me."

After another brief meeting with a caseworker and the unit manager I was able to reach my daughter-in-law Jeannie at work. Thankfully she accepted my collect call. I couldn't get Mary Ellen or Amy [an old Tucson friend and colleague in justice and peace work]. I got my attorney's number from Jeannie and talked to his secretary Sharon. I requested Bill check into my transfer and that

Sharon or Bill get in touch with Amy to inform the support network. I told Jeannie that I'd try to get back with Mary Ellen around 10 p.m. tonight, hoping she will be at home at that time expecting my call. I want her to have Amy notify Nick, SOA Watch, Denny, and if possible the Disciples News Service and local media, along with local supporters. And she needs to be clear about *which* La Tuna facility I'm at. I have address and telephone information to share regarding both the La Tuna prison administration and myself. I gleaned this from the letterheads on notices posted on bulletin boards near the office.

This facility *has* a handbook. Here it was about the first thing I received. I've read but not digested it. Don't know if I care to since there are written policies and then there are the real ones to live by that will capriciously change from time to time.

The routine and administrative emphasis is different here. Neither makes much sense. While some things are similar, I have to get used to new times, rules, and so forth. Prison has its own ways.

I did complete letters to Mary Ellen and Marvin that I started last night, adding news about my transfer on page two, and put them in the camp mailbox.

The following poem was inspired by observing the early evening sky on this first day at La Tuna Prison:

Light In Darkness

Sliver of moon
crescent in blue
Floats suspended
in iv'ry hue

Above twilight
vastness of space
Guides the steps of
the human race

Light in darkness
leads on the way
Chased by the dawn
of a new day

March 26

Awake at 4:15 a.m. Breakfast is from six to seven. Report for census and work at 7 a.m. PA in medical at 7:15. I need to ask some questions. Will FPC El Paso forward my mail? I need to get information and start an approved visitors list. I am interested in participating in or starting a poetry group here. I need to see the education person.

There are some beautiful small trees at the entrance to Camp 2. Perhaps it's a specie of mesquite. Very gnarly and interesting shapes. Standing about fifteen to twenty feet high. They give shadow and shade from the western afternoon sun at the main entrance. They are poetic. They are a metaphor for the twists and turns of all those who enter here. They also remind me of Dad's painting of the dancing trees.

These steel-toed shoes are not as comfortable as they seemed yesterday. Nevertheless they are an improvement. My foot misery is surely lessened with them.

Back to the A&O menial tasks today.

Wrote to Nick and Louise after talking with them on the phone. There were a couple of other things I wanted to share. They were as surprised about my move as I was. Nick has written the Fort Bliss general but hasn't sent it yet. He said he has some revision to do.

Mary Ellen sounded less stressed. She has a new resident in her assisted living home. I had so much information to share in a brief time I'm afraid I wasn't a very good listener last night.

I'm doing amazingly well, I think. Yesterday's surprise was a real energizer for me. I'm only sorry I have to start from scratch on acquaintances again. I have met a dozen or more already. Some know my story.

They have a camp choir here. I might consider joining it. I hear that they occasionally go off compound to sing at nursing homes and for other community groups. There is at least one more clergyman in here and, I'm told, many men from Tucson. There is a lot to learn and many new people to know.

I wrote to Mary Ellen, our daughter Julie, and Community Christian Church in Arizona City today. I enclosed visitation forms for my family along with instructions on filling them in and returning them. I can't have visitors until they are approved. This will take some weeks. Because the step of a pre-sentence investigation (PSI) was bypassed in our case, even family members must be investigated before they can visit. We are permitted ten approved visitors beyond immediate family. No clergy exceptions.

As far as mail goes I may receive letters, newspapers and magazines clippings, photos (no Polaroids), and paperback books. Complete magazines and newspapers, and hardback books, must be sent by the publishers. I haven't received anything yet. I'm told that what was sent to El Paso will be forwarded. I'm looking forward to receiving something. Mail is a lifeline for any prisoner.

I was initially processed by a PA in medical this afternoon. She was more forthcoming than the one at El Paso and I will be getting my two medications at the pre-prison dosage starting tonight and eventually, she says, a full blood work-up and physical.

I don't seem to miss the news, newspaper or TV, even though I have been a regular consumer of them on the outside. I have seen one paper, watched the Oscars show Monday night, and about three minutes of the CNN News last night before turning in.

The news I would *like* to hear about is what's happening to my friends in prison around the country. I wonder what *their* experiences are like these days. I do know the momentum is building for the SOA Watch DC event next month. What stories we will have to tell each other next November. Two things seem sure. This experience is a sacrifice and it will be powerful in its effect. I have faith that, as the Apostle Paul says, God will use our weak witness to confound the strong [1 Corinthians. 1:27].

March 27

I have been working in food service for the last two mornings. Spent time in the library this evening. They carry the *El Paso Times, New York Times, Arizona Republic, Time,* and *Newsweek.* Picked up a copy of *Walden* and reread the essay "On Civil Disobedience" which is printed in this edition. It's amazing how relevant Thoreau still is today. I look forward to rereading *Walden* as well. La Tuna is no Walden Pond.

I met an inmate with interests similar to mine. Gordon Harris is 71. He's trying to learn how to write good short stories and has written poetry as well. I talked with him some about starting a poetry group and maybe one on short story writing. We could write and share with each other; provide encouragement to each other; grow in our craft while we are here. Probably there are others who would be interested if it was offered. Harris has taught poetry in other prisons. He told me, from experience, the downside of attempting this. It's not encouraging.

Harris shared one of his short stories with me. "How I Became Rich in Prison" is a moving piece growing out of his personal experience.

March 28

The sun is coming up and the birds are singing. It's my first weekend in prison.

I went to my first religious service here last night. During a testimony time I shared the Bible verse that was in my thoughts upon waking last Sunday morning; a surprising verse on the day I was traveling to El Paso to surrender at the prison—Psalm 118:24, "This is the day the LORD has made. Let us rejoice and be glad in it." In reading over this psalm, especially in the New English translation, the context is amazingly appropriate. However, I would have never chosen it in a million years.

The brothers here who stepped out to lead the service have

some depth. They tend to go on too long and some have a proof-text method approach and string scripture passages together that fit their purposes. They have an authoritarian style. It is typical of many fundamentalists in my experience.

I would like to see if it is possible to introduce another approach among these brothers without disturbing what they have going for them. I was impressed by two or three in particular. They would grow in a more open rather than such a measured method. I guess this means I am opinionated. I obviously have something to learn from them. One inmate's use of the prayer circle holding hands was a mite long, but the circle and hand-holding aspect is powerful in this prison context. There appears to be some maturity and wisdom in some of the brothers.

I asked for prayers for my 20 colleagues presently in prisons around the country. The word about why I am here is beginning to get around. Those I've shared my story with have told others. I'm becoming known by the grapevine.

Gordon Harris is the most interesting man I have met so far in these few days. He is an ordained Baptist who has spent a lot of his life in the administration of small Christian colleges. He has taken me under his wing and is introducing me around. He served time in higher security prisons before arriving here.

Today Harris asked me to read and comment on his stories. He has had five theological and academic books published but no short stories. It seems we share a lot in common.

His job is as the chaplains' assistant and other work as assigned. This includes all the custodial tasks of keeping the chapel clean and in order.

Harris has given me his critique on the nature of various services held in the chapel. His description of one chaplain's homilies was precious. A typical sermon would have three points, he said, with all the depth of the following outline: "1. Mary had a little lamb; 2. If you have fleece white is as good a color as any; and 3. The little lamb was a follower."

I did briefly meet the Catholic chaplain. He understood my

reference to the assassination of six Jesuit priests and two women at the University of Central America in San Salvador. Harris doesn't have a good opinion of his homilies, but the service has traditional substance, he says. Harris attends the different services on a rotating basis as a part of his job.

I had a long conversation with Mary Ellen on the phone yesterday evening. She said *The Disciple* magazine article I was expecting was about half a page with my picture. "It was okay," she said, but was apparently disappointed with it. She seems to be doing better.

Mary Ellen said she had made a lot of calls about my move. She has talked with Amy, who mentioned that Paddy had put a story on the SOA Watch web site and wondered if I wanted to do the same. That would be a way to keep active in the movement while in here. I'll send her something soon about my transfer. That's something I could write and send off later today.

[Later] Here it is:

Welcome to Fort Bliss

> It was March 23 and eighteen of the SOA 25 were self-surrendering to federal prisons across the nation.
>
> A group of El Paso citizens gathered at the Army's gate with signs and every television news crew in town. The MP's were edgy even though one of our number reassured them our intentions were peaceful and would be brief. Eventually El Paso Police arrived and questioned our presence on city property "without a permit."
>
> As time for me to report approached we gathered in a circle. I shared two poems I had written. One, "November 16, 1997," speaks of our action at Fort Benning that day. The other, "The Gardener," muses about "who will tend this garden while I'm gone?" I told those standing with me that they were the answer to my question. They placed their hands on me, commissioning me for my time in prison.

That night the peaceful vigil at Fort Bliss made the evening news. The staff and inmates already knew who I am and why I am in prison. Within 36 hours I was moved, handcuffed with a belly chain and shackled, to another prison on request of the powers that be on Fort Bliss. The Army doesn't believe in free speech even *off* military reservations. The darkness doesn't like the light of day.

I was expecting six months in Bliss. It was less than two days.

My colleagues and I will continue to speak from prison. Many of us will be fasting while work is being done in Washington April 26-28. The truth shall not be silenced.

March 29

My first Sunday in prison. On the outside I'd be on the road for Arizona City as on most Sundays of the last eleven years. They are a courageous and faithful group of people. My thoughts are of them this morning. Here the Christian religion tends to be charismatic, fundamentalist or Catholic. There is no alternative for me besides individual prayer and meditation. The thought has crossed my mind to promote an alternative, but how does one do that without introducing a divisive spirit? We don't need a divisive spirit among us. My organizing tendencies could prove a problem not only for me but for others. I must hold back, go slowly, and learn "the lay of the land" before making *any* proposals here. After all this is just the last day of my first week. Twenty-five weeks to go.

I am apprehensive of what my brand of religion would do if we directly related our daily experience to the Gospel. There's so much resistance to my theology on the outside I can only imagine the resistance directly under the thumb of Caesar. Perhaps something informal could take place. I need to wait and see if something like a Christian Base Community might be possible. That is to say, a small group gathering together to approach Scripture not as remote and cloaked, but as immediate insight and power for our present experience and condition.

My thoughts have also been of Marvin's health and I'm curious what he might say this morning to his congregation about his brother in prison. I miss talking to him already. I'll have to get his telephone number from Mary Ellen the next time I talk with her.

I'm without addresses and telephone numbers. My memory of such things isn't helped by the stress of my circumstance. I'm experiencing a considerable amount of disorientation. For example, most number sequences I want to remember are just an unusable jumble. This place is playing with my mind.

Mary Ellen did get the package back that I had sent to myself with paperback books, addresses, phone numbers, and some other items. Father Roy was mistaken about this being allowed. But then the rules have probably changed since Bourgeois was in a couple of years ago. Mary Ellen also received the box of my clothes and shoes from the BOP. She wasn't expecting this. It was shocking and frightened her. She said it seemed as though I had died and she was being shipped my personal effects.

I've just had my sermon for the day. Harris introduced me to Jim Bob Elder, a Texas businessman and, by his own description, "a yellow dog Democrat." He once served several years in the Texas House. He's a member of the Church of Christ. "I'm morally conservative and politically liberal," he said. Jim Bob is a charming man. He held forth on several issues with great conviction.

Harris continues to introduce me around. He invited me to drop by his room sometime today. He resides at Camp 1.

I certainly look forward to beginning to receive mail. It has been delayed by my transfer. And, of course, receiving visitors would be nice but the process even for family members will probably take several weeks.

Yesterday I got some extra sleep, wrote and read, as well as watched the two NCAA final four games in the evening. While I was watching, one brother came up and asked if I was on television news a few days ago. Others saw my photo in Tuesday's El Paso paper. So there are some who are making that connection.

I spent some time in the library and in the chapel (which has another library). The chapel is a good place to read when small groups aren't meeting there. It's a place of quiet, away from the noise of the camps, the wind, and the smokers in out-of-doors areas, and the omnipresent clicketyclack of typewriters as inmates work on their case appeals in the prison library.

The prison population is scheduled to be counted by the officers several times a day. Then there are those additional counts they decide to call. Prisoners must be in their cells at these times. Our abode is variously known as cell, room, and house here. Take your pick.

Tonight I'll get a second pair of trousers that are being hemmed by a fellow inmate. That will give me two pair that fit. Perhaps I can do some laundry. I don't have much yet. But with only two of most things I can't wait long. Maybe the scheduled clothing distribution will take place tomorrow. Whenever that does happen there's a chance that I can get the normal limited issue of clothing. That would sure make life easier.

A neighbor stopped by to get acquainted. We had a brief conversation. He flat can't believe I'm in here for a misdemeanor. He never heard of such a thing. He reinforces for me the piddling amount of time of my sentence in comparison to others here. He had 84 months and has already served 64. "It's all down hill from here," he said of what remains for him. My six months is only a fart in the wind. Although, I must admit, it doesn't seem that way to me just now.

There are items I need from the commissary. I must see if my account has been transferred from El Paso. I'll check with the counselor on Monday.

I also need to watch the ulcerated place that has started developing on the top of my right big toe. It's caused by these shoes. Perhaps I need to make an appointment at the dispensary 6:30 a.m. sick call tomorrow to have it looked at and attempt to get some better shoes that won't do this. I think this has happened because my arthritis causes this toe to "hip up" making it rub against the work shoe's steel toe. I have heard about how much of one's prison time is spent with such seemingly petty personal concerns as my big toe. This is because, unlike life on the outside, it's often impossible to solve these nagging problems on your own in prison.

There has been a lot of unsolicited advice about angling for one of the better work assignments. What a good job is in prison depends on who's talking. As on the outside, pay is the biggest factor for most. It goes into your commissary account once a month. The least one can expect is $5 a month. The greatest is $1.25 an hour. That is for jobs in the prison industry, Unicor, up on the hill where all kinds of brushes are made. Oh yes, there is a prison industrial complex. On the other end of things there is a horticultural unit in the fields where crops are grown and then plowed under; orchards cared for and the fruit allowed to drop to the ground.

For many this pay is their *only* source of income. Besides the purchase of personal items it is tapped to pay off fines and other debts. It can prove relatively expensive paying the company store prices for every little thing you need or want from its very limited selection. Men also use commissary accounts for bartering services, like hemming up pants and getting a hair cut, from other inmates. I have never even thought about this very practical daily aspect of prison life before. Duh. Now I *have* to think about it.

I have no interest in competing with other inmates for the good jobs. I don't need the money. I guess I'm just not political enough. Ha Ha. But I will need to watch out for my own interest in regard to my physical limitations.

Tomorrow is the start of my second week. I almost have my feet on the ground. There's still much to learn just about the routine. It'll take another week for that at least. I'm on callout for the A&O orientation session—seventeen speakers in one day, Harris tells me—in the chapel. How apropos.

I keep being awakened early. This is not that unusual for me even in the quiet back home. Some of the men with food service duties have to leave the camp for work about 4:30 a.m. There are a couple of rounds for head count during the night. My old bunk mattress sags in the middle big time. This is making my legs go to sleep. I have to keep turning over and rubbing their numbness away. Then there are the multiple broken springs that poke out of the mattress that must be adroitly avoided. I have tried to pad them with old towels and an extra sheet. I even sleep on top of the bedspread with just a blanket over me so these extra layers of linens can add some protection. I learned this strategy by observing how other inmates cope. But these protectors shift around as I shift around. I have to reposition them at least once a night. There is very little snoring noise on this corridor. Surprisingly little. I don't have a watch in here, so I have to ask an inmate who has one or walk up the hall to the unit office to see the clock on the wall to know what time it is. I could request permission to purchase a watch from the commissary. That would be yet another bureaucratic hassle. Begging is not something I do for myself. I'd rather get along without one.

We've had some rain overnight. Perhaps that will continue today. There are no raincoats to get from one place to another. Right now I don't have *any* kind of coat or hat.

It's almost six. Time for breakfast. We line up outside the west dining hall door for all meals and wait to be admitted by an officer.

[Later] Now it's near the close of my first Sunday in prison. My congregation in Arizona City has been in my thoughts and prayers throughout this day. I've written them a letter tonight.

I participated in a service this morning that was very lively. The Reverend Brown of El Paso has been coming here for some time now. He is a good preacher in his own traditional style. He brought a message of hope and the possibilities of new life into lives that have need of this message. He dared us to have a dream in accordance with God's plan. He challenged us "to cross the line" to greet our dreams like Jesus did. I was, of course, struck by his phrase "cross the line." That's what landed me here. Rev. Brown served up hope in large doses. God bless him.

I am settling in. I have met some wonderful people here despite the fact that, like me, they are all called criminals. Many have helped me, the new kid on the block, get acclimated.

My mail hasn't caught up with me yet. Hopefully it will this week. I'm anxious.

March 30

Mary Ellen told me in our telephone conversation that our son Paul leafletted passersby on the SOA issue at the Michigan State Capitol in Lansing recently. He put together the leaflet himself and talked to people about why his dad is in prison. To my knowledge Paul hasn't done this kind of thing before. I also learned that the SOA Watch video *An Insider Speaks Out* was shown at the recent Board Meeting of The Christian Church (Disciples of Christ) in Michigan. I served as their associate regional minister there for almost six years in the seventies. It pleases me that these and other efforts are taking place. They are happening because we are in prison.

I have written Paul tonight. I included the poem I wrote in Tucson the last time I tended my garden before my incarceration.

The Gardener

As I stand here watering
        the geraniums red
As I drop to bended knee
        humbled to weed this bed
I wonder who will tend
        this garden when I'm gone

Love cooperating
        with faith in nature's design

Watches anticipating
continued growth as God's sign
Yet I wonder who will tend
this garden when I'm gone

Our Saturdays and Sundays are generally free of work assignments. Though I have been working right along I haven't been assigned to a job yet. It takes a couple of weeks for all new guys. I have been doing yard work, picking up cigarette butts and such, and have done both cleaning and food preparation in the food service department.

I plan to watch the NCAA basketball final tonight. I haven't watched much TV. Just a couple of games, *60 Minutes*, and a few snatches of CNN Headline News.

I have been doing some reading and writing.

March 31

I received my first mail yesterday afternoon. A long letter from Marvin and a copy of his latest sermon, and a card and note from Tucson friend Rosemary Lynch. It was wonderful to get this outside contact after more than a week in prison.

Orientation set again for today. They also have me called out for lab work this morning. Perhaps I'll get an issue of new clothing today. Or it could be Thursday. One lives in hope. Also I checked and my commissary funds *have been* transferred and this is my once-a-week commissary day. Laundry to do soon. An inmate can have the camp laundry do it. This involves "paying" a service fee through the commissary. Or opt to do it oneself in the self-service laundry that has some individual washers and dryers. This requires purchasing detergent from the commissary. Take your choice.

I experienced several moments of an intense claustrophobia last night about 9 p.m. An irresistible sense of panic came upon me unexpectedly out of the night while I stood alone in the yard. I have never known such fear. I wanted to flee immediately. "I *have* to get out of here *NOW*!" I thought. This was an unreasonably distressing, and fierce, full-blown panic attack. It took my breath away.

Carol Richardson warned all of us it would be this way and that it wouldn't get better. Hers was a helpful warning. I recognized what was happening and asked for God's help to deal with it. I reminded myself why I am here. I have a job to do far beyond picking up cigarette butts. My prayer for assistance was positively answered, and the panic passed quite speedily, thank God.

This brief episode will probably return during these months. I will need to deal with this demon very directly and seek God's help immediately. One's mental state in here has a tendency to swing. I can only imagine what it must be like for those serving many years not months.

While I was writing to Julie and Paul, an inmate stopped as he walked by. Jay is a young man who was in the Army. He knows about the SOA. He said he read the article about it in *Esquire*. He had some army buddies who served as trainers there. It was clear by his comments that he is very aware of its true nature. Jay's brief visit was an instant encouragement.

The brothers in here are mellow; respectful of older men like me. The BOP staff, other than their daily seemingly calculated siege on our self-esteem, are usually not aggressive toward us if we are not aggressive toward them. It is a low security prison, but these officers work both here and up the hill at the higher security La Tuna Correctional Institution. Sometimes some don't shift gears. A very few are just mean-spirited and sadistic SOB's.

I admit that I have not been entirely candid with my family about prison conditions. While things have been better than I had imagined they would be, that's only because I was anticipating far worse. Still it's no picnic. So far the most negative experiences have been precipitated by the officers not by the inmates. This is the reverse of what I expected.

It hailed pretty good here this afternoon about one. Then it turned very cold last night and we had snow way down the mountains to the east and north of the camp.

Despite the low temperature the guards kept the swamp coolers on in the dorm units all night. This is to keep us from leaving our beds? Men scrambled to lay their hands on another blanket. We are supposed to have only one. One doesn't keep a man warm in conditions like these. Men put on more clothes if they had them. I didn't have an extra blanket or extra clothes. It was a really cold night.

I still don't have a coat or hat but borrowed a coat from Harris for the morning. He works inside. I had "butt patrol" and picked up trash *all* morning. It's a job that would normally take an hour tops. But the local wisdom here suggests stretching each task out as long as humanly possible. The longer it takes the better.

This afternoon, since the BOP doesn't have a coat and hat to issue me, the officer told me to stay inside rather than work outside and I had more time to write letters. I hope to write my wife and children and congregation at least once a week. Because I tend to lose a sense of time I have started keeping a record of letters written to them. It's difficult to keep straight in my mind what I have written to whom and when. Just another symptom of stress.

I like this prison better than FPC El Paso with one exception. The food quality and variety here is much worse. It's a sure recipe for gaining weight. The lack of choice makes it very hard on diabetics.

There are vending machines from which inmates may purchase sodas and snacks. All the wrong ones for me. So I made a conscious decision not to purchase the debit card credit from the commissary that one needs to access them. There is usually sugar-free soda available at the drink fountain in the dining hall at meals. And we can legally take one piece of fruit with us from the hall after each meal. There are refrigerated water fountains. There are some better snack alternatives available at the commissary. So that's the way I'll go.

CHAPTER 2

April: Dealing With It

April 1

Just spoke with a young inmate from Tucson searching for deeper spiritual foundations. He started last May trying to read through the Bible and better understand it. He asked if I would be willing to get with him to discuss the Bible. I told him, "Yes, I'll love to." It's an opening for the both of us.

The young man asked me what I thought of Rev. Brown. As I think on it now, Brown goes beyond a particular style of preaching. Beyond his style is his substance. He has biblical substance. And he understands something important about what men here need. He certainly brought a message of hope last Sunday.

I had the beginnings of a routine physical, including dental, today. The PA is ordering additional blood tests, an electrocardiogram, and a session with an eye specialist, as well as the general practitioner. It's obvious to me, knowing they are not usually this thorough with other inmates, that they seem to be taking greater care in my case. Why? Perhaps the letter from my doctor and a check on my transfer from my lawyer is making some difference. One never knows. But then this greater attention may or may not materialize.

It will be interesting how my session goes with the BOP team [counselor, case manager, and unit manager] on Friday afternoon.

I got some word relative to when I'm required to pay my $3,000 fine that I need to have checked out by my lawyer. So I will call Walker's office tomorrow. This will be discussed in my scheduled team meeting. The question is when and how is it to be paid, whether I can wait to pay it, or whether the BOP will insist on deducting money out of my minuscule commissary account. The judge said we have six months from the trial date to pay it.

I tried to reach Mary Ellen earlier tonight but didn't. I will try again later.

A copy of Randy's op-ed in *The Arizona Daily Star* arrived today with Amy's letter. It must have appeared between March 23-29. The clipping wasn't dated so I don't know.

I am concerned about Randy's experience in Safford. It's not a camp but the higher security correctional institution and terribly over-crowded. In comparison this place must be a cakewalk.

April 2

I finally got a coat today. It turned very cold after I arrived here. This brand new lined jacket came with the personal help of a fellow inmate who is looking out for me. No hat yet.

I'm sitting outside at a table at almost 8 p.m. It's a little chilly, even with the jacket, but for some reason this is a good place to journal. I was here for the first time last night.

My morning pages have most often become evening pages here. I start my work days so early that morning pages often aren't possible.

I received a mother lode of mail today; over 20 pieces plus 3 books. A Maryknoll office is sending three books I preselected from their catalog every month I'm here. They made the generous offer to all the SOA 25 and I took them up on it. I have almost finished Henri Nouwen's meditation on Eucharistic living, *With Burning Hearts.* It's a great book for prisoners. I hope to share it first with the young Tucsonan. I hope he'll be open to a Catholic author. There are excellent insights in this piece that focuses on the disciples' walk to Emmaus [Luke 24].

The other two books are going to be interesting. One is about

20th century martyrs. The other is *Sharing the Word Through the Liturgical Year* by Gustavo Gutierrez with his commentary on all readings in the three year cycle. I'll be dipping into this each week I'm here and afterward.

I wrote the letters tonight that I most wanted to get in the mail. There is no mail collection or distribution on the weekends so I'll have a couple of days to catch up on a backlog of responses to my other correspondents.

I have a thought in mind for a poem about the shoes I was issued. They are used. They have the imprint of another inmate's feet. They are very worn. The non-skid soles are so worn down that I have to watch out for wet floors. I have already slipped. There's absolutely no grip left. But what interests me most is the question of *who* wore these shoes *before* me. This idea came to me yesterday or the day before. Perhaps if it ruminates a while then something will emerge.

It has become something of a struggle dividing time between personal relationships, letter writing, and reading. My personal commitment to letter writing sometimes gets in the way of relating to other inmates. But I am determined to answer all my mail. It is a good way to remain active in the movement and make the most of my incarceration. Nevertheless, I am aiming for some kind of appropriate balance to emerge. As strange as it might seem to those on the outside it's clear that I will stay busy. I consider myself fortunate in this regard.

April 3

I had my initial team meeting today. The good news is that my release date is September 20. *Hallelujah*! Now I have a specific date to wildly anticipate.

I was told by another inmate after this meeting that the BOP does not allow family or friends to pick up released prisoners. It insists on purchasing a ticket and puts them on a bus out of here. I'll check more on that. There are many things one hears that must be checked out. You can take little at face value and even the well-meaning live by and repeat certain myths.

In addition to the expected bureaucratic questions the unit manager asked why I did what I did that landed me in La Tuna. He said he had seen something about the SOA "a couple of times on TV." This gave me yet another opportunity to further educate these staff members.

Regarding the installment payment on my fine a promise to pay the full fine, prior to the court's July deadline, wasn't good enough for them. They said I had the right to refuse to participate in the installment program but the record would show "refusal to pay" without explanation. What they "suggested" was $25 to be deducted monthly from my commissary account as payment on the fine starting in May. They will deduct that amount sometime between the first and fifteen in May, June, and July which is up to the time I expect the balance is paid to the court. Obviously I will need some kind of receipt to prove the remainder *has* been paid or they will continue to make the deduction. Inasmuch as I didn't see the $25 a month as a big problem I signed the "voluntary" agreement. I do need to get a copy of it to send to my lawyer and the Tucson defense fund. I'll ask the counselor about that possibility next week.

They worked me pretty good today in food service. I was on my feet far too much. My legs are still numb tonight due to pinched nerves caused by prolonged standing. It's going on to 9 p.m. now. I am concerned about permanent damage to nerves in the area of my disk rupture that would necessitate surgery and cause further permanent damage. Not only that, I have a very painful arthritic right knee because of the same reason. I need to be up front with this concern with both medical staff and others in charge. I put in 7 to 8 hours of work, almost all standing, today. I shouldn't do that. I can't do that again. I'm trying to be cooperative but I must be insistent regarding this medical problem I have for my own health both now and in the future. This continuing numbness has convinced me. It would be better in the long run for me to refuse to work and be sent to "the hole" up the hill if it comes to that. Since there is no sick call on the weekend I will have to wait until Monday to see a PA about this.

I was told just this afternoon, at the team meeting, that I will have no definite job assignment until after medical clearance. Then tonight the callout sheet announced my status has been changed, as of tomorrow, from A&O to food service. So much for believing what they tell me. I thought I would have two days off work for my back and knee to recover. This is maddening. The BOP seems to work at keeping inmates off balance. The night officer suggested I show my team paper to the food service supervisor tomorrow but to be sure to show up there on time.

I tried to get through to the Johnsons in Arizona City today to no avail. The phones are so busy at night it's almost impossible. Some men stay on for hours. We have four phones for almost a hundred men. As in El Paso, all calls must be collect. The telephone company and the prison make out like bandits on the backs of inmates and their families in their sweetheart contractual arrangement.

Because of the physical demands of this day it was one of my most difficult to date. I learned my physical limits and I need to be my own advocate in this regard.

April 4

I appeared at food service this Saturday morning at 5:30 a.m. because of my transfer from A&O to food service. The supervisor said the only opening he has is in the dish room. I told him of my back problem—again. My problem isn't washing dishes. My problem is standing on my feet for any length of time. He said I'd start to work on Monday. I'm still up in the air on this assignment because nothing more was said. The good news is that I have today and tomorrow off work. I will go to sick call first thing Monday morning and try to get a medical limitation put on my work.

This poem came before breakfast:

Used

How new was he
    As new as me
Who wore these prison shoes

The prints of toes
    Are in these soles
Who wore these prison shoes

They are much used
    They are abused
Who wore these prison shoes

The steps are mine
    Now in this time
Who wore these prison shoes

Today I answered the remainder of the week's mail. I will write to my family again.

I connected collect with Nona and Bill and had a good talk with them. They tell me it's amazing how the word about the SOA and the imprisonment of the SOA 25 is spreading. The church received letters of support after Suzanne's article was published there. I'm glad I finally reached them so they could report to the congregation tomorrow, Palm Sunday. Nona asked for information on the newest video so they can get a copy to share and suggest to others.

I keep hearing about the rapidly expanding knowledge of the SOA because of our imprisonment. A University of Texas journalism student wants to interview me. He mentioned in his letter that the Valdez editorial in *The Arizona Republic*, earlier this year, was reprinted in a very conservative Austin paper. This gives me hope.

I got some extra rest this afternoon. I have also been reading *Martyrs*. It has chapters on selected 20th century martyrs. They include the six Jesuits priests and two women, Romero, Biko, and King. I'm also learning about some not-so-well-known ones.

It's good to have a weekend off. I can do without the dance of prison labor for a couple of days.

April 5

Daylight savings time started so we sprang forward one hour this morning. That's particularly hard for an Arizonan to do since Arizona doesn't indulge in DST. Most men participated by skipping breakfast. That wasn't any great sacrifice. Saturdays and Sundays breakfast consists of cold cereal and stale danish. They'll catch up with greasy calories at the 10:15 a.m. weekend "brunch." I got up and arrived at breakfast as usual about 6:30 (5:30 by my inner clock).

Harris, who is a breakfast regular, had a couple of funny stories for me this morning so it was worth it. He supplied good laughter to start the day.

I'm planning to go to both the Protestant and Catholic services today. I hear that neither chaplain is a good preacher. Despite popular opinion this is *not* all there is to a service of worship. I want to meet the Protestant chaplain and also go to the traditional Catholic Mass. In my denomination we celebrate Holy Communion every Sunday too. It is always a spiritually nourishing experience for me.

I have placed the list of the SOA 25 between the pages of this journal so I can bring them individually to my awareness each day. I wonder about how they are in *their* journey of prison witness. Eighteen of us are about to complete our second week. Two others are in their third month. The remaining five await their dates for incarceration. Oh, the stories there will be to tell among us. I recall the power of stories from the SOA 13 that were told in November two years ago as we prepared to cross the line at Fort Benning for the first time.

It's a clear day as the sun rises higher over the mountains to the east. I'm sure disoriented direction-wise even though I know the sun comes up in the east and sets in the west. So north must be this way and south that way. But those directions don't seem right somehow with the lay of the landscape. I arrived in the back of a barred van and got all turned around at the start. The camp is laid out catawampus to the compass directions which doesn't help. A part of this inner confusion is how I-10 angles on a diagonal through this area southeast of the prison. There's a lot of traffic this morning. The sound of humming tires and motors is louder than usual. The highway traveler must go northwest toward Tucson, I think, before turning more directly west.

If I were home this morning I would have cut two long canary palm branches from one of our trees to take with me to Arizona City to decorate the Palm Sunday service. I would be starting north out of Tucson on I-10 just about now.

[Later] I participated in two very different services this morning. I was invited by the Protestant chaplain to offer the opening prayer and be the narrator in a reading of the Passion Story from Luke. The service seemed to me to be lacking in grace and spiritual food was meager. The good news is that the Catholic Mass was all the other was not. I'm sure not every worshiper would share my assessment. People's needs and perceptions differ. This response of mine says more about me than the services.

The hymns chosen for the Catholic Mass spoke powerfully to me. Two were "Here I Am, Lord," and "Though the Mountains May Fall." I was particularly deeply touched when we sang the first. In truth I was too choked up to sing because it seems such a strong affirmation of why I'm here. The chorus is inspired by Isaiah 6:8:

> Here I am, Lord. Is it I, Lord?
> I have heard you calling in the night.
> I will go, Lord, if you lead me.
> I will hold your people in my heart.[1]

Participating in the Eucharist was the high point. During the intentions, which tend to be only personal petitions, I asked prayers for "the people of Chiapas and other places in Southern Mexico presently living under a reign of terror." I noticed that the chaplain included concerns for peace and justice in his pastoral prayer later. The sign of peace passed in the chapel has a deep meaning in this context among captives, too. It all spoke to me and my condition.

I imagine I will continue to go to the Protestant service but my primary spiritual nourishment will come from the Catholics. I feel at home with them.

The Mass reaffirmed my commitment and whole reason for being here. And I thank God for it. I plan to participate in the Good Friday liquid-only fast and the Catholic service that day.

With my letter to Mary Ellen tonight I'm starting to include pages of my journal for her to keep for me. I just want to get them out of here. There is absolutely no security for personal possessions. This includes my journal. It could be confiscated by the BOP at any time. I will number the pages consecutively so I'll know if all pages make it out.

The correspondence I'm receiving is very helpful to me in many ways. Several have sent me articles and information that keeps me in touch with others in this movement—like a list of the SOA 25 and where they are incarcerated, addresses and phone numbers of the two SOA Watch offices, news about Chiapas, and so forth. Inserts provide spiritual sustenance.

Many people don't realize how cutoff a prisoner is from things he cares deeply about. I am totally dependent on what is being sent in to me. For example, I couldn't bring in a phone and address list with me. So I'm having to create one from scratch a little at a time. I'm also creating a separate mailing list of all my correspondents.

After almost two weeks of incarceration I'm doing better than I feared I might. Though there are no fences, bars, or barbed wire, this is no "country club." As a fellow inmate remarked recently: "This place *looks* like a park. But it's no fucking park." He's right. I'm in prison.

Prison is prison. We wear dark brown work clothes and black

work shoes with white socks. We could be mistaken for UPS men except for our blue belts and the fact that we aren't free to go anywhere. Those in food service wear whites to work. I share a 4-man room with only one other and I have a bottom bunk. The mattress is old, worn out, popping springs, and the bunk springs sag. After two weeks I'm still in the process of an initial physical examination through the dispensary. I do have some diabetes medicines but I need a greater restriction on work assignment due to my arthritis and back problems.

The good news is the public response to our imprisonment. We should thank Judge Elliott for helping close the SOA even though that wasn't his intention. I'm hearing this in letters from total strangers as well as old friends.

The bad news is that I don't have any approved visitors yet. Even my wife. Beyond family I'm trying to get five visitor friends approved from both the El Paso Area and Tucson.

April 6

I started out the day with breakfast at 6:00 and then sick call at 6:30 to schedule a medical appointment. I told the PA I have back and knee problems. She said I couldn't have two problems at one time. "I can do only one at a time," she said in a huff. "You choose." I chose back.

This is just another example of the insaneness of this system. Both problems stem from the same thing. With my chronic back condition and arthritis I can't be standing for hours working. I may have to get my attorney involved in this before it's over. If everyday is like Friday it could be disastrous. I have an appointment for my back at 12:30 p.m. today.

I don't know how helpful the PA will be. She was certainly surly this morning. I may also need to see the unit manager. It's *not* that I am unwilling to work. I *am* willing but I have physical limitations.

[Later] Well, the PA *did* give me a work restriction for

"prolonged standing, bending, carrying over 20 pounds," for 3 months. "Until we check you out," she announced. She's ordering an X-ray, which will probably show nothing. In the meanwhile I have to give a copy of this restriction form to my food service supervisors and carry another around with me at all times to produce on demand as needed.

The PA says Dr. Eisenstein's letter is not in my file despite the fact he has sent one to El Paso and another here. I have a copy but they don't. They won't accept it from me. That's "against policy." If I can get this straightened out then perhaps things will go more smoothly the rest of the way.

I will pursue getting my attorney to help get my doctor's letter into my medical file by sending it certified with a return receipt. Obviously I will need this to keep appropriate limits on their work expectations. I called Walker's office this afternoon but he was busy and his secretary gone for the day. I was invited to call back tomorrow when Sharon will be in.

I received 14-15 letters today. Many included important movement information. One from Mary Ellen, Amy, Paul, and Marvin among them. Mail is distributed once a day, Monday through Friday, at a mail call in each camp. Inmates gather outside the camp office and an officer reads out the last name on each piece of mail. It is passed to each recipient one at a time. Men live in hope of receiving something. I am getting so much mail these days, while most inmates don't get any, that a fellow inmate at mail call today angrily suggested, "You need your own fucking box."

Tomorrow I have A&O orientation most of the day in the chapel. It had been canceled last week for some reason. Prisoners are not due any explanations.

I'm now into my third week. I'm beginning to have informal "counseling" sessions as fellow inmates drop in to talk. I'm a listener, and process facilitator, not an advice-giver.

I am assigned to food service and will have Fridays and Saturdays off until further notice. Right now I'm one of the table cleaner-uppers for the three meals each day Sunday-Thursday in the dining hall. Inasmuch as there are many more inmates than table space there is a flow of men in and out requiring each table be cleaned several times at each meal. My work consists mainly of cleaning tables, window sills, filling napkin holders, salt and pepper shakers, and the like for now. Some sweeping, mopping, and window washing. The princely sum of 12¢ an hour is to be added to my commissary account for this work.

I picked up some white shirts and pants from the laundry. This is my work uniform. It's also a way for officers to easily identify food service people whose hours vary widely and may appear to be lollygagging around when they should be at work somewhere. In whites there aren't so many questions from the officers. They know we have different work schedules.

This first day officially on the job I was approached by an inmate who knows I now have access to the kitchen and storage areas of food service. He asked for me to get something specific for him. I told him, "Sorry, I don't participate in that," as nonchalantly as possible. He can pursue other sources. I think he was somewhat taken aback by my directness. I have to nip this in the bud before I start getting "special orders" from my fellow inmates. I will not be a part of what appears to be a rather routine and small-time food pilfering loop.

April 8

With the addition of a day-long orientation session and commissary I didn't get around to journaling yesterday. I did write several letters, including one for the first SOA 25 newsletter that is being put together by Sara. I sent her my two prison poems.

This morning I awoke early, as I usually do. Finally I got up about 4:45 a.m., dressed, and straightened my bed. I'm now awaiting the 5 a.m. count before brushing my teeth, placing my metal folding chair on top of the mattress, putting all my stuff away in my locker as required, and going to work at 5:30 a.m.

There are the officers walking by with their flashlights doing their head count now.

Daily scheduled counts are at 12 midnight, 3 a.m., 5 a.m., 4 p.m. (we are required to stand up for this one), and 10 p.m., with census (the inmates call it "senseless") at 7 a.m. and 12 noon, when all inmates must report in person to the Camp 1 office and our presence is noted. Rather than census on Saturdays and Sundays there is an additional count at 10 a.m. All inmates are to be in their cell for all counts. Special counts may be called at any time. The BOP must assure themselves we are still here.

Yesterday a new officer swept the camp and confiscated a ton of personal items. This action is called a shakedown. I lost my drinking cup because it was on the window sill and not in my locker. I wasn't aware of this rule. That doesn't matter. This guy is a hardass recently transferred from Leavenworth who doesn't want to be here. Now, because of racist remarks he made to a black inmate his first day, he doesn't work here any more. I've heard he remains up on the hill at FCI La Tuna.

April 9

I wrote Mary Ellen and Marvin again. I asked Mary Ellen to send a money order for the commissary. It can be enclosed in a letter to me, payable to "Kenneth Kennon 88105-020." Including the number is mandatory. It will be automatically removed by the mail officer and put in my account. All incoming inmate mail is opened and "inspected for contraband." I still have more than $50 with most one-time items I will need already purchased. I am trying to stay away from between-meal snacks so this additional amount will do me for some time. My biggest expense is proving to be postage stamps. Then there will be a $25 deduction toward my fine starting next month.

Marvin reports he's working on his *Mark* manuscript again. There is a sense of urgency in his letter that is unsettling. I'm still waiting to hear what will be done about the return of his cancer. I worry about him, and my sister Lynn, knowing that if any family emergency develops while I'm in here I will be cut off from them and unable to respond. Lynn's condition is chronic and worsening. We almost lost her some years ago. Marvin learned his cancer had returned right after my trial and sentencing. I pray a lot for the health of all three of us.

April 10

Wrote 12 reply letters yesterday and got another load, including our prepared state and federal income tax forms. I need to sign and put them in the mail Monday. It's great to receive letters and keeps me busy responding. It takes up a lot of my "free" time. I do have specific suggestions when they ask, "What more can I do than pray?"

I have taken some time off from letter writing to do other things like other writing and reading. The opportunities for meaningful conversation with other men is increasing and I don't want to be so engrossed in writing that I miss those opportunities.

I had to laugh out loud when I received a big puzzle book from Amy this last week. I do like crossword puzzles but, as strange as it may seem, I don't know when I would have time for such a thing in prison.

I stayed in bed longer this morning because this is my day off. It's Good Friday. I'm fasting today as a spiritual discipline. Before the two Good Friday services begin I'm writing, doing my weekly laundry, and replying to letters.

Louis Freund, a long-time artist friend of my parents, sent me a catalog of his paintings from his 1991 show and one additional larger color reproduction. It's wonderful to have them in here. There is an intimate connection made with Mother and Dad when I hear from him and his wife Elsie. Louis will be 93 this year. Elsie is a little younger. In her 80's still I think.

There was a big collection of inserts from Bill and Nona, a letter from Stig and a copy of the Arizona City newspaper of April

1 with Suzanne's story about the SOA and me. It was large and prominent with photos. Also *The Arizona Disciple* with a brief article sharing my new address. Bill enclosed three Sunday bulletins, including one for their Easter service coming up. Little did I realize "The Church Mouse" would be in prison with me. [A weekly bulletin cartoon drawn by Bill Johnson.]

After I visited with Harris last night he brought me a gift. This pen I'm using. It's easier to write with it. Not so much pressure is required and the larger pen is easier to grip than those available from the commissary. It was a gift out of the blue. He had brought me a fine hat earlier. Harris has been a good friend and an interesting person to talk with. He has been all over the world and is an inquisitive person who dares to do new things. He will have a lot of time remaining to serve after I am released.

I noticed two days ago a single bud opening on a yellow rosebush in the flower bed outside the dining hall. There are several bushes there and this was the first blossom of the season. Other buds are coming on. The bed was fertilized and watered last week. I couldn't help but think of Mary Ellen. Her favorite flower is the yellow rose. I think there's a poem in here somewhere, but it hasn't arrived yet. The sight of this flower was certainly nostalgic. In this warm sunshine they will opened up in a hurry. I will have to keep my eye open to the beauty of this bed.

Fred is a long-timer with a bad back who sees it as his mission to create a lawn around our dorm unit. He is assigned to landscaping, but he does this on his own time. Fred told me that when he came there was no grass at all on the east side. He has kept replanting and coaxing bermuda to spread out. Finally the BOP gave him some seed and fertilizer. He has been busy ever since I came getting this lawn going again this spring. It's greened up pretty good now. It is Fred's contribution to a better environment for all of us. This work must give him some sense of worth and accomplishment.

I'm sitting out on the patio. It's about 7:30 a.m. and still a little nippy. The sun is warm on my back. A slight breeze is cooling to my face. I can clearly hear the traffic on I-10 moving in the distance. It's very busy this Friday morning. The compound is mostly deserted. A little coming and going. Most of the under 200 men are off working. This is a day off for a few of us. This means we will be working on the weekend.

I remembered, at the last moment, to take my medicine bottles to the dispensary. They have to be put in the refill slot before the PA finishes the early morning sick call. I would have run out later today and there's no refilling on weekends. I should be able to pick up the refills tonight at the 7 p.m. pill line. And, I remembered, I had to report for census at about 7 a.m. So much for the "freedom" of a day off. Census again at noon, count at 4 p.m., and so on and on. I had to get up and get moving. Then I mistakenly thought when all the other men had got off to work I would shave and take my shower. No can do. That's when the orderlies clean the bathrooms and showers. I'm just not into this prison routine yet. Each of these experiences teaches me the realities of prison life.

I was saddened to learn from correspondence that FCI Sheridan, where Chris and Paddy are, had been in a 24-hour lock down since they arrived. I don't know how long that lasted. These women and men in FCI's obviously will have a more difficult experience doing their time than those of us in FPC's. I assume it's the difference of La Tuna FCI, up the hill, and La Tuna FPC. There's a disparity in the quality of daily life for inmates in these two places.

April 11

Well, my days off were shifted around again. I took off the morning only to be called in later and have my days off changed. The supervisor who first gave me Friday-Saturday came on at noon and told me to go ahead and take off the rest of Friday, but come in on Saturday and have Monday-Tuesday off. They may change their minds again. Each supervisor seems to do his or her own thing regarding the work schedule, according to his or her own needs, without consultation. We're only inmates after all. Why sweat it?

I did fast yesterday; water only until about 8 p.m. when I took a few ounces of cranberry juice. I feel better today because of it. I attended both Catholic and Protestant Good Friday services. Again the Catholic was more my style. At the Protestant the fundamentalist brothers were in charge. Seven different ones held forth on one of the Seven Last Words, each giving a sermon that was wide ranging rather than a short reflection. Another, who introduced the other brothers, told us before and after what they should have said, according to him. The chaplain was there. He was silent until all this much talking was over and then lead a communion service that was mercifully brief. The service lasted two hours. We certainly felt properly crucified by the time it was all over. But will we rise?

The counselor, who opened the envelope containing the tax forms from my lawyer in my presence, said he would have to approve the mailing in the federal issue envelopes that were enclosed, and to see him about that rather than just putting the forms into the envelopes. I'll have to wait until Monday.

I did get my medicine prescriptions refilled yesterday. I will have to see the PA on an early morning sick call to have them rewritten the next time. I assume they will check my blood sugar at that time. That may be only an assumption.

Yesterday afternoon I watched the last few holes of the second round the Masters from Georgia. There are several guys in Camp 2 who are interested in this upper crust and bourgeoisie pastime so I got to watch too.

Then in the beautiful cool of the evening I sat outside on a park bench near the dining hall, watched a full moon rise out of the east, and visited with a man about my age from New Mexico. He's a Native American who was charged with using tribal funds for his own benefit. He said it was a matter of retribution stemming from intertribal politics.

I introduced myself as having a Hopi son-in-law and telling him a little about our family in Keams Canyon, Arizona. He did most of the talking after that and I did most the listening. Obviously he has been needing someone to unload on. This proud man has met with pointed discrimination here and told me about a couple of specific incidents. It was sad to hear how he has been treated by BOP officers. Most call him "Chief." I had earlier seen him around and said hello, but after this evening we are at least acquaintances if not friends.

I also got some extra rest and continued reading *Martyrs.* Some of their stories are better told than others. There are some amazing accounts of exceptional men and women in this book. They are inspiring. Now they are present with me in this prison.

I have enjoyed seeing the robin red-breasts here. They were a true sign of spring as I was growing up in the southern Missouri and very scarce in southern Arizona. But there have been many migrating through here. Many of the trees have leafed out over the last couple of weeks, but some still have only buds. The Mexican elders have begun to flower. They have small clusters of white flowers. I'm watching the birds soaring in a pale blue sky outside my window, which faces the courtyard between the two camps. This is a relatively broad area of lawn and trees. It's one of the beautiful views available to us prisoners if we have eyes to see.

Yesterday morning I also enjoyed a lengthy conversation with my friend Harris. He said at the close that it was good to have an intellectual conversation for a change. This struck me as somewhat of an elitist attitude. Harris and I have many experiences, commitments and interests in common. He has something of value to share with me and vice versa.

Conversation here *is* often shallow and some of the men's vocabulary is limited and coarse. The other day Jim Bob said he counted the cuss words in one sentence by a man as a foursome noisily played dominoes in the cell next to him. I forget the number, but Jim Bob reported that in a single sentence this man used motherfucker as *every* part of speech.

In a letter to Mary Ellen yesterday I had to apologize for not communicating with her as often as I should. She expressed some anxiety about not knowing what is happening to me. There's some disorientation in here when it comes to the passage of time. It is a different world. I suppose I need to keeping a better record of when letters are sent and phone calls made.

Easter Sunday, April 12

I have received several Easter cards and letters leading up to today. My congregation even sent ahead the worship bulletin they will be using this morning.

A card from the Ursuline Sisters Convent in the Bronx expressed a hope: "May Easter dawn in your heart." And it did. That is an especially touching line for me; the very idea of letting Easter dawn in my heart in prison.

I have been recalling my time in the Holy Land two years ago—the Via Dolorosa, the hill on which Jesus was crucified, and the empty rock tomb in the garden not far away. Those vivid images help me keep a grasp on the reality of those days as well as get a grip on these. And there is something about being a prisoner myself this Easter that deepens all those impressions and brings them to life again. A resurrection of sorts.

I have been reflecting on the fact that God calls us all to be doers of the Word and not hearers only, deceiving ourselves (James 1:22). With that call there comes this promise: "Those who look into the perfect law, the law of liberty, and persevere, being not hearers who forget but doers who act—they will be blessed in their doing" (James 1:25). That promise is fulfilled by a faithful God who never leaves us or forsakes us.

I worked the three Easter Sunday meals. All in all it was a memorable day. Easter dawn this year found me dressed in my food service whites like an angel beside the tomb.

April 13

Yesterday was a different kind of Easter. I attended both the Protestant and Catholic services. I participated in Holy Communion at both. I worked the meals in the dining hall all day. My days off were changed to Monday-Tuesday. And now, this morning, I hear that they will probably be changed again. It's a part of being assigned to food service.

My right knee is doing better this morning for the first time since that long day on my feet a week ago Friday in the kitchen. I had begun to wonder when it would straighten up and quit hurting. It isn't entirely painless, but it seems much better.

I put a card in this morning's mail to a friend whose husband, a long-time friend, died March 30. I finally got her address and a card from the chapel.

The tax forms are ready to mail, but I still need the counselor's okay before posting them. He arrives at work a little later in the day.

A Committee for Clemency for SOA Protesters was formed by some Seattle attorneys. They have already submitted a request to the Department of Justice with affidavits and have contacted congressmen seeking to push the process ahead. I don't expect early release from this initiative. However there are several positive aspects of such an effort, when one takes a comprehensive view, not the least of which is raising the awareness of members of Congress.

I wrote to Oprah Winfrey yesterday following up on the Chicago Religious Leadership Network on Latin America project to get the SOA issue on her show. Wrote several other letters, including another to Arizona City.

I also wrote Mary Ellen information about visitation. No approvals, even for her, yet. Visitation days and hours differ from prison to prison. Here visitation is Saturdays, Sundays, and federal holidays from 8 a.m.-3 p.m. Visitors can come both weekend days and stay as long as they like between those hours. But once they leave that's it for the day. They can't come and go. They check in at the entrance to the administration building and then inmates are called to the visiting room. There are vending machines there with snacks and sandwiches of questionable quality, plus soft drinks, chips, etc. Visitors can't bring anything in. So they need to bring a roll of quarters if they plan to use the vending machines. Inmates can have 4 or 5 visitors at one time maximum. Rules include one kiss and hug at the start and at the end of the visit, maximum. If I am working when a visitor comes I will be called out. Visitors take priority over scheduled work. This is by far the best BOP policy.

Spring is everywhere for those who have eyes to see. Swallows have built a nest out of mud and other materials in the entryway to the self-service laundry. I noticed it Friday as Harris and I sat there talking. I had just previously noticed the presence of the barn swallows. I think that's what they are. They are forked tailed, black with white breast and orange under their beaks. The nest is empty this morning and I don't see them flying in the area. Perhaps they have changed their minds about their choice of location due to the human traffic. I'll watch to see if they return.

Then there are the roses in the quadrangle bed. So far the bushes blossoming are all yellow. There was only one blossom and buds coming on Saturday and then on Easter, as if on command, there where a multitude of buds bursting forth to welcome the resurrection. This morning I noticed some iris coming to flower in another bed near the administration building. The grass in really greening up after the attention of fertilizer and deep waterings. Most of the trees have leaves but there are others, seemingly of one variety, still with only buds. I wonder if they are of a flowering variety. I will know in a few days time.

At breakfast this morning I looked up through a northwestern window that framed what makes a fine composition for a painting. Outside were the dark branches of a tree with 6 or 8 black birds moving among its branches and behind the pale blue of the early morning sky. What a lovely photograph or painting that would make. There was something of freedom and hope in the scene.

This is the second such "picture" I have noticed through these windows. I wonder if other inmates are aware of such things. There are a few artists among us surely. I haven't noticed painters in the hobby craft room but I have seen some drawing going on in the cells. There are some excellent paintings by inmates of past years hanging in the administration building.

April 14

Yesterday was a day off but I helped Jack with the dining hall at lunch and supper. He was all alone again today.

This pen Harris gave me certainly doesn't last very long. It's beginning to go. Of course I'm doing a lot of writing. But I expected it to last longer than this.

I had a good letter from Marvin, Julie, Amy, and about 20 others yesterday. Some more dispatches from StarNet regarding Chiapas. Amy sent two copies of my 1997 op-ed piece and a copy of my little article regarding my prison transfer that has now been posted on the SOA Watch web page. I had a woman write me from New Hampshire who had evidently read it there because of her reference to "garden tending." I had first thought she was in El Paso on March 23, but I don't think so now that I know this item is on the internet. It's hard for me to get my mind around how fast information can and does travel using the present electronic technologies.

The swallow pair were back in their nest last evening. But they are not there this morning. A variety of rose bushes are now blooming. They are lovely.

The deprivation of these prisons makes one wonder how anyone leaves them with a shred of humanity remaining. It's an absolutely stupid system of so-called "correction." In truth, at this level of men who haven't been involved in violent crimes, it is simply warehousing human beings for political and business purposes. It is a quite costly policy in more ways than one. It's a wonder, and a credit to the human spirit, that men survive such long-term degradation. The indomitable human spirit sometimes miraculously wins.

A man stopped by my room yesterday afternoon as I worked on answering letters. He wanted to know why I am receiving "stacks" of mail. As it happens he trained at Fort Benning and is well aware of the SOA. He is serving a 10-year sentence and was given a $4 million fine. He's paying it off through the BOP at the rate of $10 a month. He had figured out how many years it would take him. At $120 per year he will be long dust.

I am having more and more men stopping by asking how to spell a word, or curious as to my writing and letters, or for informal "counseling," or to just share their personal stories. I have even been able to use what I've learned at Our Place, Mary Ellen's assisted living business, as information for those facing similar needs in their families.

Back to work tomorrow. I'm doing laundry. I decided to get my whites done at the camp laundry. I will probably spend most of the day letter writing. I've used *all* my stamps, but today is commissary. I'll replenish my supply this evening and have them to place on tomorrow's outgoing mail.

I started a poem about the birds today.

April 15

Tax Day. The forms were mailed to the IRS yesterday. Hopefully Mary Ellen will be able to pay the taxes today from the other end.

The birds here are into mating and nest building. Especially noticed them yesterday and their activity continues today.

The poem that came yesterday occupied a good part of the morning. The first three stanzas are pretty good but the rest that I wrote just didn't live up to the initial inspiration. Here's a rewrite that I think is more successful.

Timing

They are as darts piercing
a crisp morning sky
Swallow-tailed and black backs
just streaks flying by

White breast winged messengers
with orange under beak
On this spring mating day
a nesting they seek

The timing of nature
has spoken its word
Not only to humans
but every small bird

When I shared this poem with a young inmate his comment was, "You'd never know this was written in prison."

Generally speaking the poems that come to me are short; typically three or four stanzas of four lines each. Longer ones usually, in the end, seem contrived coming as they do from the left brain rather than the right.

I enjoy sitting on the south concrete slab that I call a patio. I'm at one of the tables in early morning after breakfast to write in the cool of the dawn with the warmth of the sun on my back. It's certainly not my garden at home, but some of nature's wondrous mysteries are also present here to observe and to inspire.

I've decided to send the letters I've received, and replied to, home. I will discard the envelopes and send them in batches in a big envelope I can purchase from the commissary.

Back to work today. I'm told I will have different days off next week. The BOP supervisors in food service keep screwing up the schedule. I didn't get my days off this week because of it. They need two men on the job doing what I do at every meal. They can't seem to figure it out. But then they are the bosses and if anyone suffers it won't be them. Gee, I'm beginning to sound like a whiny employee.

April 16

I'm sitting on the patio again this morning. It's colder. It turned so last night. I could have used double blankets again, but no such luck.

More than 30 letters and cards arrived yesterday. They are especially interesting in their variety. For example, one came from a Bruderhof community in New York. Another from a Disciple in Maryland. Yet another from a staff person at a church in Topeka.

Tucsonan Mark Holdaway sent lyrics to two of his SOA songs. I have shared those and other items with some of the men here.

I'm about finished with *Martyrs*. On the last chapter. Some are indeed excellent. I suppose that the next batch of books will be sent to me next week. Maybe this. I have forgot what I ordered. But then I have less time to read than I thought I would before arriving.

I went through all answered mail yesterday preparing a package to send home. I was able to discard the envelopes and some of the cards. Still the postage is going to be considerable. I haven't been able to see the mail officer to weigh it for me.

I just had an impromptu counseling session on the fly with Carl who is finding it hard to cope with hypocrisy. He's fed up, he says, with some of our neighbors here speaking and posing as pious on the one hand and doing wrong (lying, stealing, out for themselves) on the other. We were interrupted. Different kinds of things just seem to pop up quickly, without warning, whether I'm ready or not. I need to be already ready.

I stopped to have a lengthy conversation with an inmate who wanted to know more of why I'm in here and to share some of his story. It's best not to pry into other men's affair but simply wait until they wish to share something. This is the policy I follow.

My niche in the camp is still developing as the days go by. Guys have heard some things and finally their curiosity cannot be contained and they approach. And then there's the part regarding my clergy status, too, that brings me others. The stereotype probably repels still others.

I haven't been able to catch my counselor for word about visitor approvals, if any, either. It's a matter of patience. For us inmates most things are a matter of patience.

One problem here is that there are no real counselors in this place save among ourselves and some of us aren't so good either. I overheard two men talking about why a certain officer had been recently assigned as a counselor in our camp. One asked, "What are his credentials as a counselor? The other's answer was, "The warden discovered him in the bathroom measuring the water in the urinals."

No wonder the hope is so shallow. There are few purveyors of hope here. Almost none. The system crushes it to the earth. And there is an organized resistance by authorities to any open initiative to promote hope among us. Where does one look? Obviously, beyond Caesar's system. God is veiled here too. Even the institutional chaplains are reined in. The authorities would never tolerate *real* freedom of religion. That would be uncontrollable. The SOA 25 are a case in point.

April 17

This morning I have a callout to get back X-rays for which I have to go "up the hill" to the FCI. It's going to be a long morning. I don't need X-rays but the BOP is "diagnosing" my ruptured disk. What a waste. I am told by other inmates that this trip will entail a lot of waiting around.

Jack Sutton, a diabetic on insulin, was having low sugar sweats and reported to the dispensary to get his morning fingerstick reading yesterday. No strips. They are "out." The PA suggested he "eat a Snickers."

I drafted a letter, and a second draft, to DPF *NewsNotes*. I'm not satisfied with it, but I need to get this one in the mail soon. It goes like this:

> Dear Disciple Peacemakers,
>
> It was Albert Camus who expressed his disappointment with Christians because of their silence during the Holocaust. The world, he said, expects Christians to speak out clearly and pay up personally in such situations.[2]
>
> In the summer of 1996, thirteen Christians and others of good will started serving harsh prison sentences as punishment for re-enacting the massacre of six priests and two women in San Salvador by graduates of the School of the Americas on Fort Benning where the SOA headquarters is located. They were calling our attention to something terribly wrong in our own country. With their bodies they said, "Enough!"
>
> I was ashamed not to be among those witnesses. I too was calling for the SOA to close. I had written letters, made phone calls, visited my congressman, participated in local education efforts and peaceful demonstrations, prayed, and even fasted for forty days on the U.S. Capitol steps. But putting my friends and colleagues in prison because they were active peacemakers was the last straw.
>
> When Martin Luther King was in the Birmingham jail a group of the city's ministers asked him what a good minister like him was doing in jail. His reply: "Why are good ministers like you *not* in jail?" I felt like one of them. So in November 1996, I was a participant in a peaceful walk into Fort Benning. And again in 1997.
>
> Someone must speak. Someone must pay.

[Later] I finished up *Martyrs*. The "Afterword," discussing the meaning of the word "martyr" and related matters, is especially enlightening. It's a subject that I would not have considered so fully without this reading in the midst of my present circumstance.

The majority of the SOA 25 are assigned to FCI's. That's the security level above FPC. I am reviewing my list and recalling them to my heart this morning.

Lil Corrigan's letter brought some information. The USA Amnesty International annual conference passed a resolution late last month calling for the closing of the SOA and has sent it on to the Amnesty International Secretariat in London for their consideration. Many Amnesty folks had early on felt that the resolution didn't have a chance. They were wrong. There appears to be some momentum building. The April actions in Washington will be yet another indication and it's coming up a week from Sunday.

I have yet to see my counselor in camp this week. Therefore I haven't been able to find out anything about my visitor list status.

April 18

Never got back to this last night. Spent the entire morning, after breakfast duty, getting X-rays at the FCI medical clinic up the hill. What a hassle. First sitting outside on a breezy porch in the cold (40°-45°F) for an hour and a half waiting to be admitted to the prison. Then going through R&D, changing clothing, passing the metal detector scan, and waiting some more. No strip search this time. I had been warned that was a part of the normal routine. Didn't get back to camp until after 11 a.m. There were six of us for X-ray. They are checking on my back condition. Not taking my physician's word for it, I suppose. I'm not sure what X-rays will show. I had MRI's for diagnostic purposes in the past.

It's cool on the patio this morning. It was supposed to get down to near freezing in El Paso.

Received over twenty letters and cards yesterday. Some are dillies. Another from Marvin. Jo Nelle sent me a bunch of stuff that was obviously seen as contraband and sent back or confiscated, but she did get me a full copy of *The Disciple* for April with the news article about my incarceration.

One letter was from a 21-year-old volunteer at Annunciation House in El Paso. I have already written a reply. He says the volunteers there met March 24 and decided to further organize El Paso to close the SOA. This grew out of the March 23 vigil at the Fort Bliss gate. This is another positive springing from my idea to arrive in this area a little early and make contact with local peace-loving people beforehand. The very successful event just prior to my self-surrender was put together on their own initiative. No doubt I will be following up with these folks as the days and weeks pass. I made several suggestions though they will have their own ideas. I am thankful for these fruits of my imprisonment. God is good.

I received a list of five approved visitors just now. They are Rev. Robert Allen, Sr. Joan Brown, Louise and Nick Rauseo. These four live in this area. The other is our youngest son John. I spoke to Joan. She's coming tomorrow after 11:30. I attempted to call Louise and Nick. No answer. I noticed in his church newsletter that Bob is out of town until tomorrow so I'll write him about his approval. I need to wait until Monday to see my counselor especially regarding Mary Ellen. She sent in the form, but it may be lost in the system. Also Punch Woods and other friends and family. Of course Mary Ellen is the one I most urgently want approved. Hopefully her paperwork hasn't been lost but only delayed. My counselor was sick last week but they say she'll be back Monday.

I'm not sure what such visits will do to me emotionally. But I have taken all else in stride so far. I have had only one moment of panic about being here.

Harris spoke to me about the needs of his 92-year-old mother. I was able to share a lot of information with him including a variety of options. He was going to talk with his sister. This morning Harris said his sister had taken his Dad, 95, to look at a "retirement home," but his Dad's predictable response was, "I think we can still make it on our own." His wife is not even able to get out of bed on her own. I had suggested she might benefit from physical therapy. Harris is finding it very hard not being able to respond to his parents' increasing needs. They were a top priority on the outside but in here he can do very little.

I have heard from Marvin that he expects to be treated with a new medication for his lymphoma. I told him that if the prayers of prisoners "availeth much" then healing is already underway. He writes he has had a book of poetry shipped to me.

April 19

I confronted my BOP supervisor regarding my days off work. I haven't had a day off since a week ago Thursday. While Monday and Tuesday were my days off I worked due to a supervisory snafu of changing my days when it was not necessary or even advisable. Now they have been changed again to Wednesday and Thursday. Now I'll have to wait another five days.

I had a good phone talk with Mary Ellen late yesterday afternoon. She tells me Tucsonans Ila and Jerry are back from their trip to the highlands in Guatemala. Out of Coban they met up with two Franciscan Brothers working in the *campo*. The Brothers asked them if *they* knew of the SOA 25 in prison in the U.S. What a small world. The Brothers wrote a letter to President Clinton that Ila brought back to post in the States. Mary Ellen said Ila would send me a copy. Jerry was one of the over 600 line-crossers last November.

This chilly wind on the patio is about to chase me indoors. . . . It did. It seems unusually cold for this time of year. It reminds me of the cold rainy days in April and May of 1994 on the U.S. Capitol steps during the SOA Watch 40-day fast in Washington.

I wrote a four-page letter to Marvin. He had, in Marvin-fashion, suggested that I write rather than call because then he could re-read my letters. I know I deeply appreciate his letters, too. There is something of a lasting value in them. I recall how wonderful it is, even today, to have the correspondence of our deceased parents and others to re-read. Still I miss his voice.

Mary Ellen said that she hopes to go to Arizona City next Sunday, April 26, with Frankie. I must write to the congregation again later today even if it's a short letter. She also talked about coming with John to visit the first weekend of May if we can get her on my approved list by that time. I will check with the counselor tomorrow and get another application form for her if necessary. At least John has been approved.

I must be looking and open to receive another poem again this week. It seems that I must remind myself to be open and expectant. Often when I do this they arrive. Perhaps there's a new focus for poetry that will present itself; new images that depart from those that have been the most numerous since my breakthrough last summer. Perhaps something on the order of "Hypocrites" or "November 16, 1997." I do not know what it will be, but I must ask the Muses for the gift. The powers of dissipation are oppressive in this place. Still one must continue to live in the hope and promise of the creative power of God. So far I have been able to keep in touch but not in the same flow as on the outside.

I have the feeling that I need to return to Paul's prison letters to teach me a focus that will be productive. I am concluding these pages so I can get out my Bible. I will turn to *Philippians* first.

April 20

Thorn Dancers

Silhouetted on pale blue sea
this resurrection morn
Grackles black in acacia tree
dancing among sharp thorn

Joan Brown, a Franciscan sister living nearby in Sunland Park, New Mexico, was my first prison visitor. She came yesterday about noon and stayed until 3 p.m. We shared in the Catholic chapel service together. She has a wonderful singing voice. Everyone at the Mass was encouraging her to come *every* Sunday. We had a good visit and discovered several crossing points in our lives, including farm worker ministry. She is of the same order as Mary Kay Flanigan, another of the SOA 25, incarcerated in Pekin, Illinois.

Between the time I got off work and Joan arrived I wrote the poem above. It has been in my thoughts on and off ever since I saw this image framed in one of the dining hall windows early Easter morning. The "sea" of the poem is the sky. The branches, foliage, and birds were all black, silhouetted on the pale blue dawn sky in the west. It was a well-composed beautiful picture. I was not immediately aware that it was an acacia tree they—the grackles—were perched in. I'm still not sure these birds are grackles. They are totally black with yellow eyes, having rather long tails and a sleek iridescent appearance. When the male displays he can ruffle up his feathers and appear to be three or four times as big. They have several calls that are quite melodic. I toyed with calling them ravens in the poem. That image seems to fit with the word "resurrection," but these creatures are different than ravens in temper, voice, and instinct. And the raven carries certain symbolic freight that distracts from the message of *this* poem. The name "grackles" is distinctive though perhaps not accurate. I don't think I can look up information on birds here. I'll check the prison library.

I changed one word even though I had sent it out to someone in the other version. I'm a little torn between "singing" and "dancing." They were doing both. Perhaps there's a second stanza for this poem so both of these celebrative action words may be utilized descriptively.

This morning is not as chilly as yesterday and it's nice in a jacket on the patio. Last night there were two brilliant stars on the eastern horizon. One is probably Venus. I imagine the other is also a planet. The sky is wide in this place much like Arizona. One can see over vast distances.

I'm sharing my books with other inmates. Books that are good by my tastes are in extremely short supply here. I expect to leave most of these I'm receiving in the library when my time is up. I do look forward to receiving the next bunch. While I could keep busy writing, reading is a good break.

My counselor says she has never received Mary Ellen's visitation application. So I called and informed Mary Ellen. She is going to try to get hold of the form I sent Amy, if it hasn't been filled in yet, to hurry up the process. But I am putting another in the mail to her also.

My counselor also notified me that the mail office was complaining that much of my mail is addressed to "Reverend Kennon."

"That is not allowed," she informed me. "In here you are just Inmate Kennon."

I explained that people have been calling me that for 40 years, but I would let them know not to when I answered their mail, which is all I can do. I did tell Mary Ellen to ask Amy to put this information on the SOA Watch web site and share it with others. No more "Reverend." I want all my mail.

This is an interesting little-known fact of BOP policy. Just *another* attempt to take me down a notch. Well, it won't work. Harris had already told me of this policy so I'm not surprised. He had the same problem with people calling him "Doctor" for 40 years and had been amazed that I was receiving mail with the clerical appellation.

I have run completely out of stamps until I can go to the commissary tomorrow. Hopefully Mary Ellen's money order will have been received and posted to my account by then. She mailed it a week ago today. The package of answered mail sent home took ten stamps of my weekly maximum purchase. By policy I can't purchase more than sixty a week. I guess that means I've sent more than 50 letters this last week.

April 21

The story is told of one of our number in food service who started to enter the men's room when the supervisor reminded him, "Be sure you wash your hands before you go back to work."

"I'm not going back to work," the grubby Mr. Wright replied, "I'm going to eat."

"Like water on sandstone" is a phrase used in the introduction of a book of Native meditations that jumped out at me when I read it. I find it a magnificent metaphor. When people like myself passionately seek change in the world our vision is not of "water on sandstone." Yet it is an image that those of us who live in the western United States readily understand. Many of us have experienced some fascination of canyons being created, shaped, and constantly reshaped by the rush and even the agonizingly slow dripping of water on sandstone. The ultimate example is the Grand Canyon. Nevertheless we are impatient. We want change *now.* This impatience shapes our tactics. It is a very short view. We need to learn the lesson of canyon-making from the Creator of all things. The One who is forever doing a new thing. If we do then our hope shall have an eternal view. And we ourselves may then painstakingly participate in the shaping of history like water on sandstone.

I learned from an internet copy of a Columbus (GA) news story, sent to me by Amy, that Roy Bourgeois has refused to cooperate with the BOP. Ever since self-surrender he has steadfastly refused to work for them. So he has been in the hole since day one and may remain there for the entire six months.

I would have been faced with a similar dilemma almost immediately had I stayed at El Paso. I could not have spent my sentence working for the U.S. Army at Fort Bliss. The only alternative would probably have been the isolation of "the hole." Ironically I would have been sent to La Tuna. That is, the solitary confinement block at the FCI up the hill.

Roy's position as founder of the movement gives an added

significance to his action. There is something to say for Roy's decision. I know that solidarity in tandem with such an action is likely to strengthen it, but I am not at that place at the moment.

One of the priorities of any grassroots national movement is its community building and decision-making. The nature and mission of a movement and its requirements are very different from institutional procedures and processes.

I think we did have the right idea in the sanctuary movement of the 80's, among those of us in Tucson, to accept and even celebrate the diversity of responses to the same situation and goal. It was problematic but successful in that case. The SOA Watch is the same in respect to people entering and participating in the movement who come from many different places philosophically, religiously, politically, and by experience. It's no doubt best to keep it as open to the participation of all as it is now. This means if Roy wishes to defy the BOP as a matter of conscience, and I don't, both decisions are in their own contexts okay. Both contribute to the goal. Any other judgment is to require one orthodox approach that all must walk in order to be faithful to the goal. That's self-defeating.

I guess I am uncomfortable about Roy's decision. Upon reflection this seems to stem from both a personal concern about Roy and from the fact that his decision challenges my own. The question of the effectiveness of his "tactic" comes in a poor third. That is not really the question. It's a matter of conscience for him not a matter of tactic. He has spent years incarcerated as a prisoner of conscience. It's where Roy is in his spiritual journey. God bless you, Roy. You are faithful to your vision.

Today's mail: Five letters only. None of which had "Rev" in the address. Perhaps the mail officer is denying me my mail already even though I wasn't told of this curious policy until yesterday afternoon. Perhaps it's a fluke. Tomorrow should tell. If I am being denied my mail I will go to the unit manager.

There is a man in my camp who, immediately upon learning of the BOP's prohibition against addressing me as "Reverend" by correspondents, has started calling me "Reverend" whenever he sees me. I have never put any stock in being called "Reverend." I've always encouraged people to call me Ken. However, in this present context, I take some delight in this man's use of it. It is his small satirical act of resistance.

I called Jean. The El Paso Area support group meets tomorrow and I want them to have word about this prohibition for their meeting. I requested Jean put it out to her e-mail network. I also wanted the local group to know that Roy is in solitary confinement. The BOP don't take kindly to his uncooperative attitude. They will find additional ways to make his life harder while he is in the hole. It's what they do best.

Today brought a blessing. Because a neighbor departed for a halfway house I was able to move a better mattress and a bed board onto my bunk. I think I will be sleeping better. What I've had since day one reminded me of the thin mattresses on sagging springs one used to expect in Boy Scout or church camp only worse. This older body requires more support. The mattress is far far from good but it is better. And the board will be a real help to my achin' back.

April 22

Well, of course, they woke me up to work at 5 a.m. on my first day off in two weeks. But, in fact, I was already awake by habit. Then, of course, I have sessions on callout all day in the chapel for pre-release information which I don't need. Sessions are scheduled for 9 a.m. and again at 1 p.m. So what else is new?

I watched the Women's World Skating Championship on ESPN mostly because of the interesting story the only other inmate in the room, Hector Cortez, was sharing about the saga of his back injury, botched BOP surgeries, and other stories of his experience in the federal prison system. Hector is the man I passed on the sidewalk my first hours here who told me, "I have been sent by the CIA to eliminate you."

When I just wait, more and more men approach me when they are ready to engage me in conversation. Now even Hector with his weird macabre sense of humor.

I'll have to watch my mail again today to see if "Rev" is getting through.

My bed is much better, but still I'm having aching legs. I don't know why or what's causing that. I thought it was the sagging bed. Evidently not.

I'm doing my laundry before the 9 a.m. callout. This day isn't going to be as duty-free as I had hoped. [Later] Actually the morning session was for fifteen minutes, and the afternoon one only about an hour, so I was able to knock out a lot more letter replies today.

Mail this afternoon included an oversize thick paperback book of Van Gogh drawings. It's one of those coffee-table volumes. I have no coffee table, so like with many other things, I'll just have to make do. Mary Trotochaud sent it. She is one of the SOA 25 who is awaiting sentencing on a second charge. Mary asked me prior to my imprisonment what kind of book I'll like. I said a book of Van Gogh art. Mary is a potter. She had this one in her own personal library and sent it. It is very special to me. I turned around and wrote her right after reading her letter. I wrote about the glorious sense of community that is present in this movement. I was genuinely moved by her letter and extravagant gift. There's such a closeness among us and now that community continues to broaden out and include more and more from far and near.

Mary Ellen's letter said that our denominational publishing house had called and wants me to review Bible study manuscripts for beyond 2000. I need to reply. Although I have enjoyed doing this in years past the answer is no. I have other priorities just now. Perhaps they felt it would give me something to do in my spare time. I have no spare time. I think I have had a particular perspective on Bible study to contribute and have done so in the past. I have no idea what difference it has made. Over the years there has been no feedback to reviewers. One doesn't know if their time has been wasted or not.

I didn't get an afternoon nap so I'm already sleepy and it's only 6 p.m. Perhaps I can answer a few more letters or read some. I'm afraid if I read I'll just go to sleep. I have a self-imposed rule not to go to bed before nine. It's a strategy to keep depression at bay.

The germ of an idea is in my head for a poem on the name of this prison camp. In answer to my question my cellie told me *la tuna* is the Spanish name for the fruit of prickly pear cactus. I haven't thought about it much. Is there a connection between this prison and a cactus fruit? My cellie says a large *la tuna* is very sweet to the taste. That can't be it. I wonder how or why this prison got this name?

April 23

Only one month after entering I have started a series of callouts for presentations called pre-release preparation. This is designed to prepare convicts for life on the outside. Yesterday the whole session was on how to make out a personal check, nutrition, and fitness. Another session this morning. Attendance is mandatory.

I'm sending a letter of solidarity to Roy through a third party. Prisoners are not allowed to write directly to other inmates.

Supporters of SOA Watch in this area held a meeting to plan and organize for a more active local resistance. I'll probably hear details from someone this weekend.

Long-time friend Bob Allen writes that his people at First Christian El Paso took my suggestion and are getting a copy of the newest SOA Watch video and will hold a congregational seminar on the subject. I have received letters and cards from a covenant group in this congregation ever since I entered prison. I will probably see Bob for the first time on Saturday.

April 24

Over the last few days it has become clear that I need to be working on several articles: 1) the next issue of the DPF *NewsNotes;*

2) Peace Network newsletter; 3) perhaps an op-ed piece for *The Arizona Daily Star;* 4) a piece/letter for the SOA Watch web page; 5) *The Disciple;* and 6) the SOA 25 newsletter. The question is what tack these should take. Most will be brief. All 800 words or less. Some only 100-150 words. Each with its own particular focus.

1. One aspect that needs emphasis regarding SOA is Chiapas. Connecting its mission to what's happening there now.
2. Another aspect is the nationwide SOA Watch activity generated and spurred by the imprisonment of 20 of the SOA 25, the coming sentencing of five more, and the Washington actions April 26-28.
3. A third aspect is the prison experience and communications from the outside with specific examples, at least by type.

Yesterday I wrote to the Democrat candidate for Congress in my district. My Tucson friend Rosemary had his headquarters address on some inserts she sent with her letter. I have also thought that I should write to Jim Kolbe, my Republican congressman, while I'm incarcerated. Content is an issue. I have met with him and his staff personally several times, and I've written letters to him, on this issue for years now with no apparent positive effect.

Also I wonder how to interest media sources, and which media sources, in coverage during my incarceration. I have no media list or addresses, so I need to ask Amy to consult and supply.

Back to work today. I gave blood at the lab this morning. What for? Who knows? Because of my experience so far I feel it's not healthy to ask too many questions even of the medical staff. I do need to go to sick call Monday regarding a refill of my prescriptions.

At the pre-release session this afternoon I did pick up a useful piece of information. I found out that those being released "to the street," like I will be, *can* have their family pick them up here or the BOP will give me a bus ticket to Tucson. It's those released to a halfway house who *can't* have a family pick-up. All other things in the session didn't apply to me. I waited to ask my question after the session was over. I'm an odd duck here.

I am aware of a different mood setting in today for which I seek God's help. It's probably depression as these days go on one after the other with little or no change and pretty much confined to the pettiness of this existence with no escape in sight. This is where the Spirit's help is needed and I'm sure visitors over this weekend will be a welcome relief as well.

The NBA playoffs are on. I watched most of one game last night and about a half of one tonight. They don't much interest me but I don't want to go to bed so early. It's a giving in to depressive spirits. And right now I'm letter-writing-out having written over 20 since yesterday evening. So I imagine I'll watch a part of another game later. First I'll look at the Van Gogh book for a while. Maybe I'll read that whole thing before I get out of here.

April 25

A Conference on Chiapas today in Washington starts four days of action. SOA Watch will be in Lafayette Park tomorrow and on Capitol Hill Monday and Tuesday. My fast starts in the morning and will continue until Wednesday morning. Come to think about it, I'm not going to have to worry about running out of my diabetes meds on Monday because I can't take them during the fast anyway. I must keep up drinking water during those days. Lots of it. It would be wonderful to be in Washington for these events. However our being where we are is giving some impetus to these events.

I'm expecting to see Bob today and maybe the Rauseos (or one of them). I'm guessing that Bob would come on Saturday rather than Sunday. I'm looking forward to hearing about Wednesday's SOA Watch meeting in El Paso.

I watched a real West Texas jackrabbit late yesterday afternoon in the scrub brush east of the camp. His ears were almost as big as he was.

These grackles are birds with interesting features and gestures.

They have a "royal," haughty manner, sleek and sophisticated in their bearing. Their long wide tails appear to be used as a rudder or aileron, like an airplane, when they are in flight. Rather than horizontal in position they appear vertical. Grackles are plentiful in this place this time of year. I haven't noticed any of their nesting places. Perhaps I haven't been observant enough. Some are still in the mating mode. The male displays are interesting to behold. They puff up and spread out almost tripling in size. These birds are large to begin with. Some almost the size of a small hawk. They have beautiful and varied calls. I am watching and listening to four high in a tree across the quadrangle doing their thing this morning. The males are trying to outdo one another. One is displaying on the tippy-top branch. Now there are five.

[Later] None of the visitors I expected might come today did, but I had a surprise one. My son John. He got here about nine and stayed until almost noon. Jeannie [his wife] was waiting at a nearby motel where they had spent the night after driving to the area. He said it was 300 miles from the far southeast corner of Tucson at Houghton Road and I-10. That's a little less mileage than I thought.

We had a lengthy conversation. It seems we had no lack of something to say. He shared a lot and so did I, including things I had not shared with the family before. He could see that I was doing okay. He still can't resolve in his mind why I'm here. He says no one can. They can't believe the sentence I received for my very peaceable act of walking across a white line painted on the asphalt in a funeral procession. Well, that's a part of their education about the nature of the beast among us. It's clear we're making some headway. If we weren't, they would just ignore us. They can't ignore us.

John told me that he was about to get laid off his construction job due to lack of work. He really likes his job, feels appreciated, valued, and likes his bosses. Jeannie is trying to talk him into joining with her to manage the Burns house of our assisted care homes, lessening the need for other employees and assuring a better return on the income there. Jeannie stepped forward when I came to prison and has been a real help to Mary Ellen. John's not sure he wants to do it at this point. But he could speak freely about it. He worked as a caregiver for us before he left to go into construction work. He's a very good people-person. It seems to come naturally for him.

He thinks Mary Ellen was having a hard time dealing with my absence, but that Frankie and others in her long-time women's support group were helping, and he was being more intentionally around for her.

John wondered what I was going to do in the fall at Fort Benning. I told him I would be going in November but had not yet decided if I would "cross the line" again at that time. I have intentionally decided *not* to decide this issue until after I finish this tour of duty. I need an opportunity to have some perspective on this prison experience.

I shared with John that I couldn't get a longer sentence since six months is the most that can be given out for this petty offense. That seemed to reassure him. He said he didn't realize that. He had thought a second sentence would automatically mean a longer sentence. This information didn't do away with his anxiety but it seemed to lessen it.

I told him the hardest part of all this is for me is the effect it is having on the lives of my family. Especially his mother. That has to be evaluated after the sentence is completed. The other hard part, which I did not discuss with him, is the very serious health problems my sister and brother are experiencing. I'm worried about what might happen to them while I'm incarcerated. Of course, I can't know that. Nevertheless it is a source of anxiety for me. The fact that Lynn hasn't written to me yet is a case in point. I have written her only two letters. But then I have received none from her. Is it because she's physically unable, doesn't know what is say, or knows what she thinks but has decided to keep it to herself because she doesn't believe I should have put myself in this position? I don't know what she thinks. I don't know how she is.

April 26

The demonstration in Lafayette Park is about to begin. People are gathering. Here Harris and I are beginning our 3-day fast in solidarity with their action there and together with others among the SOA 25. I haven't heard just who. Anne Herman, who is serving her time at Danbury, had suggested it. I assume Roy and Carol are participating. I learned of this idea first from Carol in a letter before my self-surrender. She and Anne were already inside at the time.

I will take this fast, as usual, one day at a time. The Good Friday fast made me feel better. Probably a weekly fast for one day would be a good thing physically as well as spiritually. But I haven't done that.

The day is starting out a little chilly and with a slight breeze. Scattered clouds. The birds are singing. I changed into my browns so I'm ready for visitors if they arrive before ten. If not, I will have to change back into my whites and go to work. I have no idea about who may show up today. Maybe several. Maybe none. If the local folks coordinated that would be nice. This is just my selfish desire to have at least one visitor each of the visitation days.

The vast majority of men in here *never* have a visitor. In most cases their families are too poor and too far away to come. I've learned, for example, that one man's wife is in a nursing home in Boston, his daughter is also in New England, and his son lives in California. Almost all of the visitors on any given visitation day live in the immediate Texas/New Mexico area.

I can't help but painfully notice the very poignant scenes of all the little children who come to visit their dads with their mothers. Some of these dads have years to serve before being released. Although, in many cases, these men may have "brought it on themselves," their spouses and children are victims of our society's seemingly insatiable appetite for longer and longer incarceration, no matter what the costs.

I will go to the Mass today and take my visitors with me if I have some. That is permitted. I do look forward to the nourishment of Mass each week. So much so that I don't want to miss it.

I'm still basking in my visit with John yesterday. He and Jeannie have returned to Tucson. It sure was good to see and talk with him.

There are three little yellow daisies blossoming from a single volunteer plant on the lawn nearby. There's another plant a couple of feet away that hasn't come into flower yet. Things are pretty quiet. Some men are doing their laundry but few are stirring. There were more men at breakfast today than usual. The word got out that we were having homemade cinnamon rolls. They were made this morning by the man who owes the United States a $4 million fine. He's a good baker. They looked so yummy. Alas, for me, if it wasn't the fast today it would be the diabetes.

April 27

Well, I wonder how yesterday's event went in Washington? How many resisters showed? Today and tomorrow on Capitol Hill are important citizen lobbying days for the movement. This spring their visits in congressional offices will be punctuated by the imprisonment of the SOA 25.

Nick came for a visit yesterday afternoon. He is always quite interesting to talk with. Our interchanges make me realize the lack of depth to most conversations on the inside. For me, so far, most of such talks have been with Harris. Then I'm not one to strike up a conversation with strangers even on the outside. I tend to be uncomfortable and bored with merely polite chit chat.

I caught a phone open last night and called Mary Ellen. She didn't get to go to Arizona City as she'd planned because an employee didn't show up for her scheduled shift. Mary Ellen was at Paula's wedding Saturday and talked to a lot of our old friends. Judy called her from Utah this last week. She had just heard about my imprisonment.

Mary Ellen didn't get the visitor application form until Friday and hasn't mailed it back. So, obviously, she will not be cleared in time for this weekend. Nevertheless, I need to check with the counselor and see who *has* cleared so far. Perhaps Mary Ellen's first form has surfaced. Miracles do sometimes happen even in this crazy place. She talked about Our Place and asked what I thought about John and Jeannie taking on the management of the Burns house.

As I entered my second day of fasting I had an idea for a poem emerge. I am working in the dining hall three meals a day for all three of these days of the fast. I sit there with my glass of water or I'm cleaning up after others have finished eating. The idea came to me that this situation is a parable of a universal reality. Some are at the table eating their fill while others who are hungry are assigned to clean up after them. In such a short fast as I am on the sense of hunger remains. This brings the image home. If I could be a good observer of the pangs of hunger in an atmosphere of plenty and put it into words I'd have something.

I found six postage stamps on a table in the dining hall. No one was around. I talked to one inmate thinking they might be his. Nope. So I put them in my pocket. They were so obvious, near my coat which was on the back of the chair across the table, I wonder if someone left them there on purpose. Perhaps someone will mention them at lunch.

I expect quite a bit of mail today. That usually happens on Mondays. It's so good to be able to stay connected while in here with the continuing witness out there.

April 28

Clear morning. Breeze from the opposite direction today. North. The daisy plant that started with one flower, then three, has eight this day. I enjoy observing these little changes, since so much of our lives here lacks beauty. It is in so many ways quite ugly.

[Later] There were several very good things about yesterday

and today. An excellent visit with two friends. The arrival of three more books plus a NKJ Bible. I had requested the Bible from a religious group in California who sends Bibles free to prisoners.

Went to sick call only in order to get my prescriptions renewed. At the afternoon appointment my blood pressure was a concern so the PA, in consultation with a doctor, is starting me on a medication tonight. That's when I can get my three prescriptions. My blood pressure was a little higher than when I first came in. Is it stress? Is it an effect of my fast? Today is the last day and I have less energy but still doing okay. I have been drinking a lot of water and one 11.5-ounce can of Ruby Red Grapefruit and Tangerine drink per day. I would rather have 100% fruit juice, with no sugar added, but then one must make do when they are in prison. This is the best available at the commissary. It does spike my energy level. 140% daily Vitamin C, 1% sodium, 3% potassium, 190 calories, but 47g of sugar. It tastes good, of course.

I started reading the new Henri Nouwen book, *The Road to Peace,* posthumously put together by John Dear. I was particularly interested in a comment in Dear's introduction. Nouwen had once suggested Dear use his time in prison creatively to reflect and write. Dear had explained why prison was not an ideal, not often even a possible place for such activity. Obviously Nouwen, who was never in prison, didn't understand the usual environment a man must contend with on the inside.

Conditions must vary a great deal from prison to prison, but it's certainly not conducive to creative work. That makes it all the more mysterious that Paul was able to write, even think, inside the prisons of the first century. I'm having to search for the method by which I can do that. These mornings here on the patio, after I get off from working breakfast, are the best time and place I've have been able to find. But I am also always interrupted many times in the course of this reflection time. I need to write some articles to send to periodicals so I hope to discover an adequate way to do this soon. This may be as good as it gets.

This fast is, in a way, more difficult than the two long ones I've experienced. This time I am fasting in isolation. At Texas Christian University, while usually fasting alone, at least I was on the institution's chapel steps and relating to passersby. That one was thirty-three days, water only. At the U.S. Capitol I was sharing every day with others as we were focused on a common goal. I was one of a core group of eleven fasting, water and six to eight ounces of fruit/vegetable juice daily. The small amount of juice helped to keep our basic body chemistry in balance. The core group was on the Capitol steps from ten in the morning until six at night, seven days a week for forty days. We held signs, passed out information leaflets, lobbied in congressional offices, and talked with passersby. Some other people fasted the whole time in other locations around the country. Others fasted for varying lengths of time. Still others lobbied their members of Congress and spread the word in their own communities, but did not fast. Harris is sharing this fast but it's different somehow. He does not seem to be fasting for the same reason as I am. At least he hasn't verbally expressed that purpose when we've talked during this time. I would certainly have liked to know what's going on in Washington. I'm sure they are very busy. I do expect to hear a lot about it in the days to come.

I started my fast after supper on Saturday so I will end it after supper tonight. I have some fruit I have been taking to my cell when available at the meals I have skipped. My cache consists of a banana, two apples, and a tangerine. I also have flour tortillas, mixed nuts, and Fritos from the commissary. So I'll choose from this bountiful store. Probably fruit and tortillas.

The other thing different this time around is that I have had to be in a large dining hall surrounded a lot of food and 200 men eating three times a day during this fast. The first days are the hardest because you still have your hunger. Actually any days after about the third day is much easier because you eventually completely lose your craving for food. This situation has been an acid test for a faster.

April 29

I found out late yesterday afternoon that Mary Ellen was okayed for visitation April 23. Six days ago. The counselor had told me I had no new ones. Punch has been denied and she wouldn't tell me why. "I can't reveal that information," she said. Earlier she had told me that he had an FBI number she had to check out. Mary Ellen discovered from Punch that an FBI background check was done at the time he was named to the President's Council on Hunger in America. I told Mary Ellen to suggest that he get in touch with Congressman Kolbe's office about this. Jim is a long-time member of the Food Bank board. That's where I got acquainted with him before he was elected to Congress. An inquiry from Punch on this would bring the SOA and my imprisonment to his attention again. I've already tried several times to get Mary Ellen on the phone to tell her of the approval but to no avail. I'll try again later today.

Read more than half of Nouwen's *The Road to Peace.* I especially appreciated his account of the Selma March in 1965 and the funeral of Martin King in 1968. These are worth the price of the book. This morning I read a section on "Christ Will Come Again" which is especially thought-provoking, focusing on "The Parable of of the Last Judgment" in Matthew 25. He calls it "The Day of Recognition" when we realize the standard by which our lives will be judged. He also emphasizes the judgment of nations and the goals to which nations give themselves.

Nouwen tends to write, in some instances, like the author of the Gospel of John. Yet, in the midst of all that mystery, there are sky rockets bursting. I was rocked by the power of his talk to the National Catholic AIDS Network at Loyola University in Chicago in 1994.

Completed the fast last night. Started the medication for hypertension this morning.

I brought my metal folding chair into the self-service laundry this morning. Each man, if he's lucky, has one in his cell. The breeze is picking up and it's very chilly. So as I wait for the machines to noisily do their thing I'm in a warm place where I can read and write in relative peace. Today and tomorrow are days off work.

This afternoon I am ordered to report to the Education Department. Evidently they *are* going to insist I prove I finished high school. They won't take my word for it. I can't just present a diploma. They must write off and request evidence from the institution. They insist on all men working toward getting their GED while here. Generally speaking this is a good thing. However I've heard of inmates with advanced degrees forced to go to GED classes. It's just another of those hassles one must endure. One man, who is being released next week, has been ordered to report for his first class this week. It makes as much sense as everything else related to this place.

I got a letter from a 10-year-old student who said his Catholic school in Washington, DC, was teaching him right from wrong, a postcard from Marvin with Van Gogh's "The Sowers" on the front, and a note and packet of material on the SOA Watch Washington events that Yvonne Dilling posted on her way there.

April 30

Yesterday was another especially good day for me. It proved to be a day off that, comparative speaking, was very satisfactory. The only interruption, other than the normal prison routines, was a brief meeting with the education director relative to my education level. He said he would verify my two degrees from TCU. I don't know why he was so nice to me. That's not his reputation in the camp. Was it my overwhelming charm or my physical resemblance to a horned frog? Who can say?

Today, my second day off, I have the pre-release program at nine. I'm not aware of the subject of this session; perhaps the last part of job interviewing that we didn't complete two sessions ago.

I finally caught Mary Ellen at home last night. She had been in Phoenix all day working as a member of an Arizona Department of Health Services Task Force on a comprehensive rewrite of State rules and regulations for adult health services. She has really battled political forces trying to force small providers, like us, out of business in favor of large corporations through shaping provisions in this new law. It's a part of her mission.

She is planning to be in Flagstaff in a couple of weeks for the Governor's Conference on Aging and to see Julie and family.

Mary Ellen probably won't be able to come to La Tuna now until Memorial Day weekend, but we could have three days of visiting then. This weekend, which she originally was shooting for, has presented an opportunity. I told her she shouldn't pass it up. The Arizona Disciples Regional Assembly is to be held in Scottsdale. They are showing an SOA Watch video and inviting her to speak. It's an opportunity to thank them for their support, bring a personal report from prison, and encourage their continuing action in regard to the SOA. She's already planning what handouts to take with her. The Region has been very supportive. My incarceration has served to open some minds of my fellow Disciples to this human rights issue like nothing else had been able to do.

In our telephone conversation I learned of the assassination of Guatemalan Bishop Juan Gerardi last Sunday. Mary Ellen read me the news article from *The Arizona Daily Star.* There's official regret expressed and, no doubt, a lot of official cover-up in progress there. The slaughter just goes on and on. The Guatemalan Army has learned its counter-insurgency lessons well. The killing continues.

In Nouwen's account of the fearful time following the Selma March when folks were trying to escape Alabama in one piece, he says,

> As we were finally approaching the state line, Ronald [one of his passengers] said, "You know what my philosophy of life is? An old man on the march told me: 'Risk in faith, decide in hope, and suffer the consequences in love.' That's my philosophy of life. God is with me and now I

> know it." And when we finally arrived in safe country, he suddenly said, "You know, I think I'll go back next week to help my people. Now they're going to suffer more than ever before."[3]

Such fearless witness strengthens me.

CHAPTER 3

May: Life in the Birdcage

May 1

Another 15 or 16 letters yesterday. Louise Rauseo sent me copies of three poems I wrote before prison: "November 16, 1997," "The Gardener," and "Hope." The last was published in a recent Disciples Peace Fellowship *NewsNotes.*

Hope

There is inside us
a deep longing
a longing set to the music
of days of weariness and struggle

a weariness born from the struggle
with ourselves as well as others
it is a longing for justice
for peace, for love in our lives
God, will it ever come?

Yes!

I had forgotten she had that one. I'm glad to have them all. Now I can share them through my letters.

They mowed the lawns yesterday. Unfortunately my two little

volunteer daisy plants and all their beautiful blossoms were pulverized into a thousand tiny pieces by a John Deere riding mower and scattered in the wind. So much for uncontrollable beauty in prison.

The air is almost still this morning. The first time in many days. The sun is rising over the Franklin Mountains and is already brilliant and warm. I think the day will be pretty hot before the afternoon is out.

I am awaiting the Bly poetry anthology with great anticipation. Yesterday I started on *Tribes of Yahweh* and *Beowulf.* The copy of *Beowulf* here isn't the translation Marvin quoted from in his letter. What a difference the new translation makes.

Amy sent me a copy of an internet message from Guatemala regarding the assassination of Bishop Juan Jose Gerardi, auxiliary bishop of the Archdiocese, and point man for the Catholic Church human rights office. He had just made public the results of years of investigation into human rights abuses that were very critical of the Guatemalan Army. The Army took action. I will ask the men to pray for him and for the people of Guatemala this Sunday at Mass. He had his head bashed in by an assassin at his residence last Sunday evening.

The men here are entirely cynical about any possibility that ordinary people can change anything and make it better. They are in this regard, like the majority on the outside, without hope in the world. It's the people of hope who insist on trying. And, to a great extent, the people of faith.

Back to work today. I may have no visitors this weekend. I've heard from most that they will be away or busy elsewhere. Mostly away. Nick is the only possibility, I guess.

The Arizona Disciples Regional Assembly starts tonight. I will be interested in getting Mary Ellen's take on it next week. She is participating tomorrow.

While the grackles have not made their appearance this morning the swallows have been darting in and out.

May 2

The mail bonanza hit again yesterday with 20-25 pieces. A letter from Cliff Pine had an announcement of the hour-long "Inside the School of Assassins" program on the Las Cruces PBS channel next Saturday at 3 p.m. I received a copy of *The Soul Is Here For Its Own Joy*, edited by Robert Bly, from Marvin.

Harris handed me a short story he wrote to read and for comment. I read it last night. I need to see him about it this morning.

I have learned that the late April meeting of the SOA Watch supporters in the El Paso Area drew about fifty folks. They created an area SOA Watch and organized three task groups: legislative, public education, action. Several are already planning to be in Georgia this November. Three of this number have been visiting me regularly.

May 3

We inmates enjoyed a rare La Tuna fringe benefit. A fireworks display celebrating Cinco de Mayo was launched from the county park just east of the FPC. We took our folding chairs out on the lawn at the back of Camp 2 and had the best seats in the big house. We had a completely unobstructed view of the spectacular show. The men oohed and aahed like children, including me. It was a good evening emphasizing the wonder that still resides in all of us hardened grown-ups.

My young Tucson friend was on the patio this morning alone, so I approached the subject he brought up with me when I first arrived here—Bible study. We have never followed up on it. Since then I have got this NKJV Bible. I gave it to him. The study Bible was put together by people not of my theological perspective but, knowing his Tucson church connection, probably more of his experience. If he sends for a copy to replace this one, as he said he would, I can give it to someone else. The opportunity will present itself.

The Arizona Regional Assembly was in my thinking all this weekend. I'll try calling Mary Ellen later today or tomorrow to hear about it.

It's so warm on the patio already this morning I'm going to have to remove my coat. No chilly breeze today. As yesterday the temperature will no doubt be in the mid-80s or higher. I haven't heard a forecast. I don't expect a visit today but Nick might come. It's letter writing day again. I'm quite a way behind.

[Later] I talked briefly to Mary Ellen tonight. She got home late last night from Scottsdale. She spoke to the Assembly briefly Friday night and had an interest group on Saturday that saw an SOA Watch video, plus one on Chiapas. This was not the exposure to the entire Assembly that I hoped for. Oh, well. People in authority still put institutional concerns first. There nothing surprising about that. But, under the circumstances, it is disappointing.

Our young granddaughters Amanda and Katie were at Grandma's when I called. They sang "Jesus Loves Me" to me over the phone. It was a sweet and beautiful gift for a prisoner.

In his morning walk around the track today a way to share his father's story flooded in upon my friend Harris when he wasn't consciously thinking about it at all. He said he had written down a list of seventeen very specific stories that, when told one after another, would tell his father's story. It was a tender magical moment. I tried to encourage Harris as much as possible. It was a breakthrough for him; the reception of a blessed gift of the Great Creator.

As for me, the much reading and writing along with the routine nature and incredible loudness of this place has, it seems, steered me away from creativity. I must very intentionally draw back to the openness, to the reception of the creative, and push aside the blocks. I believe there is a whole other level of poetic expression awaiting me.

The Catholic chaplain had to be away and the guest priest at Mass was not with us in spirit. He started Mass by grousing that this was the seventh Mass he had had to do that day. Poor baby. He was in a bad mood. He simply went through the paces. The lectionary passages were on persecution and the good shepherd. Despite his attitude this man had a good homily. He developed the idea of the symbol of the sheep in the First Century context and what it means in reference to Jesus and his followers. A clincher would have been to tell the story of Guatemalan Bishop Juan Jose Gerardi's assassination last Sunday. That would certainly bring the Gospel home to now. But he didn't. Not only that, he didn't allow us to participate in sharing intentions, so I couldn't add it. After he said, "The Mass has ended," I daringly raised my hand and asked if I could share an intention with my brothers. He allowed it and I asked my brothers to pray for the assassinated Bishop and his people in Guatemala. During the singing of the final hymn that followed this visiting priest disappeared out the door without so much as a word to anyone.

May 5

Cinco de Mayo. I received some very interesting pieces of mail yesterday including a copy of our (SOA 25) pre-sentencing statements from the court transcript that have been published together in a 40-page booklet by the Maryknollers as *Speaking Truth to Power.*

I shared the booklet with Carl to read. He's 22-year-old Texan in here on a drug charge. He is trying hard to straighten his life around.

Several men have and will be leaving this week, including Jack Sutton who I have worked closely with in the dining hall. Almost all are on their way to halfway houses but Jack is being released to the street.

Jack said he'd see to it that I got his Saturday and Sunday days off. I said, "No thank you. I'd rather have weekdays." That means I can add some weekend time off when I have visitors. Jack had never thought of it that way since he never had any visitors.

If I'm lucky I might get all mine approved before I'm released. Obviously this is a measured bureaucratic way to harass me. It's the experience of other inmates that this system will always find a way of "getting to you." If it's not one way it's another.

I am going to spend the rest of the morning on answering my mail.

May 6

The most notable happening yesterday was that Harris came to my cell and read aloud the first chapter he's written for his book about his father. It's a chapter about an alcoholic rural mail carrier who sobered up and later had a life-shaping influence on his father when he was young. It's a moving bit of writing excellently put together. As I told him, when he asked, I wouldn't change a thing. If all of his chapters are as good as this one he's got one interesting book. Harris is really excited. And he should be.

Hector Cortez stopped by and talked. He is something of an enigma. At the end of his personal litany Hector called the government "coldblooded" and "ruthless," two very appropriate descriptive words. While Hector tends to be extravagantly melodramatic, his evaluation should be listened to with some seriousness.

I have an appointment with a doctor at the dispensary at 8:30 this morning. This will be routine. It is not because I'm sick. It's the initial examination that should have been done a month ago. They are still "checking me out" through their system. As long as nothing changes concerning my meds or job I'll be okay. One is always concerned that they will do some cockamamie something or other.

Carlos Gonzalez, who is about my age, finally had much needed surgery yesterday for a cataract removal and lens implant in his left eye. He's been trying to get something done for months. His other eye is also clouded by a cataract and needs the same procedure. He has been steadily going blind. Ever since I arrived men have been offering him their arms as he moves from place to place, and up and down steps, so he can navigate around the prison without injury.

I have talked with him in detail about what he can normally expect from the surgery inasmuch as I had this same operation very successfully last December and plan to have my other eye done this coming December. Hearing my positive experience encouraged him.

Carlos also has a chronic heart condition for which he needs an angioplasty procedure. Nothing doing on that. This is one way a prison sentence of a few months or years can become a death sentence.

Carlos was really upbeat yesterday because, after a great deal of legal pressure by his lawyer and family, the eye operation finally happened. Within twenty-four hours the improvement is dramatic. His situation is characteristic of the so-called medical care here. There's a budgetary incentive *not* to treat the men incarcerated. This is to say nothing of the thoughtless and publicly applauded vindictiveness given as a moral justification for non-treatment of prisoners. I don't know the whole story but I do know that medical uncertainty is one of the worst aspects of imprisonment.

According to Carlos he is an innocent man who landed in here by way of a plea bargain on a conspiracy charge with a federal prosecutor. He's taking the fall for a drug-related crime of his youngest son. This incarceration kept him from following through with surgical procedures he needed to have performed at the time of his arrest. The BOP, he said, previously would not allow him to have surgery done while he's in custody. He had pled to be allowed to personally pay all his own medical costs so he could receive treatment. The BOP simply won't have inmates telling them what to do. Regardless. Period.

Old cons counsel new ones, "Whatever you do, don't get sick in prison."

May 7

I'm sitting at my spot on the patio this morning watching the grackles wading, bathing and drinking in a large pool of water created by a lawn sprinkler that was left on overnight.

I took a day's hiatus from letter writing. Only wrote one. Read quite a bit in the Van Gogh sketch book. Started a letter to Amy and Marianna to be read at the band concert benefit for Tucson SOA Watch later this month. I decided to check on possible additional approved Tucson visitors, including Amy and Marianna, before finishing it.

I got some extra rest. It was mostly a day of rest. I went to see the doctor. My weight is down. My blood pressure is in the normal range now. I had started drinking coffee regularly and I cut that out. They have never checked my blood sugar by a fingerstick here at La Tuna; only at El Paso in March. I suppose they could have got such information from a blood draw that they did do. But I was told that was to see if I have AIDS. The doctor briefly listened to my chest. That was it. He said they would check me in another month. Whoop-de-do.

May 8

The mail delivery has been late for the last two days. Rather than delivered in mid-afternoon it was about six. One letter from Melissa, a friend from sanctuary days, who now resides nearby in Las Cruces. She included her phone number and I called. As a part of our conversation she said my old friend Gary MacEoin will be in El Paso next week for a book signing. He wants to visit me but, as I told her, unfortunately prison visitation rules makes that impossible.

A nice long letter from Marvin. Among other things he tells of a Van Gogh show scheduled for the LA Museum next year. He wonders if I would like to see it. Of course I would.

A list of my visitors as of a month ago was delivered to me yesterday.

This is an out-of-date list. Why send *it* to me? Why haven't Sr. Jean Miller and my Tucson friends been approved? Apparently they process approvals when they feel like it. Which is seldom.

Fascinating letters tonight. One from the Guatemala Human Rights Commission/USA members include Jennifer Harbury and Sr. Diana Ortiz. It brought me to tears to read their message and see their signatures. Receiving letters from victims of SOA graduates reminds me precisely why I am here like nothing else possibly could.

Keith Watkins, a retired seminary professor, wrote that one of his colleagues used to speak of "the presence of absence" as a powerful witness sometimes. He said that's what my absence at the Arizona Regional Assembly was recently.

Dan Oliver wrote that Richard Hamm, the General Minister and President of my denomination in the United States and Canada, spoke of my faithfulness to what I believe at the Northern California Regional Assembly. I don't take this as personal flattery but rather as an indication that this witness has a positive effect.

This all points to the power, by God's grace, of prison witness—"a presence of absence" of all twenty-five of us. It is, at least in part, what the Latin Americans mean when they recite the names of the victims of the SOA and respond with *Presente!*

I spoke on the phone with Mary Ellen. She still hopes to come Memorial Day weekend although she only recently realized that it's not the last weekend of the month.

I also spoke at length with Yvonne at SOA Watch Georgia. It was a good thing I called when I did for several reasons. I found out that apparently of the twenty already in prison only Randy and I can make collect calls out. If that's true then the experience of the twenty is varying widely. She said I am one of only some who seem to be receiving most of their mail and not having items removed. It did appear that a 2-day priority packet from the lawyer from Seattle was held up. It was mailed May 1 and I received it the evening of May 7. The lawyer failed to address it in the "legal mail" format required to keep it from being inspected by the BOP.

I wrote a reply to the Seattle Clemency Committee and need to go to the library to get copies made. Inmates can get copies made for legal purposes only. They deduct a per page fee directly from your commissary account. I'll do that now. It's so windy I'm almost being blown off the patio this early evening anyway.

May 9

The little daisy plants that were mowed down are trying to make a come back on the lawn. I spied one blossom on one plant this morning.

Very little is stirring. The men were up late last night as on all weekend nights. Some were talking on the phone until 3 a.m. just up the hall from me. Usually the "no call after 11 p.m." rule is enforced by the officers. I was more bothered last night than usual. Usually I can roll over and not be disturbed despite the noise. Other men have asked how I can do that. Well, I couldn't last night. Racket is a basic ingredient of prison life.

I can't seem to get my mind going on a poem. Perhaps I'm just not waiting expectantly for one. I find that I have to be in a receptive listening mode for their arrival. I haven't been doing that lately. It's difficult when you're constantly interrupted with conversation and noise. There's nowhere here where I can be in solitude. Even in solitary, I understand, although I've not been there.

[Later] Bob Allen and Louise Rauseo came for their first visits. Bob in the morning. Louise with Nick in the afternoon. They said Joan is coming tomorrow. I went to the Mass tonight because there will be no service tomorrow. The chaplain will be away.

May 10

Mother's Day. A choir of fifteen men are serenading their mothers in Spanish. I understand it is a traditional event. They are gathered around the phone outside the clothing room. One after another they call their mothers collect, wish them a Happy

Mother's Day, hold the receiver while the choir sings, and then end their conversation. Some of them do not have mothers they can call but, nevertheless, participate for the sake of the others. It's a tender scene amid hard prison life.

Yesterday at 3 p.m. the 1-hour-long documentary *Father Roy: Inside the School of the Americas* was broadcast on the Las Cruces PBS Channel. Eight men viewed it at Camp 2. I had seen it previously. It was quite powerful for the men who saw it for the first time. I was playfully hazed for being "a TV star." I appeared on the screen for all of about ten seconds.

I had several conversations following the telecast. Some who missed it wanted to know when it would be shown again. Of course I don't know that it will. And, in here, that's not easily learned.

For the first time since I've been here the guard had to awaken me this morning. Though I was up and down some, I had rolled over one too many times. I went to bed a little later last night because I was pumped by the discussions that followed the telecast. I spent some time on the main smokers' porch listening to interesting stories and laughing at the humorous banter. One man finally had quite enough of hearing from others of my "celebrity." He put down the reason for my incarceration by saying that was nothing. He was in "for jacking off in a post office."

May 11

I put out 12 letters last night but I'm way behind again. This is "an occupational hazard" for SOA prisoners. I did a long letter to SOA Watch on several issues and sent the information with enclosures.

I made the mistake of working "too fast" this morning and finished ten minutes "ahead" of time for this turkey. He found something else for me to do and kept me overtime. It's like he's paying me the whole 12¢ per hour out of his own pocket. He trains the men in bad work habits and he thinks he's doing what he should. It's an insane practice. Among all the bosses he's singular. He continues to earn his low reputation. He could never hold a job or employees on the outside given his attitude and management methods.

I was working by myself this morning and will continue to do the work two or three normally do the rest of today and tomorrow. Doc is off today. Jack was released last Friday. No new men have been assigned. We have been having a very few arriving. Men are leaving at a steady pace it seems. A few more each week. One today. One this coming Friday that I know about.

Well, I'm going to start in on some more letter replies.

[Later] Overheard in the hallway tonight from men returning to the camp from their GED classes:

"Did you learn anything in school today?"

"Oh, all kinds of shit."

"Well, I'm so fuckin' happy for ya."

This is a typical prison conversation with a twist. It struck me as so typical that I just had to get up from reading a book on hope and write it down.

[Still later] It's breezy and quieter than usual here on the patio but it's still a long way from quiet. Nevertheless I often come here to continue my journaling in the evenings before I go to bed.

Last summer, as I was working my way through *The Artist's Way,* I realized that I must make some firm decisions, give my writing projects a time line and a deadline, and commit to completing my historical novel project. Perhaps that involves doing some of the writing here despite the fact that this environment seems an unfit context for such creative work. I do have Harris's example of its possibility although his job situation, including his work haven in the chapel and its uninterrupted blocks of time, is quite different than my daily reality. My time is cut into prescribed chunks every work day and I don't have the same sanctuary for writing.

Nevertheless it is important that I confront my procrastination on my biggest project and get on with it. It's too important to go undone. I have the sense, and always have, that it will require a sea change to accomplish it. I can't do it piecemeal. That's probably just “block” thinking. There’s no reason that it can’t be accomplished a piece at a time. But can I overcome my resistance to do it this way? Yes. If I commit myself to a time goal even if it has to be adjusted somewhere down the line.

May 13

I received several pages of contact photos of the Washington action from an Albany man. It’s not like being there, but it’s a pleasure to see the images. There are shots in Lafayette Park, at the Pentagon, and on Capitol Hill. While I know a good many of the people there are many more I don’t know. There was also a letter from Bernie about her experience of the Washington events. Another letter with enclosures from Mary Ellen. I got my first letter from my niece Cora from Japan.

Harris read me his third chapter last night and we had a long conversation on the patio after the commissary closed. He’s doing an outstanding job on his book about his father. It has universal appeal.

After lunch today my counselor called me over to the entrance to the administration building. “Mr. Butler asked me to straighten out the denial of Mr. Woods,” she said, or words to that effect. Mr. Butler is the camp administrator; the top dog of this camp. She said there were two Charles Woods with the same birth date on the law enforcement computer. Obviously the other is in some sense unsavory. She tried to get me to describe Punch physically. She said I was no help. I am absolutely terrible at physical descriptions. So it was no help. I asked, “Do they have the same middle name?” Duh. No. I knew Punch had included his middle name on the application. She said she’d “take a chance” and approve him as though it was some big favor she’s doing me. Obviously Congressman Kolbe’s staff made an inquiry. It’s still *who* you know that matters. I wrote to Punch this afternoon with the continuing saga of my visitor list which still is, if you include Punch, only 5 out of 10, plus 3 family members.

I wrote about 20 replies today. I'm all replied out at the moment so I will probably read and watch the NBA playoffs tonight.

I am enjoying reading the text of the Van Gogh drawing book sent by my potter friend. It is such a pleasure. I have learned details about what materials he used in his drawing—there were several—and how the pencils, charcoal, chalk, etc., were produced and where. He used milk to "fix" his drawings. Though he used many tools, he preferred a carpenter's pencil. The experimentation that Van Gogh did with his materials reminds me so much of Dad's way of working.

May 14

With wispy clouds in the sky this morning the dawn rose pink upon the prison camp. The beautiful beginning of what promises to be the same old day. But then, who knows what it will bring? I recall the psalm verse that was in my mind when I awoke March 22, the day I flew to El Paso to enter prison the next day: "This is the day that the LORD has made. Let us rejoice and be glad in it." That was a surprising thought to have in my mind at that time. It still is stunning. It was a gift that such a thought intruded on an otherwise dismal day.

There has been so much one-on-one talk of the SOA in here that I have learned new and better ways to briefly explain the situation. This prison experience has been helpful in that regard.

Harris read me yet another chapter of his unfolding book, "Bringing Home the Bacon," yesterday afternoon. He's very successful at crafting his story.

On May 1, the same woman who mailed me an inspiring quote last month sent another. ". . . [I]n your darker hours," she wrote, "take nourishment from Albert Camus' insight: 'In the depth of winter I finally realized that within me there lay an invincible summer.'" I especially need that word today.

May 15

I haven't been able to get Mary Ellen on the phone in two days. She is probably in Flagstaff at the Governor's Conference she told me about. I don't remember those dates.

Many inmates gathered around the television last night to watch the last episode of *Seinfeld.* I watched about half of it but found it boring. So I sat down and read several more pages of the Van Gogh book. I completed the long introduction and the first notes on the drawings themselves which include his first year of his work. He had a relatively short career as an artist [1880-1890].

The new help in the dining room isn't much help. He's "a lick and a promise" kind of guy. I had to follow up after him and redo many of the tables and napkin holders. He and the other inmate left with dirty tables still needing attention. He's been on the hill for years and has three months remaining to serve inside. I hope to find a way to get him to do at least a good enough job that I don't have to redo it after him. I'm not his supervisor, and I don't intend to be, but when things are left in a mess it gets me into trouble. I would just as soon not get scolded for poor or non-performance. How we do our jobs does affect the quality of our life as a community. Who wants to sit down to a dirty table to eat? None of us. At least we would prefer a clean space.

Carl Gooding is in his twenties. He weaves crucifixes and crosses by twisting and tying thread by hand. The "chain" as well. He does an excellent job of it. He was a small-time drug dealer and learned this craft "to keep from going crazy" while doing previous time in a Texas county jail. He makes a little extra money at weaving with orders from inmates and their family members. I had asked him to make me a cross with red and natural (straw-color) thread. Carl brought it to me last night finished. It's special because he made it. He won't let me pay for it. "God sent you to me just when I needed you," he said. "You are a godsend." Carl's a Catholic seeking more than a "jail-house religion," as he would put it. He has sought me out in the past, and we have talked when he initiated it, but I had no idea. I have decided to call it "The Cross of St. Paul," since I'm feeling more of a kinship with the Apostle. It will always be a reminder of these days.

May 16

I got a card and note from Mary Ellen giving me Julie's Flagstaff telephone number. She suggested I might call Friday night or Saturday. So I did call and got through last night. I talked quite a while to both Julie and Mary Ellen. Evidently Mary Ellen enjoyed her conference. She met and talked with a lot of people including some congressional staff aides. She continues to be very active regarding the SOA and the SOA 25 wherever she goes.

Dylan singing and on guitar with Luis on harmonica gave an impromptu blues concert last night on the patio. They used to play together up on the hill. Now they are reunited here in the camp. They are very good musicians. Luis' harmonicas are wearing out and he has only a couple of keys he can play on the two remaining. Unfortunately the policy on musical instruments has changed. While men can keep any already on the inside no new musical instrument can enter. Another punishment. Last night Dylan and Luis were playing for their own pleasure but many of the rest of us also enjoyed it immensely.

They denied Jean Miller, a Sister of Charity, visitation rights. You can't be too careful about these Catholic nuns. Maybe she can get reconsidered like Punch. This counselor of mine is going to transfer to FPC El Paso soon and the one who will be dealing with me, at least in the interim, is more sympathetic—I think. He went out of his way to get Sr. Joan Brown approved one Saturday when my counselor wasn't here.

A woman in Illinois, who was a winter visitor in Tucson, wrote that she had read about me in a Tucson newspaper story last January. She has been on a recent trip to South Africa and offered to send me Nelson Mandela's autobiography. I shamelessly took her up on it and told her of my 1988 fast at TCU seeking divestment at my alma mater.

Mary Ellen is coming for her first visit on Memorial Day weekend. I've written to her about the visitor dress code. No shorts, sleeveless shirts, or sandals. I suppose they don't want us inmates to get too excited.

May 17

Clouds look a little showery this morning. Mostly overcast and therefore a bit cooler. Yesterday was the warmest day since I've been here. They turned the evaporative coolers off in the heat of the afternoon. Then they froze us out by leaving them on all night. Just like the BOP.

Harris read me his sixth story on a bench near the dining hall. He said that after mental preparation it took him about three hours to write. It's another good one. He puts out high quality stories. I'm impressed.

I noticed yesterday that the two dorms, with a slight variation, are in a cruciform and wondered if there's a poem here.

Nick came to visit around Mass time. We went to the chapel together. He says he will pick up Mary Ellen at the airport and bring her here Saturday. She will stay at their house. Louise will be gone so she will use her car Sunday and Monday. Louise will be back later Monday, so Mary Ellen will have a chance to get acquainted with her, too, before she flies back Tuesday.

Nick said Gary MacEoin got a fax that Roy's out of solitary. Nick is going to try to find information on the web and send it to me. He was at Gary's book signing. I've known Gary ever since we worked together bonding out Salvadoran refugees from INS detention in El Centro, California, in the summer of 1981.

No *60 Minutes* tonight. The TV was needed to watch *MORTAL COMBAT!!!* The policy is that whoever has been in the TV room the longest gets to choose what channel to watch. This practice is usually followed and avoids conflicts. I am for that. But I'm certainly not into manufactured mayhem like *Jerry Springer, WWF Smackdown,* or *Mortal Combat,* among others that draw big crowds here.

May 18

A minor miracle last night. I have answered all my mail. This has not happened for six weeks. But another Monday mother lode is expected today.

I have time this morning for reflection, reading, and perhaps other kinds of writing. I wrote 70 replies, at least, last week. Oh, my achin' fingers. Though it is a chore I thoroughly enjoy it. It's a direct way to remain active in the movement toward true peace.

I had a random Breathalyzer test yesterday morning. Another first. I wasn't drunk.

Last week Mary Ellen sent me a computer printout of a bill I recently received at home totaling over $70,000 from a Tucson hospital for my heart transplant. Mary Ellen thought it would be good for a laugh. It was. She called and informed accounts receivable I hadn't had a heart transplant. As a matter of fact I was in federal prison at the time. Oops. Sorry. Computer glitch. Ain't technology wonderful?

Not long ago I received a jury duty summons at home. Mary Ellen called the county court to tell them I would not be appearing on the date as ordered. "Why?" they wanted to know. "Because he's in a federal prison." That must be a sufficient reason. I was excused.

May 19

I received a poem yesterday afternoon inspired by noticing a case worker through her office window poring over her paperwork. That appears to be all that we inmates are in this system.

Paperwork

No little boys here
with bloody skinned knees or stubbed toes
No little boys here
healing hugs or wiping our nose
It's less messy that way

No wounded souls here
seeking forgiveness, grieving blows
No wounded souls here
reaching out, risking other noes
It's less messy that way

We are paper men
computer punched analyzed woes
We are paper men
just numbers in digital rows
It's less messy that way

We are paper men
mere blips on society's screens
We are paper men
bytes of the statistical means
It's less messy that way

The case manager called me into her office later. It seems some media outlet wants to interview me. She wasn't even sure whom. The BOP needed my okay plus a written release later. She will tell the appropriate officer who will set up an appointment and get back to me. Of course I said yes. I'm interested in telling my story. I wonder who it is?

In an internet printout I received from Tucson, dated May 6, was this message:

> Following discussion at their recently concluded semi-annual meeting, the bishops of The United Methodist Church adopted a resolution urging President Clinton and Congress to close the School of the Americas as an act of solidarity with the poor and marginalized of Latin America. After hearing testimony from "the lips of our Latino constituents," the bishops concluded that the school is "perceived by the marginalized to be a source of oppression and a symbol of violence."

Hooray for the Methodists.

May 20

I have a medical callout this morning at 9:30. What for? Routine, I guess.

10:10 a.m. Signed release to speak with Richard Boren, *Texas Observer,* Austin, Texas. Time of the interview is not set yet.

A guard told me at lunch that I have "more mail than Camp 1" today. His statement was hyperbole but still quite a few. Monday through Wednesday this week I have received over 50 letters and cards from more than 30 different states. The thing that got me was the variety of people and their messages. There is one from a 78-year-old nun in Nebraska who said she wished she could be in prison with us. That can be arranged. There is a student at Union Theological Seminary who was at the Fort Bliss gate the day I surrendered who wrote, "In a time when so many of us search to become a disciple of Christ, your insistence on justice, healing, and love spoke louder than any of my books or early morning lectures." There was the letter and artwork from a second-grade girl in rural Pennsylvania, a member of the Bruderhof Community, who ends her letter by saying, "I hope we get to be good friends." What a blessing. The beauty of such messages sometimes bring tears to my eyes. Praise God for all things bright and beautiful.

I spoke to Jim Bob about the *Texas Observer.* He says it's a monthly liberal magazine that's been around for decades and has had reporters who have gone on to be "big names" in the business.

Letters to Contemplatives, sent from the Florida Center that Mary Earley is related to, arrived today. Mary requested they send a copy to all SOA 25. To me it is an unexpected witness to contemplatives. Obviously mine has been a stereotypical view. William Johnston writes a word of caution to those who would be contemplatives: "Do not think you are choosing a primrose path of dalliance. Far from it. There is no mysticism without renunciation; no mysticism without the cross." It was statements like these that kept me reading and I'm glad I did.

May 21

Day off. I was rudely awakened at about 4 a.m. Instead of rolling over I got up, dressed for breakfast (6-7 a.m.) and went down to a bench by the rose garden in the quadrangle again. As the light began to dawn I listened to the songs of the birds. We have some new ones here now. They arrived in the last week or so. I don't know what they are. I haven't discovered any bird books in the prison library. Too bad.

Completed reading *Letters to Contemplatives.* It gives me quite a very different slant on the contemplative life. The author mentions a couple of books by Japanese authors I want to look up when I get out—*Silence* and *The Bells of Nagasaki.* Johnston translated them. One of the things about Nagasaki I hadn't heard is that the A-bomb exploded right over the Cathedral where hundreds of Christians were praying at the time. That book is written by a survivor of the blast who, at the time he was writing, was dying of leukemia due to the nuclear radiation.

I'm looking forward to the arrival of some new books, including the Mandela autobiography from Illinois.

The men are talkative this morning on the patio. A lot of back and forth. Jim Bob asked for written materials about the SOA. I'll take some to him later today.

Earlier this week an inmate in my camp left for a halfway house. He has a singular kind of reputation here. The rumor is that he was in for embezzling millions of dollars from "the church." He is a lawyer and a minister of a non-denominational church. A good ole boy of the South. He presented himself as a paragon of religion, teaching inmates the gospel of abundant life; that is, God wants you to be rich and if you're not there's something wrong with you. Some fell for his schtick but more hated his guts. One asked if I knew this man's method of learning which money was his and which money belonged to God. "No," I said. "He throws all money into the air. All the money that does not fall to the ground is God's." These convicts couldn't stand his self-righteousness and slickness in recruiting a small cadre of loyal followers while he was here. He was able to do this largely by offering assistance in pursuing their legal cases. The day he left there was a spontaneous rejoicing in the camp. A cheer went up in our wing. Literally. Some dope dealers have a strict ethic. As one said, "He ranks right up there with baby rapists."

May 22

I talked to Mary Ellen briefly. Just checking in prior to her first visit tomorrow inasmuch as she has no way to get hold of me if she has a question. Everything is on schedule. I will be interested in knowing how it's coming with Jeannie and John managing the Burns house. Is he happy with the arrangement? This is more than I've thought about the business in two months.

I did some letter writing yesterday but also got some extra rest and read a lot.

The lawn has been mowed again. The little yellow daisies, that did make something of a comeback after the last cutting, have been chopped to smithereens again. Oh, well. With all the watering and weeding by the inmates in landscaping the lawns are looking pretty good, except around the edges. But I did like the wild beauty of the daisies.

I read another chapter in the Van Gogh book and I'm about through as far as the text is concerned. I would love to have a similar book of his paintings. Not all the text has been of interest to me. But I was interested in Van Gogh's experimentation with different materials for drawing and historical and scientific notes on the origin and composition of these materials. Those items relate to my thinking about Dad; his experimentation and experience. I see crossing points between Dad and Van Gogh despite Louis Freund's comment, on the day of our interview a few years back, rejecting my suggestion regarding Van Gogh's influence on Dad's painting. Louis flatly said Dad was a cubist. I think Dad's art was more complicated than that.

May 23

The Memorial Day Balloon Race is on. The launch site is at the county park just east of the prison. I read in the newspaper that the organizers expect about 65 participating this weekend. They are of all shapes and sizes and very colorful. The balloons seem somehow out-of-place floating freely above our prison.

Mary Ellen will be flying into El Paso this morning.

Poem idea:

Wise Up

Please and thank you
    on impostor tongues
Syllables of sadist's glee
Just a way to get to me
Civility
    a weapon becomes

They trip the tongue
    sweet and rippling
Words with magic power fraught

Just as Mother always taught
But now are meant
to be crippling

May 26

I didn't journal during the last three days while Mary Ellen visited. This was her first time here. It was wonderful to see her, to touch her, to be with her, to speak of things that concern us both.

Mary Ellen talked some of what transitions we might make following my release. I haven't thought much about such things. Almost nothing. But it's clear that I need to do that. I mentioned that I need to write Denny and let him know that I won't accept a reappointment as chair of the regional Commission on the Ministry. My term expires June 30. Two years served minus jail time. I want to change directions and priorities.

The only thing certain is that I am going to Fort Benning in November for the vigil. I have not decided about crossing the line yet. As a matter of fact, as I told John, I've made a conscious choice to hold off on a decision about that until after my time has been served. This doesn't have to be decided now. Such an incarceration has so many implications for personal health and family responsibilities that I need to revisit with the benefit of some perspective. It would be an easier decision if it were just me, but this commitment puts a burden on Mary Ellen.

We talked about my re-entry into the outside world. I hadn't really thought about it beyond gatherings with supporters both here and in Tucson. Mary Ellen suggested our going away together for a time. Julie and Daryl have offered their place outside of Flagstaff. She also raised the possibility of my spending time there writing. This was a new thought. She suggested that the business changes necessitated by my absence could become more permanent to free me up from those responsibilities. Obviously I need to be thinking more seriously about all this. I do want to go see Marvin as soon as I can unless he can come to me. I'm also thinking about whether to resign as pastor of the Arizona City congregation. I've been there since August 1987 and have considered leaving that part-time position before now to pursue my writing interests.

If I wish to do something regarding writing projects then I need to set myself some guidelines and deadlines for certain accomplishments. Perhaps I will want to add an update to my *Generations* poetry notebook for the family for Christmas adding new ones to the treasury.

Mary Ellen's helpful questions got me thinking in a more comprehensive fashion about what I'll do with my life when I get out of here.

She thought I was angry when I shared my frustration about the injustice of this so-called justice system. Well, I am angry. It's in the vein of righteous indignation as well as personal feelings. I aired them to her because I haven't had anyone to share such things with for a long time. Such a sense of outrage, it seems to me, must be shared personally not over the phone or in correspondence.

[Later] I learned at about 8 a.m. that my interview with Richard Boren of *The Texas Observer* was scheduled for this morning at 9 a.m. Boren had been to see Randy at Safford FCI already. He was interested in my personal story—why I'm involved, my experience in prison, and prison conditions. I had an hour with him in the visitors room. He took some photos and taped the interview. I know him from Tucson. He said he was a free-lance writer for the *Observer* and hoped to do pieces on this subject for other publications as well. He was very low key. He usually writes on environmental issues and that's how he knows Randy.

I had a good conversation with Rich yesterday morning. He lives in the next cell down the hall. I discovered he is a poet. We'll do some sharing. He has been writing a long time. He comes from a family of writers. He has a brother and sister who are published poets. Another brother is a screenwriter in Southern California.

May 28

I had a medical callout yesterday morning. Still no fingerstick test since I've been at La Tuna, but two blood draws. Yesterday my blood pressure was in the normal range.

Today I got a card Mary Ellen had sent the day before she came to visit and I wrote her a letter. Her visit was a great gift to me. I confessed that I put up a protective front to some extent because I have four months of this to endure. I feel the need to hold my emotions in check in this environment in order to survive. Despite the camp's benign appearance to an outsider this is still a prison. I also told her that although I wouldn't have done anything differently in regard to what got me here I am regretting the extra burdens and grief that it has put on her shoulders. She is handling it in the same good fashion she always does difficult circumstances. Nevertheless, I am sorry for the suffering I have brought upon her because of my commitments. There is a personal cost to this. The only worst cost would be *not* to have done it.

I did write to Paul to let him know I want him to come in September as he is planning, but that he should consider coming after Lee's birthday. Lee will be 13 on September 20. It is a rite-of-passage birthday for any young man I think he should not miss. I also wanted him to know I appreciate getting photos of his paintings and how impressed I am at his obvious talent. He sent me a picture of Lee and Kyle playing soccer and a photo of one of his watercolors. He is going on his annual Canadian fishing trip right about now.

Some supporters have tried to send me postage stamps to help out only to find they are considered contraband and it's not permissible. They can send money orders to me for my commissary account so I can purchase stamps. I am the recipient of some such gracious gifts.

I'm developing some new acquaintances through prison correspondence. It seems my poetry has opened some of this up. I'm grateful for the interest of a community college professor in California, a minister in Oregon, and a Catholic laywoman in New

Hampshire, among others. They have all greatly enriched my prison life.

Marvin writes that he is about at the point of putting his Mark manuscript out to readers and asked if the BOP would allow me to receive a copy of it. I wrote back to say I didn't see why not and that I am anxious to read it.

Yesterday was, relatively speaking, as quiet and uninterrupted day as I have ever had here. Of course, prison life is *never* quiet or uninterrupted.

I was called in by the new Camp 2 counselor and asked about Punch Woods. The transferred counselor did *not* approve his visitation before she left, as she said she would, and all that hassle is to be gone through again. The new counselor said he will "look into it" with the Camp 1 counselor. After more than two months I *still* have no visit approval for any Tucson friends.

May 29

I called Yvonne at SOA Watch Georgia. Roy came out of solitary by his own decision. He got "the plum job" of garbage pick up, he told her, that takes only an hour or two a day. That leaves him a lot of time to be active in correspondence and other pursuits. I asked Yvonne to send 25 copies of the fact sheet and the addresses of "the felonious five" which I don't have. I told her about *The Texas Observer* interview. She said that administrators in several other prisons had called the interviewees in for a "pre-briefing" before media visits probing for what they might say about any problems in the BOP system. That was not my experience.

I got several letters and cards again, including one from Fr. Dick Sinner of Fargo, ND. Fr. Sinner and I first met in El Centro, California, in the summer of 1981 when Tucsonans first bonded a group of Salvadorans out of INS detention. He was one of the celebrants at a Mass we had on the asphalt parking lot of the seedy motel where we were staying just after the release of ninety refugees.

For many years Fr. Sinner put up his inherited sections of North

Dakota land as collateral for Central American refugee INS bonds and was active in the Sanctuary Movement. His brother was the governor of North Dakota at that time. He once worked as a prison chaplain in Florence, Arizona, but he got fired for caring too much about the men there. That's a no-no. He had learned of my imprisonment.

Jim Bob Elder told a decidedly Texas story this morning at breakfast that bears remembering: A well-known and respected country doctor in the wide open spaces of West Texas spent his life serving people in the sparse small towns and ranches southeast of El Paso with his office in tiny Sheffield. One day two elderly single sisters from the even smaller town of Iraan, 14 miles away, came to see him. During his gathering of their medical history he asked, "Have you ladies been through menopause?" The two looked at each other, then one replied, "Not unless it's between Iraan and Sheffield."

I find it more difficult some days to sit down and write letters. But, without fail, when I get to it I find writing a personal response to my correspondents is very satisfying. No doubt some of these acquaintances I'm making will continue beyond my sentence.

May 30

Harris brought me two pens yesterday including this one. He also had a new poem. It just came to him, he says, like some do; the first stanza, then the next, and the next.

I may have a visitor today. Maybe not. Nick's away. I haven't seen Joan or Bob in a few weeks. Louise told me it would be late June before she could get back from her trip. I expect a downturn in both visits and correspondence during the summer months. We'll see.

Perhaps these can be more creative writing months. It's my focus on the SOA issue with correspondents that seems to be blocking my creative juices in other directions. It keeps my left brain so active that it dominates. I haven't learned to switch over effectively enough. More flexibility is a good goal for my life. It's one that needs exercising. I wonder how I might nourish my artist in prison? The possibilities seem so restricted. Maybe I'm not being intentional enough. I need to investigate. I have done several things already. For example, sitting on a bench near the rose garden very early before going to work at 5:30 and listening to the morning songs of the birds. Still the options seem quite limited in this purposefully cramped environment. So, what am I missing? The truth of the matter is that I wasn't taking advantage of the multitude of possibilities available when I was on the outside. So what's different here? It's a matter of mental attitude shaping perceptions and allowing myself to shut down. In this regard it's not so different from the outside world.

I've had a long talk with Lloyd while being here on the patio. I've learned more of his personal story. He's leaving for a halfway house about the same time as I will be released although he doesn't have a definite date as yet. He lived in Santa Fe for ten years prior to incarceration, but his wife has MS and is in a nursing home in Massachusetts near her aged parents. He hopes to be released to the Boston Area. Lloyd personally prefers the west but under the circumstances a move seems appropriate. He has a daughter in the Boston Area, too, and his other daughter will be moving there from Maryland. His son is in San Diego. So right now, as for years of imprisonment, he is a long way away from any family.

It sounds like my release will be September 18. The BOP here doesn't process releases on Saturday or Sunday. Since I am to be "released to the street," that is I don't have halfway house or probation required, they cannot keep me past the 20th. But nothing is certain.

My eye infection cleared up without antibiotics so it was probably viral. It had started on Friday after the early morning sick call so, of course, there was no possibility of medical care until Monday short of a life-threatening emergency. I finally got to see a doctor on Wednesday.

Well, I think I'll go inside and knock out a few more letters.

May 31

I had two visitors yesterday; Bob Allen and Joan Brown. They came separately and spanned almost the entire visitation time. Bob bought me lunch from the vending machines. I remember how shocked Mary Ellen was when I praised a machine sandwich when she was here. It's considered the best of the lot by the La Tuna vending machine connoisseurs. She was eating the same thing. If I thought *that* was good, she wanted to know, what was the food in the dining hall like? Everything is relative. I suppose it was an insight for her about prison reality.

In our conversation Joan and I discovered that we had met previously in Colorado Springs eight years ago when I went through in a Pastors for Peace pickup truck headed for El Salvador. Joan lived in the Springs at that time and was active in peace and justice issues. She was at the rally and we think she and others took the two of us to their house for lunch before we continued our journey south. What a small world indeed.

Bob and I talked about our loss of children. His daughter died of cancer at 28 three and a half years ago. Our son Mark died at age 23 eighteen years ago. Now there is an additional bond between us that emerged from talking about the loss of our children. It is a grief that is always with you.

Harris came over later in the afternoon with the tenth chapter for his book. He thought of this story while walking the track this morning and sat down and wrote "In the Bosom of God." The timing is incredible. It moved me to tears because it's subject coincides with what Bob and I where sharing earlier. It is about the death of a young man in his twenties.

I've written another letter to my correspondent who is a professor at a writing center in California seeking some publication information for Harris. I also asked her for a suggestion of a book on poetry writing. She just might be a resource that God is providing for the next leg of my journey.

CHAPTER 4

June: Prison Paranoia

June 1

This is our 45th wedding anniversary. I will try to call Mary Ellen collect today. It's a little too early yet. What a way to celebrate. I did leave her an anniversary card at home last March to be opened today.

I lost my cellie this morning. The officer woke Pablo up at 1 a.m. and told him to be ready to move out in forty-five minutes. He had requested to be transferred to a camp nearer his Fort Worth family. Garcia was in this cell when I arrived more than two months ago. Since then there has been only the two of us. He had several cellies in the two years before I arrived. He still has about that much time to go before a halfway house. He's probably transferring to El Reno, Oklahoma, but at this point even Pablo doesn't know where he's going. Security, don't you know.

I got a better pillow out of his departure and some items in his locker he decided not to take with him—a bowl, a cup, plastic spoons, pencils and pens, a fly swatter. I invited another inmate to take what he could use that was left before the BOP cleaned out the locker.

I have thought of writing some remembrance of Garcia. He never talked of why he is in and he never asked me questions. He was always helpful but never pushy. He did his thing and let me do mine. He had a sense of humor and was mature in his relations with others. His work here was as a camp plumber.

I'm going in to try to call Mary Ellen. Maybe I can catch her early in this anniversary day.

June 2

I did get her. We wished each other a happy anniversary by long distance. Elna Otter was there working in the office. She is one of the four volunteers that came forth from the community to help Mary Ellen with the office end of the business, which I normally do, while I'm away. It is truly amazing. Elna, Jane, David and Mark all are pitching in on various segments of my normal work load for our assisted care business. They generously say it is something they can do to be a part of what I'm doing. I think their giving this six months is truly remarkable.

Mary Ellen says John is planning to come visit the 7th and she's coming back the third Sunday of the month. He is having back problems again. Perhaps another ruptured disk. He's going to have tests to see if that's the case. Our long-time friend Malinda is arriving in Tucson tomorrow from Illinois for a five-day visit. Mary Ellen says they plan to have fun. In addition, the Ginger Beer Band is coming to Our Place Assisted Care Home to give a concert this week. Mark is the leader of the band. He is a full-time astronomer, an amateur composer-musician, and one of our volunteers. He is doing the billing to our residents each month on our computer.

I received some exceptionally good mail including three new books—one of selected writings of Dorothy Day, one of essays honoring Daniel Berrigan, and a third on storytelling. I've got into the Berrigan book quite a way already. It was a surreal scene last night. I'm reading about the Apostle of Peace on my bunk while across the hall the television set is going at full blast on *War of the Worlds Wrestling,* complete with the modern coliseum atmosphere of shouting crowds and the mayhem of mock violence masquerading as entertainment.

I dreamed last night that I took a group of young people to

their congressman's office for a visit. The congressman was comedian Tim Allen. I started sharing the word about the SOA 25 and the fact that I was in prison. I got angry at his flippant attitude and we were about to get thrown out when an officer woke me up at 5 a.m. to go to work at the dining hall.

June 3

I'm learning about writing from Harris' creative process. Now if I would *do* it. I am able to be a sounding board and encouragement for him. I do have a good editorial sense and a manner that does not block but encourages and nourishes his process. I know how to get him to use what he's got. And the more that we have experience together the better it goes.

I notice a small pencil drawing on the top of this brown metal patio table this morning. It's a small pot with flowers. A line drawing of simple beauty. A doodle I would guess. I wonder who's the artist? It's faint and my notebook was covering it. The human spirit persists.

I just can't put the Berrigan book down. It has some gripping stuff in it. The memories of Dan are revealing and often funny. He once suggested prison clothing as the "clerical attire for a new church." On the last day of one semester Dan took his Loyola University students on a field trip that was also their final exam on The Acts of the Apostles. They all got arrested at the New Orleans federal building for demonstrating against U.S. policy in El Salvador. Dan called out to his students as they were put in the police wagon, "Everyone gets an A!" Showing a friend the very comfortable Jesuit residence in New York, he remarked, "If this is poverty, bring on chastity." "If you want to follow Jesus," Dan once said, "you better look good on wood." And on a more direct note he has said: "We don't have peace because we don't have peacemakers, and we don't have peacemakers because there's a cost to making peace, and we don't want to pay the cost of peace."

June 4

Mark's 42th birthday. I still grieve his death. The pain is still with me. I suppose it always will be. Oh, my beautiful son, how I miss you.

Yesterday I took the day off as much as anyone can as a prisoner. No callout. An extra nap during the day. I finished *Apostle of Peace.* I feel like I know Dan Berrigan from the testimony of his friends and family. The book was honoring him on the occasion of his 75th birthday, May 9, 1996. The testimony is personally challenging. His persistent peaceful witness speaks directly to my journey and reason for being here.

Also I wrote, and put in the mail, a short article for Joan Brown's community Justice and Peace Network newsletter. She had asked me for such an article last month to include with one by Sr. Mary Kay Flanigan who is in the Pekin prison. It was a good thing I asked her to remind me in writing because it had slipped my mind. That is, what I have left of it.

Here is what I wrote. I concluded with my poem, "November 16, 1997" written the early morning of November 17 in Georgia as we waited for arraignment before a federal magistrate:

Present in Absence

Where two or three are gathered together in my name, I am there in the midst of them.
—Matthew 18:20

It is truly remarkable how palpably present persons can be even when they are absent. Those of us serving sentences in SOA prisons around the country these days are reminded through correspondence that despite our absence we are present in the continuing prayers and protests of others.

A brief note on a postcard arrived at the La Tuna federal prison in early May. It was from an Arizona friend. He had just participated in a regional assembly of my religious community. He was recalling how a colleague once spoke of the reality of "presence in the mode of absence." This came to mind, he said, because "in this way you were with us this weekend."

That prompted me to think again of that November day in Georgia. I remembered how it was when that river of witnesses crossed the line into the U.S. Army reservation that hosts the school of assassins.

As the silent procession moved forward toward arrest, a drumbeat punctuated the reading of names of SOA victims. The names of the absent ones were read aloud one after another for the longest time. And, one after another, the crowd of witnesses responded, *Presente!*

In the justice of God prisoners of the U.S. Government, as all the victims of the SOA, are present in our absence. And the day of closure for that evil institution draws near.

November 16, 1997

At the sound of heartbeats
a river flows uphill winding
among cold gray stone
as a lone hawk watches
soaring protectively overhead

A river of witnesses flowing
from the safety of silence
to speak with their bodies
Basta! Basta! Enough!
To stop the unspeakable

Tortured cries echo through
towering piney wood

as autumn oaks and maples
quiver with red and yellow
death in quiet procession

The stillness of the massacred
moves on a chilly breeze
across soft Georgian hills
their crimson clay bleeding
burnt by innocent blood

Only two pieces of mail yesterday which is the lowest number in a day since I started receiving mail. Still that's a whole lot more than most inmates receive.

Today I need to get to letter writing but I have decided that I should take my days off to do some different things like reading. I can do my letter writing on all the other days.

June 5

I changed my mind. I got several letters done and in the Friday mail. Then I started the book of Dorothy Day's writings.

The Nuclear Resister quarterly arrived. There's quite a bit in it on the SOA 25 this time. They have published a poem by Carol Richardson. I have heard she is being strip-searched every time she has a visitor. Her poem is about that.

The Search
by Carol Richardson

The two of us again,
"Just doin' her job."
I hope she won't
But she does.

Rings? Watch? Glasses?
No. No. No.
Shoes first
Shake out the socks.

She chats. I strip.
Naked. Exposed.
Stranger eyes penetrate.
Touching, unwanted
touching.

From another place
I watch it happening
Me watching not-me
Until it is done.[4]

As I have been sitting here an officer headed for the administration building with an inmate in handcuffs. What? This man works in the kitchen. He worked this morning. They paged him to the Camp 1 office just prior to leading him away. It could be most anything. He has a lip on him for one thing.

I wrote a long letter to Mary Ellen. She usually doesn't write long letters but only snatches of little notes on greeting cards. I know she is very busy so that doesn't bother me in the least. What bothers me is her sometimes indecipherable penmanship together with often incomplete thoughts on a page. It's daunting. I teased her tonight by writing something like, "Sometimes everything runs together in your little notes. No periods. No paragraphs. I spend a lot of prison time trying to decipher them. I've only got six months."

Well, I finally got a letter from our eldest son Bruce. He invited me to call collect. He's not much into writing but he did enclose five recent snapshots of his daughter Katelyn who's three and a card she made just for me. In addition to her creative artwork she wrote, "HI GRANPA! ♥ Katelyn." Now how sweet can you get?

The photos and card are going in my commissary-purchased photo album. Such messages are singularly sustaining.

And, finally, I got a letter from my sister Lynn. It's a very funny "Lynn letter," as hers always seem to be. For one thing I had written her about the trees, Mexican Elders, that stand at the entrance to my camp unit. In a pixie play on words she wrote: "I suppose if you had an avenue lined with Mexican elders it would be a pretty sensational sight."

No one else has been assigned to my cell since I lost my cellie Monday. Several men have as many as three. Right now we are having several leave each week and very few new guys coming in. But that could change overnight. It's just another of those things in life now out of my control. So I just pray for the best and take what comes. Garcia was generous in helping me get settled into the prison routine. He did his thing and I did mine. In here that's called "doing your own time."

I sent my journal pages, up to this partial one, on to Mary Ellen. I want to get all these pages home. I'm concerned they could be confiscated by the BOP.

I have almost done this pen in. I've gone through a lot of them already indicative of the amount of writing I'm doing.

June 6

Last night we experienced our first walk-away since I've been here. A walk-away is what they call an escape from a prison without perimeter walls. I was awakened, as was everyone in Camp 2, a little before 1 a.m. The room light was turned on. Two officers shook me awake and asked my name and number. It seemed to take me forever to answer them. I had been in a deep sleep. Oscar left between the 10 p.m. and midnight head counts. He's a very athletic young man, 6'1" and muscular, who did a lot of running around and around the prison track. He had been brought down from the hill less than a month ago. He was working in the food service warehouse and living in the cell next to mine. He had varying lengths of time remaining depending on which rumor you choose to believe. After they were satisfied who had walked they took everything from his locker and stripped his bed. It took a while to get back to sleep. I still feel that interruption this morning. Some believe Oscar headed directly for Mexico. They say he has family there. The border isn't that far away. We will never learn what happened to him.

Yesterday was a hairy day. First a man went to the hole for arguing. Then at short line, about 10:15 a.m., someone broke the safety glass in an exit door of the dining hall and eventually four were taken to the hole because none of them would talk and the officers think one of them did it and the others know which one. Having five men out of food service stretched our human resources. I was lucky enough to arrive after the incident and didn't personally see or hear anything regarding it. Then Oscar takes off after 10 p.m. count.

The story was retold here today of one legendary convict who walked away. He made it across the Rio Grande. As the story goes he stood on the opposite shore waving obscene gestures and cursing the BOP officers who had pursued him. What the escapee didn't realize was that his geography was a little bit off. At that place in the river he was still on United States soil. Imagine his surprise when he was captured.

And that's not all. The powers-that-be took all the small tables, with compartments underneath, from the cells in both camps. That's the vast majority in Camp 2 including mine. So I don't have a table to write on until they get around to replacing them. By BOP policy each cell is to have one. Most of them were welded shut, but because of "inmate misuse," using them to store "contraband" items like food, they are gone for now. I do have a clipboard I purchased from the El Paso commissary. That helps a little. This morning it's both sunny and windy on the patio. I'm having to hold this paper down.

My new counselor approached me at lunch yesterday about why Sr. Jean had been denied visitation rights. I told him it beats me why a Catholic nun would be denied. He didn't understand it either. Jean had called and inquired. By 12:30 he had her approved. He brought me a new visitation list. Punch Woods, Jean Miller and Marvin have been added. No one else from Tucson approved or denied, so I wonder if the other four applications I sent have been returned. Now all the El Paso/Sunland Park friends are on the approved list. Punch is the only one from Tucson. All family, who are likely to be visiting, have now been approved. So if we can get the four Tucson friends processed my list will be complete.

John arrived and we had a good visit. I had not got the date of his visit straight in my head. I thought he was coming next weekend. He seems to be doing very well. He's trying to become a better person. He's not unaware of his good points and that's positive. But he's not just accepting his not-so-good points and is looking to deal with them.

He will hear back about the MRI of his back next week. He says he doesn't want to have any more surgery but wants to find other ways to deal with his pain. Nevertheless the numbness in his feet and legs sounds serious. Unfortunately back problems seem to run in the family.

He's interested in getting more family-involved. John says this experience with Mother and with me in prison has brought home the gaps in our relationship to him as never before.

I was quite saddened to hear that the broken door glass at the dining hall has been laid at Jay's feet. The others are out of the hole as of this morning. It's said that Jay won't be coming back and will be charged with the destruction of government property over $100. It is said that could add as much as two years to his sentence. It is rumored that the others "ratted" on him, saying they saw him do it. It seems suspicious to me that the original three picked up are all socially-related and are getting off. To me it seems more likely one of them broke the glass. I wasn't there. So I don't *know* anything. Jay is so laid back it just seems unlikely to me that he would do it even accidentally. It's said the door was locked at the time. In any case, it was a case of bad judgment, an accident, and doesn't demand a 2-year prison term. If that result does come down it would be sheer vindictiveness on the part of the BOP. I hope he can get a good lawyer.

I like Jay. He's one of my earliest friends here. Very early on he dropped by my cell to say he knew why I was here, that it's unjust, and he wanted to know more about the SOA although he already seemed quite knowledgeable.

We got four out of five guys back in food service today but will be missing the one who appeared to be the most responsible of the lot. I wouldn't wish two years of imprisonment on anyone. Most certainly not for such a minor incident as this. It is obviously a big deal to the BOP who seem poised to make Jay an example.

June 7

Well the BOP is restless. One inmate having walked away they did two additional counts last night before bedtime. I don't know how many extra were accomplished during the night. I didn't stay awake to find out.

I didn't write letters yesterday. It's harder getting to letter writing since my table is gone. But I've got to get to it. I'm way behind. I read about Dorothy Day instead. It's a most challenging collection of writings.

Julie wrote about little Darik needing his first stitches. She wrote that the stitching process seemed to hurt his older brother Dyan more than it did him. It reminded me of the time when both Marvin and I were about the same ages as Julie's Darik and Dyan. We were climbing in a neighbor's apple tree. Marvin was inching out on two little parallel limbs, his feet on one and his hands holding onto the other above him. The one under his feet snapped, leaving him momentarily dangling from the one he held on to. It broke right away and he fell ten or twelve feet to the ground. It was grassy but there was a rock there, too. He bumped his head on the rock and it put a gash in it. I remember how bad I felt being the older brother who shouldn't have let him get hurt.

His blood poured out profusely as with any head wound. I got him home. We were both crying and bloody, and it took Mother some time to figure out which of us was hurt.

Julie also wrote about her African violets. I sure miss mine. They are so beautiful. Mary Ellen says there are a couple at home that need me to "yell at them" again. I wrote Julie the "yelling at the violets" story. I had a couple that would never bloom. One day I yelled at them. I told them in a loud voice that if they didn't get busy and blossom they were going in the dumpster. In less than a week buds began to appear. They rapidly became two very beautiful bloomers. I told Mary Ellen I should have yelled at them a long time before I did. I wrote Julie she might try that if she needs to sometime. But she has to mean business.

June 8

This is our granddaughter Amanda's birthday. It's also our former daughter-in-law Linda's birthday. She is married now to Dan. We still keep in touch. I'm thinking of both birthday girls today. There are several family birthdays this month.

Worked overtime after breakfast and I'm really feeling it. The boss said to wash the windows inside and out. I didn't do those that need a ladder or the outside windows that have screens, and where one must reach over three feet from the outside wall to the window, which would be death on my back for sure.

In the late afternoon yesterday an inmate had an allergic reaction to a new medicine they gave him that nearly killed him. He lost consciousness in the shower. Some thought he might be having a stroke or heart attack. He had stopped breathing. One of the staff was about to give him CPR when he started breathing again on his own. He had been given a diuretic for water retention that caused hives some weeks ago. He was allergic to it. Well, come to find out, the medicine they substituted was of the same drug family only twice as strong. They finally took him to the FCI hospital up the hill. I went into the chapel to pray for him last night. It's all I could do. He got back to his room a little before midnight. He is off work for a couple of days recovering and will be medically-monitored a little more closely for awhile. It could have been a lot worse.

I have heard of a man here who died of a heart attack for the lack of timely medical attention shortly before I arrived. There are no medical staff assigned here. They come here only at specific hours on specific days from the clinic on the hill. I have come to know men who have suffered greatly from what I would call the BOP's criminal neglect of their serious medical conditions.

Joan came for a visit yesterday afternoon while I was in the Protestant service at the chapel. I didn't respond to the page so the BOP launched a search until they found me. I couldn't hear the page in the chapel.

A new chaplain was being introduced and preached. He's a Baptist who has been a pastor and a missionary in South America and the Caribbean. One can only wonder why he's working for the BOP. His sermon, as much as I heard, had some good points and was much more gospel than we usually hear. One wonders if he will be censored and tamed by the system or fired. As strange as it seems I hope the latter. He obviously has some experience and talent. The fact that he is bilingual makes him even more effective at La Tuna.

Harris says this man either got pushed out of the Baptist Church or jumped. Having had experience in Latin America as an evangelical, one wonders what his reaction to this prison life will be. If he spends any time at FPC perhaps I'll get acquainted with him. The three chaplains we have now also serve the more than 1500 men up the hill at the FCI.

June 9

It's 6:45 p.m. I usually journal right after my breakfast shift, but I had a callout this morning for the whole morning for a pre-release session on community resources. Almost everything didn't apply to me, but I did learn more about the halfway house, probation, and other elements of the system that affect most prisoners lives for years.

I got a new cellie. This is his first time in and he's frightened spitless. All of a sudden I am "the veteran" explaining the routine of this rotten system. Adam Finley surrendered this afternoon as ordered. He had some kind of heart surgery in February. He has trouble hearing. I think he's in his 50's. He was reared in a church family, so he's not reticent to speak about religious issues. As a matter of fact it seems he's not reticent to speak period. Jim Bob had told him quite a bit about me before bringing him to my cell.

I just had to go find Finley and remind him to go get his medicines. Pill line at the dispensary is at 7 p.m. He had forgot, which isn't unusual when a man first comes in. For some of us it's not unusual any time.

Today I made an appointment for a haircut tomorrow at 12:30, if I don't have a callout at that time, with the camp barber. He's an inmate especially assigned to that job. I have the next two days off work.

June 10

After I started washing my laundry I sat down on the bench in the small covered porch area of the prisoners' self-service laundry because it's drizzling this morning. I brought the Dorothy Day book with me to read while my clothes wash and dry. I did receive the Mandela autobiography *Long Walk to Freedom* from the generous person in Illinois. I've only read a few pages in it so far.

Lloyd is reading *Cimarron Rose* by Burke, a novel newly out in paperback, first published in 1997. It includes a character who is a Latin American drug lord who was trained at the SOA. I will write SOA Watch to let them know that the issue is finding its way into the popular media.

Matt Rogers has constructed a lot of natural rock walls, concrete benches, and walkways while he's been here. And he continues to expand his work. A major project since I came is a small area between one wing of Camp 1 and the clothing room. He's built low walls with benches, a flower bed area and a lawn between. It's a work in progress though much of it has been completed. It really has improved the looks of the place. Already it has become the preferred area at Camp 1 to sit and converse, smoke and meditate. Yesterday I noticed a new handmade sign posted on the lawn. Obviously it has been informally dedicated. The sign reads: "Dead Pecker Park."

To my reading and, later, letter writing.

June 11

I'm getting acquainted with my new cellie. Adam Finley's sentence is thirty months on a conspiracy charge. He has been a crop duster, an Air Force pilot, a test pilot, and for the last decade and more an aircraft broker and expert in the certification of military aircraft. This is, he says, his "first brush with the law." Though he's from Oregon, his trial was in Tucson. He and a co-defendant had an eight-week trial last fall. I vaguely recollect it in the news at the time. It had something to do with charges of fraud and conspiracy in trading military aircraft. He doesn't believe he's guilty of any wrongdoing.

Finley's had two heart surgeries and is already having problems because he has yet to be given the three medicines he brought with him or any BOP-prescribed substitutes.

Just now I left to find him because he failed to do the census count. Finley has hearing problems that make the public address announcements all a garble for him, he says. I found him in the dispensary with the PA and asked the PA to call Camp 1 office to tell them where my cellie is.

When he came to self-surrender the BOP had not shared any information with him. Not even the location of the camp beyond "Anthony, TX/NM." This same thing happened to me. When I called El Paso FPC they wouldn't answer the most basic questions.

The person I talked to was very irritated and said, "You'll get all that at orientation after you get here."

Finley was told by the judge he was being sent to La Tuna because of the superior medical care he would receive here. What a totally sick joke.

He wasn't told what he could and could not bring. Nothing. He didn't know there are two prisons here. When he asked the cab driver to take him to La Tuna he was taken to the correctional institution on the hill. They told Finley they had no paperwork on him and sent him away without ever mentioning the prison camp. Of course the cab was gone by that time. He started walking toward Anthony and spied the camp through the apple orchard and walked to it. Sure enough this is where he was to report.

After arriving some inmates, who have served time on the hill, told him that many others who have experienced this same thing were incarcerated on the hill for months before being brought down although they should have reported here in the first place. One told him, "Count yourself blessed that they turned you away."

Finley is *very* verbal. I don't know if this will continue or if it's just a nervous need he has in these first days. This morning I moved my letter writing to the Chapel where I enjoy two pluses. My cellie isn't talking my ear off and I have a table to write on. But I may be run out of here at any time for no good reason. It happens.

I am enjoying my two days off this week and getting a little extra rest each afternoon in one-half to one hour naps. I plan to get a haircut this afternoon. It was scheduled for yesterday but circumstances pushed it to later. Just as I was about to enter the barber shop the power went down in the whole camp and stayed out for about an hour. We had light rain on and off all yesterday but the sun is out again today.

June 12

It was only by perseverance that I got my first prison haircut. I waited around for an hour, after waiting around several hours the day before, and had to give up on it. This time the guard wouldn't unlock the barber shop door for the inmate. He kept putting the barber off. It's just a little harassment some of the more sadistic officers enjoy doing. So I just left. The barber looked me up several hours later, after a changing of the guard, and said he could do it then so I went with him. The cut cost me five postage stamps.

I got a new half-page summer action piece from SOA Watch that I can use as inserts in my letters out. I will write Yvonne requesting more copies. I have no way of making photocopies here.

My new cellie went to the unit manager, at my urging, about not having any of his heart medicines. He got his most important one dispensed last night though they have "lost" his other two, they say. They found the one at the FCI. Adam told me that the unit manager came by our cell in the afternoon checking on him. He knew all the details of the problems Adam has been experiencing, including no prison ID issued, therefore no commissary privileges, no medicine, and so forth.

Quite frankly the unit manager makes sure that every incoming inmate has an added dose of fear put in him as soon as he arrives. The man sees this as his job and he's good at it.

Adam told me that he and others had been talking about how they could "get me in trouble" so I couldn't leave when my time's up. It was meant as a compliment, I suppose, but I told him it wasn't funny.

I'm back down at the chapel this morning doing this journal page and ready to write some more replies. I must remember to ask Mary Ellen to send a money order for my commissary account.

Last night Adam asked why so many in the camp like me. "I didn't know they did," I replied. It appears that he's ingratiating himself. I'm not the only one getting such attention from him.

It's particularly strange that Adam's not been given any A&O work so far and he seems to have the run of the camp. He's quick to introduce himself and get acquainted. I'm afraid I'm suspicious his real name could be Jesus Cruz. [Jesus Cruz was one of the government informants inserted into the Sanctuary Movement in

Arizona in 1984.] I need to be careful and check some things through with Tucson folk about him.

[Later] Harris abruptly appeared at my cell with a man and a table in tow this afternoon. He said the man was going to give it to someone else but he and another inmate talked him into giving it to me because "You need it for all your letter writing." The man made it but wouldn't take anything for it from me, so I guess Harris had already paid him something. Inmates have no cash. We barter by using our commissary credit and personal items we can exchange. The table-maker didn't say a word. Harris did all the talking. I thanked him from the heart. It bothers me that I don't even know his name, but I'll find out. There's probably a poem in the gift of the table. I'll muse on it.

I got called back to food service tonight while I was in the shower. So was Doc. We're both in our sixties and this BOP boss who ordered us back is in his thirties. We were told, "You men are doing excellent work. But you are only inmates. Don't you forget it. Don't ever leave this dining hall until you've checked out with me first," the little bastard said. "So you will remember this, get busy and clean those service shelves." What a power trip. With this one it's not surprising.

June 13

In a card from Marvin he says he'll start a new treatment for his cancer on June 15 for four consecutive Mondays. He calls it "the magic bullet." It is a brand new medicine only recently FDA-approved that, as I understand it, seeks out cancerous tumors and denies them their blood supply thus killing them. It's an antibody.

June 15

No journaling yesterday but did letter-writing and had my first visit from Sr. Jean of Sunland Park, New Mexico.

I was thinking of my congregation during Mass. The hymns

are so spiritually moving in this environment. They nourish the soul. This aspect of worship was heightened for me during my first long water-only fast in 1988 and that sensitivity has remained with me to this day.

One hymn we sang this week brought all the Arizona City friends to the top of my heart. The refrain is:

> One bread, one body,
> one Lord of all,
> one cup of blessing which we bless.
> And we, though many
> throughout the earth,
> we are one body in this one Lord.[5]

The tune is so joyful. So full of light and love.

We pass the peace before communion but in here there are no hugs like in Arizona City. We certainly could use them. We run terribly low on hugs in this place. There's an antidote to despair every Lord's Day dispensed in this "Chapel of New Hope." Following the passing of the peace we sing a song of faith every week. These two stanzas are very healing:

> Peace is flowing like a river,
> flowing out of you and me.
> Flowing out into the desert,
> setting all the captives free.
>
> Love is flowing like a river,
> flowing out of you and me.
> Flowing out into the desert,
> setting all the captives free.[6]

We are literally captives in the desert. God blesses thirsty days like these when we drink deep from the wellsprings of the Spirit in this desert.

Harris wrote his 14th chapter yesterday. He got the idea and had the written chapter three hours later.

I'm feeling a little better about my cellie, but remain cautious.

June 16

I'm back to being more cautious because of more unusual behavior and talk. I talked with Harris about my suspicions as I did before. I cautioned another neighbor to be on his guard until the facts are in. Finley's back to no duty this morning.

I called Mary Ellen. She and Frankie are driving over together. I finally remembered to ask her to send commissary money.

My mail included letters from Rick McDowell and Kathleen Rumpf in response to my letters to them. What wonderful people. I'm richly blessed by knowing both of them. We first got acquainted by fasting together on the U.S. Capitol steps four years ago.

Another pen is running out of ink. I wrote forty or more letters just this last weekend. I finally wrote to my regional minister saying no to chairing the Commission of the Ministry a second term. I asked him to supply the Arizona City pulpit through September so Mary Ellen and I can have a little time right after I get out.

Marvin started his new round of medication for lymphoma yesterday.

One of the young men gave an ice water bath to Lefty, who was in the entry to the self-service laundry last night. Lefty is leaving today. This baptism is a local ritual indulged in by some. Then at 4:30 a.m. this morning there was a retaliatory attack while the instigator was in his bunk asleep. He wasn't asleep for long. Neither was the entire G and H wings. And maybe E and F. The noise was not what anyone would wish to awake to any morning. I'm told that when such childish pranks get out of hand all the inmates pay for the horseplay of the few. It happened at Camp 1 not too long ago.

June 17

I received an absolutely hilarious letter from Steve. Among other things he said his congressman, "Who goes to our church and voted to cut funds for SOA," doesn't want to co-sponsor HR611 to close it "because it takes too much time away from his search for his spine." He closes with the postscript: "Remember, it's always darkest right before you open your eyes."

I also learned that Canadian winter members at Arizona City, Suzanne and Stig, participated in a demonstration with the Toronto SOA Watch in front of the U.S. Consulate there recently.

My cellie got his first letters. He has a medical callout today. Finley wasn't given any work duty yesterday. Harris made another suggestion about what's going on with him. Finley could be pumping people for his own benefit. Perhaps he's trying to discover information that he could trade for his freedom or at least a reduced sentence. I've learned he's using the same prying ploy on more people than just me. I'm not the only one who is suspicious of his motives. Yesterday I found a package of fig newtons in my locker. He had been to the commissary the night before. He said he knew I liked them. I had shared one with him before he had commissary privileges. I'm still trying to figure him out.

There are two things I'm reflecting on besides my cellie. One is that I'm often awaking with specific music and lyrics on my mind. This morning it was "Make me an instrument of your peace," The Prayer of St. Francis. We rather unsuccessfully tried to sing it last Sunday at service and here it comes back to my consciousness upon waking three days later.

Second, I have been perceiving images of faces when I first close my eyes at night preparing for sleep. When I begin to concentrate on them, try to make out who they are, they quickly fade away. They come one face at a time. Actually the images are of three-dimensional human heads. I have the impression that there have been more than one person. The last time it seemed the vision was of more than one, but one at a time. I seem to recall a fade in and out where there were more than one for a few moments. They are all in gray tones.

These images are not in any way frightening. On the contrary these mysterious experiences are incredibly nourishing to my spirit. I don't believe such mystical experience is unique but who can explain such gifts?

June 18

Another thing I realized yesterday afternoon when writing about these phenomena is that the music comes in the mornings and the images at bedtime. It didn't occur last night or this morning and doesn't come when I am thinking about it. I can't consciously manipulate their occurrence. It's a spiritual gift, pure and simple.

Harris was denied his furlough for a ridiculous reason. He's certainly no flight risk. He was hoping he could spend some time with his aged parents because of some problems they are having these days. The BOP gives this possibility with one hand and takes it away with the other. The real reason for the denial is the local administrators decided to pitilessly pull Harris' chain. They used this opportunity to remind him once again who's boss. To twist the screw. "You have nothin' coming." Due to established procedures he will not be able to reapply until his next scheduled team meeting which is next March. This means there will be not be sufficient time between then and his release date for him to be eligible. It's the classic Catch 22. The written policies have no relationship to the reality. They are there apparently only for public relations purposes. You see it again, again, and again.

A young inmate's father was killed this week in a motorcycle accident. He was told the only way he could go to the funeral in Louisiana is escorted. He would have to pay his own expenses, plus the escort's expenses and salary, if they would allow it. The old-timers say they will not allow it. They've never known it to be allowed. Nevertheless the BOP has been stringing this young man along for days now with this improbable hope. They are adding bitterness to his grief. What princes of purgatory. It's very hard to have to deal with such a loss without such charades. To make matters even worse many of his prison buddies expect him "to take it like a man."

On a brighter note, I have been enjoying the baby birds. The swallow nests are full of new ones. One prison nest has five babies. Their beaks are the biggest thing about them. Open and hungry. The parents are catching insects and flying back and forth all day. There are several nests in the compound that I know about. The birds keep the insect population under control. There's beauty and hope in this new life.

June 19

East of Eden

Baby birds
Hungry beaks
Praising words
Psalmist speaks

Mother sings
Prophets say
Grown-up wings
Fly away

This is the final form of the poem that came yesterday. The images transform it from my simple observation to a universal reality.

For some reason such construction as this 3.3.3.3. meter seems to come most often in my experience. A simplicity is called for due to length. This one moved to a rhythmic pattern that often comes to me. But why not a six-line measure or a different meter? I have no idea. This is what was given this morning.

I finished up the Dorothy Day book yesterday and got a good start on Nelson Mandela's autobiography. No writing of letters at all yesterday. Received only two tying my lowest daily total to date. Perhaps this means time to write other things during the next two months. But today I need to get some letters written. I won't get to it this weekend because I will be enjoying Mary Ellen's visit over Father's Day.

June 20

Three months from today I'll be out of here. Maybe a day or two earlier depending on the arcane calculations of prison professionals. I should find out about that at my team meeting in July.

The new chaplain came by the cell to meet Adam Finley. He said he had heard about me. I gave him one of the summer issues of the SOA Watch newsletter. I might as well educate him, too.

A neighbor brought me a Father's Day card for a son. He has only daughters, he said. I'll send it to one of my sons belatedly. Another inmate questioned me about the reason for all my mail which was yet another opening to share my story with two more neighbors. I went and got him a SOA fact sheet.

Yesterday was a captivating day. No pun intended. I'm 175 pages into Mandela's totally engrossing tome.

June 21

Beautiful quiet morning with a slight cool breeze as the sun rises warmly over the Franklin Mountains in the east.

My cellie and others claim to see UFO's in the eastern night sky. Bright lights moving erratically. Sometimes the lights are brighter, they say. Reportedly they "were seen" the night before by some. Adam got me out of bed to go see them. I never saw them in 20 minutes of looking at the sky. I wasn't the only one who didn't though several claimed to be viewing the phenomenon while the others of us didn't see a thing off the east porch of Camp 2. A mental diversion I suppose. I think someone is just pulling our leg. But then if you can't see UFO's in a New Mexican sky, where can you see them?

Last evening I read a lot in Mandela's autobiography. A fascinating story in my milieu. I've come to the place in the book where many members of the ANC are on trial for treason again.

I met Harris's sister briefly in the visiting room. She gave him yet another story idea. He thinks, maybe, his sister will bring his parents to visit today.

Another visit with Mary Ellen yesterday. She returns today. She doesn't think I'll get on with my writing unless I leave Arizona City. She might be right. She spoke again about freeing me up from business tasks when I get out of here. I don't seem to be moving toward a decision yet. I guess it's just difficult to give up what I've done for decades and take a leap in another direction.

I have been thinking of Dorothy Day's comment about the oneness of action and writing. I think perhaps there's a freeing and enabling message in that idea for me. Herself both a writer and an activist, Day wrote: "Each is an act. Both can be part of a person's response, an ethical response to the world."

Dorothy very much appreciated Dostoevsky's work. It's said she liked to quote his line: "The world will be saved by beauty."

This is the longest day of the year. The summer solstice.

June 22

A wonderful day with Mary Ellen. We met Harris's elderly parents briefly. Mary Ellen was able to get an evaluative impression of his mother and passed some suggestions on to his sister.

We talked again about the adult care business and Arizona City after prison. She reiterated that she thought I wouldn't get on the other agendas until I left Arizona City. It is difficult for me to turn loose of that connection and she knows it. I think I need to stay there for some time after my release. They have been so supportive during all my callings away from them. I told Mary

Ellen I have been thinking of December 31. I plan to be in Georgia on November 22. It's just a matter of doing it.

I suppose the truth is that this is a frightening leap not knowing what will come of it. I started to write here, "because I don't know if I can write," but that is not so. I know I can. Over the last year, particularly, my confidence in this regard has grown a great deal. One never has any assurance regarding publication, but I can write. I can write the historical novel I've had on the back burner ever since 1983. It's a matter of clearing the decks and doing it. I have received so much pleasure and satisfaction from preaching, pastoring, and social action that I have not wanted to set those activities aside to concentrate on something new and relatively untried in my life. But I have confidence that I can do it. Mary Ellen's push is very loving and gutsy. She's right that this is as good a time as any, if not better, for this move. But it still isn't easy for me.

We participated in Catholic Mass together. Frankie, a long-time friend and colleague, drove over with her. They are being hosted in El Paso. Frankie is not on my approved visitors list so when she came back to pick up Mary Ellen we were just coming out of the chapel and returning to the visitor room. As we passed by her in the foyer I took advantage of some momentary confusion of movement to sneak a brief hug. It's a no-no but I got away with it.

Now I'm almost halfway into Mandela's autobiography. It's as hard to put down as Elie Wiesel's *Memoirs* was for me. I was particularly struck by one of Mandela's statements that seems particularly fitting to the SOA issue: "The government pretends to preserve what they are attempting to destroy."[7] His descriptions of human conditions in his country during the days of apartheid remind me why I fasted on the TCU chapel steps a decade ago.

Mary Ellen and some others will be meeting tomorrow with a new editor of *The Tucson Citizen,* our evening newspaper, about the SOA and the SOA 25. They are seeking to add this paper's editorial support for closure. The possibilities appear positive.

June 23

I received two books yesterday: *The Poet's Companion* from California, and *The Violence of Love,* a selection of Oscar Romero's writings from New Hampshire. If I remember correctly both Carol and Barbara, the women who sent them, were among the more than 600 who crossed the line at Fort Benning last November.

I've found out that another correspondent, Esther who lives in Oregon, is married to an old colleague of mine from twenty years ago. They have a unique international ecumenical ministry they created called Journey Into Freedom. They publish an occasional newsletter and have sent me one on compassion and another on forgiveness. In the first Esther relates her initial experience of caring for a dying woman off the streets of Calcutta at Mother Teresa's place. Hers is a honest and powerful story.

The gnats and ants are bothering me this morning on the patio, and the sun is hotter, so I'm heading inside to write some letters.

June 24

Another lovely morning. My first day off this week. Cool breeze. Sun is just appearing over the Franklins. Birds singing. The hum of traffic picking up along I-10. Men are beginning to stir in the compound. I'm on the south patio enjoying the start of the day.

I received a letter from Aaron, a Union Seminary student working at Cristo Rey Centro Luteran in El Paso this summer. The Center is hosting student immersion in border issues throughout the summer. They are adding an SOA unit to their program. Aaron asked if I would write a letter regarding why I'm in prison and "holy obedience" to be read to the youth participants throughout the summer. I wrote him back last night saying yes and that the letter will follow in a day or two.

Finley was assigned to food service as of today. He's doing "my" job. He had another story that was hard to believe last night relative to what the counselor said to him. He also spoke at considerable length about his heart condition. He showed me a letter from the BOP Surgeon General to Judge Browning, concerning his assignment to La Tuna because of his health, in which the official painted a rosy picture to the judge of what is in fact minimal health care at best. You suppose the Surgeon General doesn't know?

The baby birds are growing apace. The first born nestlings are getting quite big and I wonder when and how it is that they leave the nest. In the one nest some are bigger than the others. Obviously they are the most aggressive eaters.

June 25

I believe this is the birthday of two of our grandkids, Joel and Katie. What sweeties. Joel is too old now to call "a sweetie" I suppose. I can't remember their exact birthdays without the help of my handy-dandy computer program. We have fifteen grandchildren. Since I have responsibility for sending out birthday and anniversary cards to family I purchased them all in advance through September and prepared them for mailing. All Mary Ellen has to do is put them in the mailbox when the day comes, which I indicated on the front of each envelope, so they arrive in good time.

This morning, between five and six, I finished reading *Long Walk to Freedom.* The story's the epitome of human struggle for justice. Its heroes are very basic fabric in a grand design. I'm going to write out a few quotes from the book before passing it on to Lloyd who has asked to read it next.

The one family of four baby swallows has to be about ready to fly. They appear bigger than their parents and are really crowding their little nest.

There's no problem in my staying busy. I only need to give myself permission *not* to be busy once in awhile. There's a sense in which life is simpler in prison. This sense doesn't make it at all desirable. I've been here three months now. I can't imagine what years would be like let alone the more than twenty-seven Nelson Mandela was incarcerated. In the closing section of his autobiography he remarkably speaks of human goodness and the importance of commitment to the human community. When Mandela left prison his mission was "to liberate the oppressed and the oppressor both."[8] That's absolutely awesome.

I am beginning to reflect anew on my experience here. Having three months down, as they say, I'm evaluating what is happening to me psychologically and spiritually. The need to do this was brought home by "a job evaluation" I received in food service. Actually it was just checked boxes regarding job performance. One of my BOP bosses had checked "satisfactory" across the board. When I first read it I was immediately disappointed and wondered why I didn't get higher marks. Not only that but my total gross pay for last month was listed—$12.12.

Then I caught myself. Why should I feel bad about either the evaluation or the pay? It was a stupid yet so human reaction. I don't need more pay. I don't care what their evaluation is. I don't plan to wipe dining tables and sweep floors as a career move. What's interesting to me is my initial reaction. It speaks to the phenomenon of prison adjustment. I recall Marvin writing me early on to "remember who you are." Remembering in this environment is not as automatic as one might expect. I have to consciously work at it. Mandela and the other political prisoners in South Africa continually worked at it through many long years.

I'm anxious to hear about the delegation's experience with the Tucson newspaper editor.

June 26

I got the copies from the camp photographer of the picture he had taken last Sunday of Mary Ellen and me in the visitors' patio. It turned out pretty good. I will be sending them to family. I've already put one in my prison album.

I started reading *The Poet's Companion* and the *Poetry Dictionary.* I wrote letters. I even drafted a letter for the border program but I don't like it. I will try again today. I need to take a different tack. It's not right for the purpose they have in mind.

The days and nights are warmer now. It's a little too warm to be here on the patio at my usual time. So I'll go inside.

June 27

There was a very large horned frog on the porch last evening. I've never seen one so big in the wild or in a zoo. It was a beautiful specimen. I chased him into the desert because I want him to remain free.

Lake La Tuna has reappeared this morning. There's an area west of our camp in the quadrangle that, when it's saturated, starts holding water at the surface. Last night a hose was left running. Voilà. Lake La Tuna.

It's a beautiful, calm, and bright Saturday morning. Many men are sleeping in. I went to bed a little early—8:30 p.m. The sun is hot on my dark brown uniform this morning and I'm going to move inside. I'm decked out in my best for visitors today.

I received two more books yesterday: *The Man Who Planted Trees* from Connie and *Risks Worth Taking* by Tim Blunt. The second is a selection from ten years of poetry and art of an American prisoner of conscience.

It was a lively and enlivening visit with Mary Ellen, Punch and Nick. I'm having to start all over again at this late date to seek approval for four more Tucson friends. I'm keeping both my fingers and toes crossed. Other than this visitor list hassle I'm doing okay. I'm staying well and gradually losing a little weight.

Marvin has had two of four infusion treatments with this new medicine. He writes that after only one treatment the pain in his hip is gone, cancer cells are breaking down fast, and the question is if it's powerful enough to "knock it into a true remission." He reports there have been no side effects beyond fatigue. That's such good news.

Mary Ellen told me the SOA Watch delegation's visit with *The Tucson Citizen* is this coming Tuesday not last Tuesday as I thought. Four are planning to meet with the editor and perhaps others. It's through Punch's good offices that this opportunity presented itself. It's wonderful what Mary Ellen and others are accomplishing on many fronts while I'm wiping dirty tables at La Tuna.

Mary Ellen and Amy have done some research on my cellie's trial in Tucson last year. News stories at that time indicated a CIA connection to this case. Ummmm? It's because I am so wide open to being framed while incarcerated that I mustn't be naive. If the powers would insist on putting me and twenty-four other peaceful citizens away for six months for walking across a little line in the pavement, to say nothing of maintaining that it's good policy to train human rights abusers to be more efficient in oppressing their own people, they are capable of anything. It would be so easy to frame an inmate if there were a will to do it. Ralph McGeehee, a 25-year veteran of the CIA, told me in 1985 when I said that those of us in the Sanctuary Movement were trying not to be too paranoid, "You can't be too paranoid."

Adam has said to me, not once but three times now, "Ken, we'll have to find a way to keep you in here." The last time, just a couple of days ago, I told him, "I don't want you ever to say that to me again." What an idiotic thing to say.

Adam is a government plant, a felon working at lessening his own sentence, or just a dweeb disoriented in this new situation who doesn't realize what the hell he's doing. His strange comments, his consistent pumping for information, his trying to get me to say what I'm going to do regarding SOA in the future, his unusual special treatment by prison officials, his disappearances from the compound where I can't find him for long stretches of time, and a string of exceedingly weird conversations with him has made me quite leery. And it hasn't let up either. Just when I think it all must be my paranoia he does or says something else that seems suspicious to me. My gut says watch out. And if I'm getting this attention from the government then I'm not the only one among the twenty-five.

Although this is a real concern I'm actually doing quite well. This issue hasn't become a total preoccupation. I'm just more guarded around Adam. This is a place where previous experience in other contexts with the ways of the world helps.

June 29

No journaling yesterday. I redrafted "a letter from prison" for Aaron and put it in the mail. It became a difficult assignment. I'm not real happy with my effort but I couldn't procrastinate any longer. I wrote:

A Letter from Prison

> As a pastor in Southern Arizona in the 1980's, and later as director of the Tucson Ecumenical Council's Task Force for Central America, I met hundreds if not thousands of war refugees from Central America. Some of the young refugees your age lived in our home for varying lengths of time. I was among those who first called for and participated in the Sanctuary Movement.
>
> Early in the 1990's I traveled in Guatemala and El Salvador for extended periods with Pastors for Peace. The militaries arrayed against the People of God in these and other countries pretended to preserve human rights and establish democracy when in reality they were trying to destroy them. They were led by military and ex-military men who were carefully taught at the U.S. Army School of the Americas in the United States.
>
> Since 1990, with others across our country, I have participated in a movement to close that military school. As have others, I have given money, prayed, vigiled, leafletted,

spoken, written, telephoned, visited members of Congress, fasted, participated in local and national actions, and been arrested for peacefully walking toward the headquarters of the SOA at Fort Benning. Now, along with twenty-four other prisoners of conscience, I'm serving a six-month sentence in a federal prison camp and paying a $3,000 fine.

At an early age my mother and my church taught me that the greatest law of all is to love God and your neighbor as yourself. Now I either believe that or I don't. Like anyone else I do that or I don't. The Scripture admonishes us, "Be doers of the word, and not hearers only, deceiving yourselves."

Archbishop Oscar Romero, one of a holy multitude of neighbors already assassinated by graduates of the SOA, explained to the People of God:

> The Christian must work to exclude sin
> and establish God's reign.
> To struggle for this is not communism.
> To struggle for this is not to mix in
> politics.
> It is simply that the gospel demands of
> today's Christian
> more commitment to history.
> [July 16, 1977][9]

Mahatma Gandhi, the great practitioner of non-violent resistance to evil in his own nation, once said: "If the people will lead, governments will follow."

The sufferings of God's People caused by the SOA are touching the heart of God. The suffering continues. It's not possible for me and others to stand in silent acquiescence complicit in continuing atrocities.

Your brother in the struggle,

I've sent all the copies of the photo taken on June 21 to family and Arizona City. I'm missing a copy for John. I'll try to have one taken with him the next time he comes.

The sun is hot and the flies are pesky so I'm going inside. Mornings may be inside for the summer.

I've been reading *The Poet's Companion.* It's going to be helpful to me. It has several poems in the text illustrative of its teachings. I must write Carol and thank her.

I had a dream just before waking about a celebration of my release from prison. I don't recall much about it except that there was a line of women dancing in celebration and one of the dancers was Idamae. She was a dear friend who died as the result of an auto accident several years ago.

I had awakened about 1:30 a.m. and remained awake for quite a time. It seemed like an hour or more. It was a very peaceful time of day to be awake. I did think about planning for the time following my release which probably brought on the dream later.

I should have my team meeting the last of this week or next week. It's scheduled for July 3 on my review form. That's Friday. At that time I hope to get a better idea about my release—what day and time of day, etc.

If I'm released early on Friday, September 18, then the El Paso supporters event could be that evening with a Tucson event Saturday evening or Sunday, leaving Mary Ellen and me free to travel to Flagstaff Sunday or Monday. But if there's no early out because my scheduled release is on a Sunday, then a Sunday evening potluck affair in El Paso seems likely with a Tucson event early in the week. Monday hopefully. Of course for Tucson we want to coordinate with Randy's plans. My hope is that those plans can be compressed so Mary Ellen and I and the family can enjoy some leisurely time together before I start back to Arizona City the first Sunday in October. Then I also want to see Marvin as soon as possible. I don't know how that can be worked. I'll have to give it some thought. I don't know if he can come here to visit this summer, if he will come to Flag or Tucson, or I will travel to LA. I'm so thankful for the good report of his initial response to the new medicine. My prayers continue for God to heal him. Oh, how I love him.

June 30

Adam gave me an opened box of raisin bran he purchased at the commissary saying, "It doesn't agree with me." He knew I was out until I can go to the commissary this evening. This morning I had some in my bowl ready to pour milk on it and just couldn't chance it. I dumped it as I will the remainder. There's absolutely no reason to take a chance even if it is an act of kindness.

Though raisin bran is for sale in the commissary, and we are not allowed milk in our cells, neither are we allowed to openly bring the cereal into the dining hall. So I, and others who want this option, "sneak" it in by putting a serving in a cellophane bag in our jacket or pants pocket. The only cold cereal they have available in the dining hall these days is Froot Loops. It has been the only cereal for weeks and weeks now. Not a good option for diabetics. I need a reasonable cereal option on the mornings they serve pancakes and French toast.

On the subject of food, I usually look forward to the broiled chicken but on several occasions it has been served partly raw. Therefore we must first check to see if our piece has been cooked through before diving in. If it's not then we just go without protein for that meal.

Tuna casserole at La Tuna is just a disaster. If inmates hear that is on the menu they just don't show up. They are smart. How can anyone mess up tuna casserole? Simple. The cooks must follow the BOP recipes to the letter. No variation allow. Because of this rule the tuna casserole is always uneatable.

The last time tuna casserole was served only twenty or thirty men came to supper. As we all alike sat there moving this bland gooey concoction around on our plates with our forks wishing it could be eaten, the inmate who's duty was to serve it up came into the dining hall and shouted with an enthusiastic flourish, "Seconds!"

ENN

It broke us up. The casserole all ended up in the dumpster as usual.

Adam was awakened this morning though it was supposedly his day off and he appeared at the dining hall at 5:30 a.m. as usual. It's not unusual to be awakened on one's day off. I have been awakened by BOP officers every day off so far. "You're on the list," they always say if you question it. The supervisors in food service don't do their paperwork well. This morning I had to work alone. Tomorrow Dylan will work alone. All because one boss scheduled Adam for Tuesday-Wednesday days off. This morning's supervisor confirmed this is his day off and he left.

After breakfast I spent a half an hour trying to locate Adam to no avail. There are times he just seems to disappear and this was one of them. I didn't look everywhere, I suppose, but I did look in all the areas one would expect an inmate could be. Places for inmates to be are quite limited.

I have discovered him in the counselor's office with the blinds shut. The blinds are not usually shut when the counselor is there.

If my misgivings are groundless this plot would still make an interesting story. There's really nothing to be done except be careful. It's uncomfortable having to deal with this uncertainty all the time.

Yesterday during a lull in our dining hall work Adam was asking about Mary Ellen's involvement in my activities. Of course there's nothing to tell. I became aware of this curiosity after he started probing for information once more. Is it all quite innocent? Perhaps. But just when my suspicions seem to quiet down some behavior of his stirs the pot again.

CHAPTER 5

July: Who Are the Criminals?

July 1

It's July. Fireworks this weekend. The sun has a way to go before it rises over the Franklins and the breeze is cool. We're in for a cold snap. It's supposed to get up to only 100° today and the humidity is high.

The first nest of fledglings have flown. I went by night before last and all five were there. I went to see them yesterday morning and they were all gone. Another cycle is turning. The parents of other nests are out with the first light catching breakfast for their young. I know of six nests. There are probably others.

A letter arrived yesterday from one of the Latin American refugee children in Amy and Marianna's summer school at Southside Presbyterian. I think she had been coached for she asked me to send a poem and what my favorite poem is. I wrote her back last night. Her name is Mayra. She told me in the letter that her mother is Mexican and her father Salvadoran. I told her I hope we can meet in the fall. I sent her "East of Eden" and "The Gardener."

July 2

Some people send really bad jokes off the internet as inserts with their letters. Sometimes one is tempted to write back and say, "I'm suffering enough already. Quit sending such stupid jokes." I'm only kidding of course. Humor is in the eye of the beholder.

It's the eyesight of some I question. One that I did like: "Heaven is British police, French cooks, German mechanics, Italian lovers, Swiss bankers. Hell is British cooks, French mechanics, German police, Italian bankers, Swiss lovers." Another: "Do you know how to make God laugh? Tell God your plans."

I got another wonderfully generous letter from Louis Freund. In it he enclosed, printed on a separate piece of paper, what was entitled, "A Reflection from Michelangelo on Dante Whom He Admired": "Were I but he—for born to such a fate, for his harsh exile, with his virtue, I would exchange the world's most happy state."

Louis writes, "In your dedication to a cause we honor you, as one who only painted pictures as a contribution." I remember well this veteran artist's series of anti-war canvases.

Last evening I read in Fred Kronen's *In Search of Peace: An American Doctor in Sandinista Nicaragua.* He and his wife live in Keams Canyon and work with Daryl and Julie. I'm over halfway through it. He tells his story of their Nicaraguan days. Though he has a political opinion, which becomes quite clear, he does not hit the reader over the head with it. It's a part of the story. It's not a political essay but a story of his experience and what he learned from it.

July 3

I finished reading Kronen's *In Search of Peace.* It is a well-told story. There are a couple of quotes that stand out to me.

> [The Nicaraguans] lived by their faith, and their faith kept them going. Those who believed in nothing were depressed and overwhelmed by events. Those with an inner conviction—be it revolutionary, religious, or that unique Latin combination of both—developed a strength of character that shined in their lives. Born of adversity, some beautiful human traits were developed and expressed. We constantly

> were learning about patience and faith from our Nicaraguan neighbors.[10]

> The realization hit me that it wasn't simply that the U.S. is rich and these other countries are poor; the U.S. is rich *because* these other countries are poor. Their servitude is necessary for our plenitude.[11]

April 28, 1988, was the first anniversary of the death of American Ben Linder at the hands of the Contras. There was a memorial service in front of the U.S. Embassy in Managua Fred tells about as follows:

> One woman . . . was carrying a large cardboard sign that read:
> "Oliver North
> 1) Sold missiles to Iran
> 2) Sent arms to the murderous Contras
> 3) Allowed cocaine smuggling back into the U.S.
> Ben Linder
> 1) Performed as a juggler for Nicaraguan children
> 2) Provided hydroelectric power for rural villages
> 3) Gave his life for his beliefs
>
> Which is the clown,
> and which is National Hero?"[12]

I called Mary Ellen yesterday morning. She told me of her small group's meeting with two editors and a reporter at *The Tucson Citizen.* They want to start with an op-ed piece. Paula was going to get Randy to do it but he suggested, since he'd done the last one, that I do this one. They'd like it ASAP. The number of words is a question. *The Star* was 800. I think *The Citizen* is more like 500-600. Mary Ellen is going to check on that. I need to start on a draft today. It must be very tight.

July 4

Independence Day has a whole new ring to it this year to a prisoner of conscience in a U.S. prison. How does that Declaration go again?

I have been contemplating *The Citizen* op-ed I need to write and get in the mail soon.

Yesterday was one of those so far rare days of deep depression I have experienced in prison. Depression is more common here, I think, than in the general population. There's a lot of extra sleeping. I refuse to give in to it. I'm pretty good at recognizing depression when it's around and do intentional activity to combat it including prayer, walking, and going to the library. So far I have refused to "take to my bed," even being sure to stay up until my normal bedtime. I don't think it would be normal under these circumstances not to be depressed from time to time.

We had one good rain shower yesterday afternoon late with some thunder and lightning. It was cleansing. But the humidity yesterday and today has made the evaporative coolers very inefficient. It's a hot and sticky Fourth of July.

No mail yesterday. It was the holiday rather than Monday. And no visitors. I expect some local visitors either today or tomorrow. There will be a fireworks display from the county park east of our camp tonight.

I wrote an additional stanza regarding a panda for Tim Blunt's *Tickle Blues* to send to a boy in the Southside Presbyterian Church summer school. He asked if I could write him a poem about pandas and remembering the enjoyable *Tickle Blues* this was a neat solution to my desire to respond.

July 6

No journaling yesterday. I worked on *The Citizen* op-ed instead. I had a constant interruption from my cellie until he had a visit.

Nick came to visit yesterday afternoon. He reported on the

group meeting regarding their congressman in El Paso. He says if they don't get a commitment this summer he will follow-up on this congressman when they are back in Maryland.

My cellie certified the plane that was shot down with Eugene Hasenfus on board in the famous Nicaraguan Contra incident.[13] "Certified" is apparently an engineering euphemism Adam uses for what he did. His business "certifies military aircraft," he says. Simply put he bought old planes from the U.S. Air Force, outfitted them for a different mission, and certified their readiness when he sold them to another government agency.

I know from press reports at the time that the Hasenfus plane had come from the Davis-Monthan AFB boneyard in Tucson, was outfitted at Evergreen and flown out of Marana. When I asked Adam if he certified that plane his eyes got big and he asked, "What do you know about that?" I explained it was common knowledge, especially in the Tucson Area. He said he "brokered and certified" the plane and his partner delivered it to Southern Air in Florida.

Further Adam said that his trouble began with "a lobbyist" for Evergreen and Southern Air "going after him." A curious story. Adam claims his business was not CIA-related, yet he gave me all kinds of information related to the Hasenfus flight when I brought it up.

He said C130s are "made for" operation in Latin America. Their specific capabilities are for touch and go operations. His trial focused on two C130s delivered to the Middle East. He says it makes "no sense" to use these particular aircraft in that part of the world. Some of the things he said about C130s were confirmed later by Nick. Nick is USAF retired.

Adam claims to not know why he's in prison. He is adamant that he did nothing different in these business dealings he was taken to trial over than in his business dealings with the government for the previous 20 years. He sees himself a true red, white and blue American.

He said there were many who saw the use of the planes as

CIA-connected but he never did. According to him he was simply re-outfitting and certifying Air Force planes for U.S. Forest Service fire fighting. At the same time Adam acknowledges he certified the Hasenfus plane and knew where it ended up.

He said Evergreen and Southern Air became his enemies. "They didn't want C130s released by the USAF" to his company or through his company to the U.S. Forest Service. He said he was also interested in obtaining 100 A10s for fire fighting and had completed all the engineering work for the conversions.

Additionally Adam said he wonders why the U.S. Forest Service insists on using such old out-of-dated aircraft for their fire fighting mission when newer and different aircraft are more suited to the job. My guess is that it has to do with utilizing these planes for purposes other than those officially acknowledged, much like the use of helicopters in Mexico that were supposedly given by the U.S. government for the purpose of drug interdiction but are being used against the indigenous villagers and Zapatistas in Chiapas these days.

These conversations with Adam have made me ponder if, in the mysterious design of God, there is a veiled divine purpose for us being cellies at such a time as this. It's a curious situation.

The birds are very busy this morning because a lot of insects are rising out of the grass. We had a good rain shower or two yesterday afternoon and early evening. So the swallows are having a field day.

While writing I have been sitting on the bench on the laundry porch watching the swallow's nest here. There are three fledglings who must be close to flying. The activity this morning appears different than in earlier days. I'll like to see them take off for the first time.

July 7

I worked an extra hour this morning and I'm more tired than usual. My supervisor says his regional boss is coming so guess who gets to work harder.

A long letter arrived from Mary Ellen yesterday bringing me up-to-date on all our family news.

I am devoting the rest of today to getting my op-ed piece written. It is a longer process without the benefit of my computer and other resources at home. Everything must be hand-written and re-written. I think I finally have a fresh approach that will work.

July 8

"Lamb of God, who takes away the sin of the world, have mercy on us. Lamb of God, who takes away the sin of the world, grant us peace."

That was the thought and song I awakened with this morning. It is sung in Mass each Lord's Day. And it was being sung in my head and heart this morning.

I'm seated on the bench on the laundry porch again today because we are getting a few sprinkles from a partly cloudy sky. It was an especially beautiful dawn. I actually stayed in bed until 5:50 a.m. this day off. They did not awaken me. That's happened only once before in all my time here. Usually I'm on the wake up list even on my days off. It's okay because I like to get up. It's a very peaceful time of day to be up and around.

I called Mary Ellen last night. She had a terrible day. Among others things there are some serious family problems and she has been without help in the business office the last two weeks because all our volunteers are away at the same time. It's a very stressful time for her. She had planned to come visit this weekend but she hasn't got a plane ticket or checked with local supporters yet. She said to call back Thursday night. I told her I always want to see her but, on the other hand, I don't want her to overextend herself.

[Later] The camp counselor told me late this afternoon that the Mullers in Tucson had been visitor approved. I asked Mary Ellen to call and tell them they could come any weekend and that

I'd love to see them. Maybe they can give Mary Ellen a ride. It's a long trip and it's always great to have company.

It's been a draining experience trying to come up with a different tack than the *Star* op-ed last year. I did get an inspiration and went with it.

One problem I faced while trying to do this was a period of two or three days battling depression. It's the first time that my depression was over such an extended period. Then last night I had a breakthrough. There was a quotation of Annie Dillard from *Pilgrim at Tinker Creek* reprinted in a magazine a supporter had sent me that released my energy.[14] For some reason her phrases "diddle around" and "raising Cain" clicked and became the beginning of my op-ed. I put this in the mail to Mary Ellen tonight:

Enough Is More Than Enough

We have quit diddling around.

We have stopped being silent in the face of suffering.

We have ceased accepting atrocity as though it should be expected.

There is a price to be paid for speaking out and standing up. Some of us have started paying.

It is not possible to have peace with justice without paying the price.

We are in prison.

All twenty-five of us, mostly in our sixties and seventies, are serving six-month sentences in U.S. federal prisons for exercising our First Amendment rights. We all are paying $3,000 fines.

We were given the maximum on a misdemeanor charge for participating in a very peaceful protest of a misguided military program of long-standing.

We are ministers and priests, business executives, school teachers, nuns, lay religious workers, university professors and students, and health care professionals.

We are residents of Tucson, Syracuse, Lutcher, Washington, North Palm Beach, Minneapolis, Boonville, Binghampton, Tacoma, Mead, Portland, Setauket, Chicago, St. Petersburg, Atlanta, Waukesha, Orlando and Roanoke.

We refuse to be intimidated by the U.S. Army.

We will not fear their misuse of the American justice system.

We will not be silent nor go away.

In the spirit of loving non-violent resistance to wrong, we will peaceably raise Cain.

We believe enough is more than enough.

Last November the twenty-five of us were among over 600 who very peacefully walked toward the headquarters of the U.S. Army School of the Americas (SOA) on an open military reservation—Fort Benning.

Our purpose was to commemorate the anniversary of the assassination of six Jesuit priests and two women coworkers at the command and hands of graduates of that military school. They are but eight of countless thousands of victims of this infamous institution's Latin American military graduates.

Our purpose was to peacefully deliver petitions from almost a million Americans demanding the closure of the SOA.

We were neither threatening in our actions nor destructive.

We walked silently and solemnly toward the "school of assassins" three miles down the road.

In less than a mile we were halted and arrested by the authorities. Our heartfelt petitions were confiscated.

During our arrest the SOA Commandante held a news conference and called us "communists." An SOA spokesperson said we would get what we deserved.

Now we are in federal prisons stretching from Sheridan,

Oregon to Danbury, Connecticut, from Safford, Arizona to Coleman, Florida.

The government policymakers and the Army are determined to go right ahead with years of bloody business as usual.

They drew a line where Fort Benning begins and told us not to cross over. But it is the U.S. government who has gone too far. They continue to cross the moral line of human decency with impunity.

We will not stand for it anymore.

Enough is more than enough.

We call on Congress to pass HR611 and SB980 presently before them. If enacted, as is, these companion bills would shut down the SOA in 30 days.

The SOA is primarily a military political school exclusively for Latin American military elites.

Today it trains 900-2000 annually in military intelligence, counterinsurgency operations, sniper fire, commando tactics and psychological operations. The SOA has actively taught torture techniques.

For five decades graduates have become the worst human rights violators in the Western Hemisphere. They have returned to their 22 countries and utilized the doctrine and tactics they have learned, at U.S. taxpayers expense, not on invading foreigners, but on their own people to insure the status quo; to support the elites and their regimes.

The SOA only pretends to promote human rights and democracy. In practice its curriculum results in the destruction of both.

It pretends to train fighters of "the drug war." In reality many of its clients are known and suspected drug dealers. A former instructor testifies he accompanied many of them to Fort Benning banks to launder their drug money.

Most recently Mexico has become the SOA's biggest

customer. A sudden increase in Mexican military elites at the SOA began shortly after the indigenous uprising in Chiapas.

The Zapatistas rose in opposition to NAFTA and other economic policies that benefit the rich in the U.S. and Mexico while increasing the suffering of the poor.

Outrageous inhumane behavior, taught at the SOA in Georgia, continues in Mexico and elsewhere in Latin America lead by SOA graduates.

While the U.S. Army welcomes, and even hosts, those who are apologists for the SOA, we are in prison today because we demand that this human misery machine be permanently shut down.

It was the Army who asked the U.S. justice system to put us away and they obliged without so much as a jury of our peers.

Our appeal will not be heard until long after we have paid their fines and served our sentences.

Nevertheless, we will be joined by an ever-widening circle of Americans of conscience, who will speak for those who cannot speak for themselves.

Enough is more than enough.

July 9

I talked to Mary Ellen a few minutes ago to tell her that the article is in the mail.

My first-of-the-month books have not arrived. I would like to get them and have them today when I have a day to read. Of course there's always letter writing that can be done.

A letter from SOA Watch arrived yesterday with an article that reports a three-judge panel of the 11th Circuit Court of Appeals ruled against us on the 1995 case. The opinion was released last week. Discussions are going on regarding a further appeal to the full appeals court or the U.S. Supreme Court. The 1997 case may have been better presented. We'll wait and see.

I am reminded by this news of the judicial support for the Nuremberg Laws of Nazi Germany. Unfortunately, in some respects, our government in these days is no more noble than Germany in those days. Save for a misguided chauvinistic hope why should we expect any different? Are we more moral? As the Germans, we have a system of laws not a justice system. Justice is God's work. It should be our own. It is not enough to simply say we are a nation of laws. Laws are often promulgated and interpreted to serve unjust and selfish political and economic purposes. Nevertheless, as a quote from Paul Tillich, sent to me on a postcard recently, observes: "Here and there in the world and now and then in ourselves is a new creation."

The "felonious five"—Bix, Mary, Kathleen, Ed and Marge—are scheduled for sentencing on July 23. Carol Richardson will be released July 17.

Yvonne sent an article regarding a congressional hearing in which Sr. Diana Ortiz testified that she had been impregnated in the gang rape during her torture at the hands of the Guatemalan Army and had subsequently undergone an abortion. My prayers are for you, my sister, Diana. The torture goes on.

July 10

Yesterday I spent a lot of time observing three fledglings that I have been watching grow. The night before all were there but it was apparent that the time for flying was not far away. Then yesterday morning there was only one lone fledgling in the nest.

As I watched the parents and the fledgling's siblings all flew around the nest, lit on it, and called encouragement to the one who would not leap into space. He indeed burrowed down into the nest so as not to be pushed out.

This morning when I went to the site one fledgling still sat in the nest. The tactics of the day before continued and within thirty minutes the last fledgling flew away.

I started the following poem last night and worked on it again this morning:

Fledglings

Taking off is hard to do
when you have never done it before
When the nest is all you know
comfort is in the familiar

Who knows what awaits fledglings
on untested and unwieldy wings
A world of risks and dangers
windy skies and breezes of destiny

A world they have never seen
beckons novices to be daring
Fearlessly launch into space
making life's next improbable leap

One thing about birds is that
all abandon cozy nests to soar
Some people never fly

July 11

It was a pretty blah day yesterday beyond the new poem. But that was a plus. I seem to be getting several bird poems lately. I think I'll call them my "jailbird collection."

I did receive the July books. They are three very different ones. I scanned them and read a little in each.

Perhaps I'll have some visits today and or tomorrow from local folk. Mary Ellen will come later in the month.

I received a long letter from Marvin. He started his two point charge July 1, adding Bellflower to his pastoral responsibility as a

Methodist minister. He wrote that his leg pain had disappeared by July 4. He had his last treatment on Monday. The new medicine he's been getting is called Rituxan. I'll be receiving a copy of his Mark manuscript.

I wrote Marvin back and reminded him that the first anniversary of our start in *The Artist's Way* had just passed June 22. He discovered the book and sent a copy to me suggesting we work through it in tandem. We set a start date and stayed in touch with each other's experience over the phone. What a difference a year has made in his writing output and mine. His comments about self-doubt are right on. If we can, as Cameron suggests, use our fears as energy for writing then something altogether positive can come from it.

I'm reading *Keepers of the Story* by Megan McKenna and Tony Cowan. The book includes some provoking quotes such as the following:

> Ramakishna was asked: "Why, God being good, is there evil in the world?' He answered: "To thicken the plot."
>
> "One of the main elements of the [Jewish] tradition is silence . . . but we don't talk about it."—Elie Wiesel, in a BBC-TV interview
>
> "What good is it to me if Mary gave birth to the Son of God fourteen hundred years ago, and I do not also give birth to the Son of God in my time and in my culture? We are all meant to be mothers of God. God is always needing to be born."—Meister Eckhart
>
> "God speaks as softly as possible, and as loudly as necessary."—Rafi Zabor
>
> "Until the lions have their historians, tales of hunting will always glorify the hunter."—African proverb

Our inmate population was down to 165 yesterday from 193 when I first arrived. The officers keep the current total posted on a chalk board at each camp to facilitate their head counts. Many more men are leaving than coming in.

While that trend continues the population at La Tuna FCI is booming. Bunk beds from here are being moved up the hill because they have run out of beds and inmates are sleeping on the floor. Old timers remember the days when this camp was running over and men were assigned to floor space in the television rooms. I'm told that many of the Mexican citizens being held in FCI's throughout the U.S. are eventually transferred here to facilitate deportation through El Paso after their sentences have been served.

July 12

Mary Ellen surprised me. She came with Bernie and Charles yesterday. They'll be back today. Bob and Nick also showed up. So I had a good old day of stimulating conversation and pleasant company.

Later I wrote letters, read a little in the new books, and visited with a new man on the block.

July 13

I had another visit with Charles and Bernie and Mary Ellen. We participated in Mass together. The gospel reading was The Parable of the Good Samaritan from Luke. I was asked to read the lectionary from Colossians.

A man on my wing came and sat down on a patio bench with me until 9:30 p.m. and talked about his case and his take on religion and church. This encounter confirms the level at which I have been accepted by some here. Ralph said, "If you were preaching at chapel I'd go." He asked why I, a Protestant minister, went to the Catholic Mass. His background is Protestant. I tried to explain. He said he might try it some Sunday himself.

Ralph's job is on the camp maintenance crew. He talked about how some of the BOP officers regularly steal equipment and materials from the prison warehouse. According to him one of his supervisors, who has his own construction business on the side, makes out like a big time bandit. For example, taking gallons and gallons of paint from the warehouse. He says once when a new lawn mower was missing the officer wrote the loss up as "inmate pilfering." "Now, what is an inmate going to do with a lawn mower?" Ralph rhetorically inquired.

While it is true that inmates pilfer some items from the government, like food, the rumor is that the scale is much more significant among officers. Officers are often quite brazen about it. There is the powerful blue line of silence that protects them from ever being held accountable. This strict code bestows impunity on every officer. Any breach will result in exceedingly bad news for the snitch. It could be literally hazardous to his health. And who would ever believe any inmate who is an eyewitness to such criminal activities of law enforcement officers?

There appears to be a strong code among inmates in this camp not to steal from each other. The incidence here is extremely rare. They have their own ways of enforcing such a code. While a few inmates get permission to purchase a combination lock from the commissary to put on their locker I never have. Of course, it is required that all combinations be the property of the BOP. Whenever officers decide to do a shakedown they have immediate access. It is usual for them to do these while men are away working. They often have one of the camp orderlies follow them around with a large plastic bag into which they dump any items they consider contraband. Items are sometimes retrieved but usually not. Sometimes items are taken purely for the purpose of harassing particular inmates.

July 15

In a letter Marvin asked me to call him. He said he missed my voice. So I did call yesterday morning. He sounds good. He's finished his treatment series. He's down to 161 and doctor told him not to lose more. He won't know the full extent of his recovery until a CT scan about September.

Marvin told me the story of a woman who took her dog to the vet afraid he was dying. The vet said, "He's dead." The distraught woman said, "Please make sure. Maybe you're wrong." The vet lifted the office cat up on the table. The cat sniffed the dog, walked around him, sniffed again, and jumped down. The vet said, "No, your dog is dead. My bill is $530." "Whatever for?" inquired the woman. "Thirty dollars for the office visit," said the vet, "and $500 for the cat scan."

We really didn't talk about much except the possibility of his coming to visit the third weekend in August. It depends on how he's feeling. He and his family will be taking two weeks vacation the first of the month. Cora will be visiting them briefly about August 12 on her way back to college in Japan.

I think I'm continuing to lose weight slowly although I haven't been able to weigh in for a month or more. My clothes are looser. Marvin mentioned that our sister Lynn reports she weighs only 98 pounds. She has lost ten pounds since January. It doesn't sound good.

I had a couple of work days by myself this last week. It isn't too bad with this lower population except for the fact that it's been so humid that any exertion takes the starch right out of you. Between extra rest and writing letters I didn't get around to journaling yesterday.

Some mail arrived from SOA Watch Georgia. There is an article from *The Benning Leader,* the post weekly, with SOA news which included the fact that Colonel Trumble, the SOA Commandante, is retiring and won't be around for us to "kick around" any more. I wonder if this is a signal? And if so what kind?

I continue to receive nourishing little items enclosed with letters sent to me that I don't want to forget. For instance this from M. K. Gandhi's South African newspaper, *Indian Opinion,* January 21, 1904:

> Sacrifice is the law of life. It runs through and governs every walk of life. We can do nothing or get nothing without paying a price for it. If we would secure the salvation of the community to which we belong we must pay for it, that is, sacrifice self . . . Every Indian must consider the question as if it affected him personally, put his hands into his pocket for the common good, give his time and energy. Personal ease and personal gain should be surrendered. To all this must be added patience and self-control. The slightest deviation from the straight and narrow path mapped out here would bring us down the precipice, not because the cause is at all unjust or weak, but because the opposition set up against us is overwhelming.

I am, of course, completely aware that when we have the Pentagon, the military industrial complex, the Congress, and the Administration arrayed against us, it is overwhelming.

Another was from an unknown author:

Great Truths About Life
That Little Children Have Learned

> No matter how hard you try, you can't baptize cats.
>
> When your mom is mad at your dad, don't let her brush your hair.
>
> If your sister hits you, don't hit her back. They always catch the second person.
>
> Never ask your 3-year-old brother to hold a tomato.
>
> You can't trust dogs to watch your food.
>
> Reading what people write on desks can teach you a lot.

Don't sneeze when someone is cutting your hair.
Puppies still have bad breath even after eating a tic tac.
Never hold a dust-buster and a cat at the same time.
School lunches stick to the wall.
You can't hide a piece of broccoli in a glass of milk.
Don't wear polka-dot underwear under white shorts.
The best place to be when you are sad is in Grandma's lap.[15]

July 16

It rained overnight. It's still wet on one end of this metal table and bench where I sit despite a cool breeze. Clouds are back to the north.

I talked with Mary Ellen a long time last night on the phone. Much information was shared. There was an editorial column in *The Citizen* last Friday. A copy is in the mail to me. My op-ed could be as early as this Friday but timing of its publication is uncertain.

Randy thinks he knows "Jesus Cruz" at Safford FCI. He smells a rat.

Mary Ellen got to Amy Monday. She's checking on my fine payment but hasn't got back to her yet. She says Amy wasn't clear what I wanted. That makes me wonder if she received the letter I sent that made it crystal clear what I want in answer to her inquiry in June. Perhaps it never left here. Things about this prison get more and more peculiar. And why wouldn't the government send me a letter telling where and when my fine should be paid? Like I'm supposed to know that? What a crazy system.

[Later] It's beginning to get dark. I have written 14 letters today and mailed them. Tonight I have tried to read but I'm too restless. I do not understand this fretfulness. But rather than fight it I have picked up this journal and pen and made my way to the patio again. At the moment I'm all alone here. The couple of people who were here left. Even the officer who was sitting on his truck parked nearby got in and drove away. There are people leaving Camp 2 and walking down the sidewalk to the self-service laundry and Camp 1. But I am amazingly alone here at this time of night. Usually this space is right in the pedestrian traffic pattern.

My present feeling is there's something unknown out there for me to perceive tonight. There's this pause in the day's occupations for silence and listening. There is a making of this pregnant space that is both mystical and way beyond the ordinary. I'm all too aware of what one can expect here. This feels like a rare window of opportunity of some kind. There's the hum of dryers turning in the laundry and the drone of the traffic on I-10 in the distance. The night time sodium lights have just come on automatically and are building in their brightness. The breeze is constant, fresh, and chilly after a slightly cooler day. There are the night calls of birds entering my awareness and now the breeze is kicking up a bit and rustling the pages of this journal. There is some inner something waiting in the wings it seems. Still no one has entered my space, though several have left Camp 2 and walked on in other directions. There's the night noise of insects as background now with only an occasional bird call in the distance. The sky is not entirely cloudless but blue above the Franklin Mountains to the east running north and south. The moon has not risen and the stars are not yet out. It is twilight at La Tuna. Now a jet plane, high above, moves from east to west above El Paso leaving its white trail. Its signature sound fades to silence in the remaining sunset. But still I don't know what I'm waiting for or when it will arrive. There's only this sense of anticipation.

What I'm encountering now is new to my prison experience. I have never had a period of time remotely like this one. I wonder if I'm finally turning loose enough to allow something new to happen. This is a silence within the constant noisy whirl of prison life.

At dinner tonight Harris was trying to interest me in an internet marketing idea for a new service. He started by saying, "It will make you a millionaire." But I really have no interest. It surprised him that I wasn't enthusiastic. On the contrary, my first thought was, "Here's something else rearing up attempting to draw my attention away from pursuing my new calling. Watch out!" His idea made me more aware of my commitment to change my priorities. I've never been interested in spending my life "making a million." That's Harris' goal, not mine.

There remains a strong sense of obligation toward the people of Arizona City Community Church. Supporting me is a courageous sacrifice on their part. Nevertheless I feel I must answer this new calling. I still have not settled on the timing of this break. The closest I can come right now is on or before January 1.

I'd like to make this transition immediately on leaving prison but I don't believe that is an option. It is, of course, my own reluctance that keeps me from that path. I don't think it would be right somehow. I knew at the time Arizona City generously insisted on financially supporting me this put me under some moral obligation. I welcomed it. Now another decision will have to be taken.

There is the issue of Arizona City's best interest. That does not require my remaining there. That much is clear. It seems to me that their options open up by my leaving. The timing of the transition is the thing. I can't recall the amount of notice my call contract requires. I think sixty days. I need to have my mind settled on this by the time of my release. I do plan to be away in Georgia one Sunday in November. So I assume that means I need to leave before then or after Christmas.

I also need to do some research into retirement related to Social Security and Pension Fund benefits. I really haven't considered that option.

It is still quiet out here. No one is on this patio but me. Usually there are smokers, talkers, and domino players. Are they avoiding the space because I am writing or was there another force at work guaranteeing me this space undisturbed tonight? Who knows? It's still my space, my silence, my restless heart. It is 9:15. Time for bed.

July 17

Carol Richardson will be released in West Virginia this morning. I understand there is a big celebration tonight in Washington.

I'm back on the patio still unclear about last night's experience. It did afford me the opportunity to think with a little more concentration about my future, my resignation, and possibly my retirement. It's a transition into a new phase of life which could prove to be the most self-fulfilling phase yet. I don't know. There are no guarantees.

Mary Ellen's suggestion of a speaking tour is tantalizing. Perhaps something next year in January or February swinging through Michigan and Ohio to see our children and grandchildren. That timing isn't the best weather-wise, but it's something that could be planned for after leaving Arizona City. There may be another January trial in Georgia. If so I want to be there.

July 18

I did my weekly shave after breakfast shift and a quick shower. I say shave but I only trim around the edges. I've had this beard ever since the summer of 1974. I'm dressed for visitors. I expect Punch.

Mary Ellen's letter enclosed the editorial column from *The Tucson Citizen* by Jill Blondin of July 10, "Justice System Frees Monsters, Jails Saints." Nothing more in the notes from Mary Ellen than she'd already told me on the phone.

I wrote 15 or 16 letters yesterday. Started reading *The Nightingale's Song,* regarding five Iran-Contra figures, including one of my U.S. Senators, John McCain. All are graduates of the Naval Academy.

[Later] I did have my visit with Punch. Rich shared a new poem and some other poetry of his; Harris read me his latest chapter, "Escape from Horse Branch"; read a hundred pages in *Nightingale's Song.* All in all a fascinating day. I worked breakfast and supper but not lunch. It's coming on to nine and my eyes are too tired to read any more. The breeze on the patio, as a foursome plays dominoes, is getting pleasantly cooler and light.

I mentioned to Punch today that I was planning to resign from my church and leave no later than December 31. This sharing came with such ease that it is clear I've "crossed the line" regarding this decision. As I told him, it's now a question of timing. Even though I would prefer to start immediately into pursuing my long postponed goals related to writing I can't do this with a clear conscience. I've come to believe my resignation will be a good thing for both Arizona City and me. There was something to be said for remaining the pastor of a congregation during this stint. The first Sunday in August is my 11th anniversary there. That's a long stretch for a part-time ministry. I have indicated to them for several years now my serious intention to depart to do other things and open up their options for the future. Nevertheless, as with other departures, it will be yet another grief of the pastoral kind in my life.

July 19

Ever so often an officer does another inane stunt that refreshes my recognition that this is a crazy-making federal prison and I am, as others, a pawn for the BOP's amusement and deviltry. This afternoon, for the second time in my personal experience, the same food service boss locked out her inmate workers when we tried to report to work on time for short line before the 4 p.m. count. The time before, as this time, she was made aware we were at the door only to refuse to come and unlock any of the three doors that are entrances and exits to the building. The first time I and others waited in the broiling sun 20-25 minutes before she unlocked a door. This time I just went back to my room and read until after the count and time for the main line serving for supper. I can't just wolf down a meal any more. I was angry. If it's not this it's some other juvenile behavior on the part of an officer. They are not all like this, thank God. But too many are. For the life of me I can't fathom what this supervisor thinks she is achieving. I was mad at myself for becoming angry at this. I think it's because if we had a choice we would never put up with such behavior and it reminds us that there is absolutely no free choice when you are a prisoner. We are at their mercy whatever their asinine antics happen to be.

Another case in point was the day another of our food service supervisors accused her workers of stealing her purse. It was nowhere to be found. A squad of investigators arrived from the hill. Inmates were being called in one at a time for grilling. A shakedown of our cells commenced. The unit manager was huffing and puffing. Heads were about to roll.

These professionals were successful in their investigative efforts. After only a few hours her purse was found. Nothing was missing. It was safely in her locker up on the hill all the time. She had never brought it down to the camp in the first place.

I did have visits from Jean and Nick this afternoon. They participated in Mass with me. These visits were just before the lock out which gave that episode a vivid contrast with the free world.

This afternoon I spent most of my time, after work and a shower, reading *The Nightingale's Song.* I'm approaching halfway in this book.

Tomorrow is another day in prison.

July 20

Late this afternoon my case manager confirmed that since my release date is on a Sunday I will be released the previous Friday, September 18. That will be my Independence Day. It seems somehow a more appropriate date for celebration this year.

There is a limited supply of greeting cards available in the chapel. I am told they are given free to prisoners by Hallmark whose founder was a felon who never forgot his sisters and brothers. With the ballooning of prison populations Hallmark could market a line especially for prisoners, their families and friends. I recently read in the paper that there are a record number of American adults incarcerated these days.

The cards we have available are not always appropriate. It sometimes appears we get a choice of the least popular ones. But I did find this particular card some weeks ago that I have been saving to send to Mary Ellen when I knew my release date. The cover art is of a deserted isle with its lone palm tree and the inside text asks, "When can we get away?" I put it in the mail tonight after adding, "Friday, September 18."

July 21

I received copies of several letters from a friend of Rita Lucey explaining the kind of experience she and Mary Earley are having as SOA prisoners of conscience in Florida. They have written to the President and one of their U.S. senators because of conditions at Coleman which includes inadequate medical treatment and male guards ogling the women prisoners as they shower.

A third worker was assigned to the task I'm doing in food service. This means we will have a minimum of two for each shift. That's the good news. The bad news is that Mr. Green does not do anything. He would require constant close supervision to keep him working. Oh well, I need to back off. Let the boss handle it. Just be ready to defend myself against any supervisory criticism because of his laziness. I refuse to complain about him. I'm doing my own time.

I learned this morning from a man who works in the dish washing room that Mr. Green stood with his hands in his pockets there before reassignment to the dining room and he had the same reputation before he was assigned there. "He's never worked in his life," this man said, "and he doesn't intend to start now."

This situation is yet another "learning experience." It's instructive that, despite stereotypes, Mr. Green is the first man in my experience here that flatly refuses to work without a direct order and supervision. When I think about it I might expect more such inmates. Perhaps men with this attitude just don't make it into camps but are kept at the higher security facilities. Mr. Green is really no problem to me. But we do need help. I certainly wouldn't want to become a Colonel Bogey, of *Bridge on the River Kwai* fame, in my adjustment to the agenda of the BOP. I still wish to do my very menial job well for my own sake and that of my fellow inmates to our mutual benefit.

This week I received a letter addressed to "Ken Kennon, Poet." That felt really good. I'm surprised the mail officer let it through.

Mary Ellen told me yesterday morning that she thinks that she and John will be coming Saturday for a visit. It looks like John will be undergoing yet another back surgery in the near future.

Regarding my release, I'm going to see if there can be an evening gathering Friday, September 18, of the El Paso Area SOA Watch folks followed by a Saturday evening event with Tucson supporters. That would free us up quickly to do family things through October 3. I return to Arizona City on Sunday, October 4. That will give us two weeks. We plan to spend most of the time in Flagstaff. The timing of the Tucson event is the most iffy right now.

Only 58 days more days and a wake-up. I'm short, as they say here.

July 22

Thunderstorms boomed through the night. Scattered clouds this morning. It will be a beautiful sunrise but not yet. It's only about 5:30.

I have to get a couple of prescriptions filled today and do my weekly laundry.

This is Paul's birthday. He's 40 today. That's hard to believe. Ironically in some ways time seems to go quite quickly.

July 23

There's a light rain shower so I'm on the laundry porch bench writing this morning.

Well, yesterday evening turned out to be extremely exciting. An inmate blew the whistle on the illegal shredding of inmate mail by BOP officers. This includes incoming, outgoing, money orders, certified mail receipts, BP-9 forms. The BP-9 forms are used to file inmate grievances and make any official requests. We have no idea how long this has been going on. Many inmates knew they weren't getting all their mail, but they couldn't prove anything. I haven't got all my mail. It appears likely now that some of my visitor applications were just tossed. That could explain some of my ongoing problems in getting them approved.

Hector, who cleans the mail office and takes out the trash, saw through the clear plastic bags some distinctive overseas mail that some inmates regularly receive shredded. On closer inspection he found that the whole bag was filled with such things. Some other items were only partially destroyed and still in the shredder. So Hector temporarily hid the bag of physical evidence, with the help of one or two witnesses, and contacted a Lt. Solis who was on duty at Camp 1. He asked if the lieutenant would be interested in physical evidence of a federal crime being committed here and if he still would be interested if the criminal were a BOP officer rather than an inmate. His answer to both questions was yes. He is an officer that some inmates see as a straight-shooter.

Lt. Solis briefly examined the evidence and called in S.I.S. investigators. He told them to bring a camera. I saw Lt. Solis, Lt. Wilson of S.I.S., and a Camp 2 female officer going through the bag of evidence in the ISM room last night. I passed by the room on purpose so I could be an eyewitness to some of what was occurring. Of course I couldn't stop and stare no matter how fascinating the occasion.

Hector Cortez had come to my room at about 6 p.m. to ask if I had been missing mail. He knows I get a lot. This morning he gave me the names of S.I.S. officers on the case—Lt. Towers and Lt. Wilson—and said he was willing to talk to media and inspectors about what he discovered.

This is the talk of the camp. We naturally feel violated. S.I.S. called Fry and Murphy down to confirm that they are current inmates whose mail the investigators had pieced together. Later Murphy said he had not received a $50 money order his son sent and he was told this money order was one that was found shredded.

Last night I couldn't get Nick so I called Jean to asked that she talk to others and contact the postal inspector and the media about this. We think if it is handled only internally it will be hushed up very quickly. I hear there was an investigation at FCI La Tuna only last year regarding the same problem. Lt. Solis, who usually works there on the hill, told Cortez that men there had been complaining to him about the failure to receive expected mail and the same mail officer was on the job.

This morning I called Nick with additional information, asked him to talk with Jean, and follow through with postal inspector and media. I gave him the lieutenants' names and the inmate's name and number.

In addition I called Yvonne at SOA Watch giving her this information and asking her to share it and call for an investigation.

She reminded me that today is sentencing day in Columbus for five SOA resisters. She suggested I call back in late afternoon their time for information. The government wants their sentences to run consecutively not concurrently which would be a very long time down. Judge Elliott is known for doing whatever the government wants. He didn't get the name "Maximum Bob" for nothing.

Carol Richardson is in Senator Durbin's office right now trying to convince him not to introduce an amendment in the Senate to cut SOA funds at this time. Inasmuch as a vote is coming up in the House it is seen as bad timing. We are sure to lose in the Senate while being poised to win in the House. A loss in the Senate just before the House vote could be detrimental. Our friends in the House believe this is the case.

I have no way of knowing what I have lost to the shredder with one exception that I'll check through with Mary Ellen when she visits.

I have a PA appointment today at 12:30 p.m. to renew my medications.

[Later] Officer Grijalva, the mail officer, showed up for work as usual this morning. He seemed to know what was up because he refused to unlock any of the rooms Cortez usually cleans. Grijalva disappeared from the office later in the morning and Officer Black, who usually does ISM work, was doing the mail.

Later in the day I got only one letter. That has never happened before. This may be coincidence or they could be withholding my mail in retaliation for my telephone calls last night and this morning. All inmate calls are subject to monitoring. Perhaps I will learn tomorrow at mail call. At this juncture bad treatment and harassment by the BOP can only help our just cause.

Although there have been rumors about what has been happening today within the BOP regarding this shredding scandal we don't actually know anything. The day after tomorrow I will be able to talk more freely with visitors, including Mary Ellen.

I finished reading *The Nightingale's Song* by Timberg this afternoon and started a biography of Sr. Dorothy Kazel, one of the American nuns raped and murdered by Salvadoran military in 1980. It was sent to me by others of her religious community.

I received a PA "once over" at 1 p.m. He added a medication regarding blood pressure. I have been drinking coffee again and diet Coke. I need to cut that out. I weighed in last night at 227. That's 20 pounds below my entry into prison. I haven't weighed that low in 25 years. If I could follow the PA's suggestions, which is impossible in here, I would lose more. "No fats, no carbohydrates, no sugar" and "increased exercise," he said. Such dietary possibilities are nil in here and he knows it. There's the reality of the prison menu and I have no decent shoes to even walk the track. So why sweat it? I just bit my tongue for the umpteenth time when he made these common sense suggestions.

Adam, my cellie, told me that he learned today from mail that he will be transported to Tucson next month for a hearing related to his case.

It's now 6:30 p.m. I just got off the phone with Yvonne at SOA Watch Georgia. The sentencing of "the felonious five" was just about what Kathleen expected but it's still hard to hear of such sentences meted out to one's peacemaking friends. They didn't get out of court until about 5 p.m. EDT.

Judge Elliott ordered the four who were sentenced with us in January serve that sentence consecutive rather than concurrently with those given today, as the government requested. All, except Kathleen, were released to self-surrender probably in about two months. Kathleen was not a part of the November action. She also requested to be remanded to federal custody immediately and she was. All were given a share of the "restitution" ($1,050), a fine ($1,000, except Ed $1,500), and court costs ($200, except Bix $100).

Father Bix (70), 12 + 6 = 18 months, $2,150 + $3,000
Ed (53), 10 + 6 = 16 months, $2,750 + $3,000
Sr. Marge (60), 8 + 6 = 14 months, $2,250 + $3,000
Mary (47), 8 + 6 = 14 months, $2250 + $3,000
Kathleen, 12 months, $2,250

All the five covenanted together to observe Thursdays as a fast day every week in solidarity with the poor for the duration of their sentences and ask others to join them. I asked Yvonne to communicate that I was with them and will start fasting next Thursday. That's about a 20-month commitment. I also asked her to tell them my hugs, kisses, and tears were for them tonight and always.

Dear God, help your people. Find a way to save your people from this on-going evil in our midst. Justice in this land is upside down. Your people cry out, and there is no justice. How long, O

LORD, how long? Bless Bix, Ed, Kathleen, Marge and Mary, your servants and keep us all safe. My prayer is particularly for Kathleen, who has already started her time tonight. Be with your daughter in a mighty way in that Georgia county jail and hold her in your care.

July 24

Harris wanted a brief bio on the five sentenced yesterday in Georgia. He said he would participate in the Thursday fasts in solidarity. I told him about sharing in a 40-day fast on the U.S. Capitol steps in the spring of 1994 with three of these five: Fr. Bix, Ed, and Kathleen.

Many believe the responsibility for the shredding in the mail room goes to higher levels and are trying to prove it. Let's hope the chickens come home to roost. We are told Grijalva is on administrative leave and the case is in the hands of internal affairs. Several have seen to it that people on the outside know about this in the hope that something will be done about it. Yvonne has shared information and will contact postal inspectors today.

It's really surprising the lengths some officers and staff in this system go to make life harder on the inmates than it already is. This federal prison is all about punishment and nothing about rehabilitation. There's so little that's positive about this experience. Most positives we experience are generated by the human beings who are called inmates. You can thank God when you run into an officer who sees more than punishment as their job. I'm amazed that anyone makes it on the outside after being here. And this is the lowest security prison for non-violent prisoners. The daily practice of this prison administration seems designed to bring us all back. I guess it's a policy that's good for business and their career tracks.

The Nightingale's Song got me in better touch with the opponents that Jesus calls on me to love in prison, related to the SOA, and elsewhere. The title is a metaphor in which the author,

Robert Timberg, recognized the characters of his book—McCain, Webb, McFarland, Poindexter and North. All are graduates of the U.S. Naval Academy in Annapolis.

> "Did you know," she asked, "that a nightingale will never sing its song if it doesn't hear it first?" If it hears robins and wrens, she said, it will never croak a note. "But the moment it hears any part of a nightingale's song, it bursts into this extraordinary music, sophisticated, elaborate music, as though it had known it all the time.
>
> "And, of course, it had."
>
> She explained that scientists had learned that the nightingale has a template in its brain that contains all the notes for the music, but that the bird cannot sing unless its song is first triggered by the song of another nightingale.[16]

This metaphor is instructive in considering the different influences in conscience formation and ethical behavior. In the same situation we hear different music and sing a different song, depending on what kind of bird we are.

July 25

I expect Mary Ellen and John this morning although I didn't get hold of her a second time to confirm. I tried to get Marvin a couple of times but missed him too. It's probably too early his time and the phones were tied up here later in the day.

We had a real drenching rainstorm last night about 6:45. The BOP called for a special count right in the midst of it which means inmates were to get back to their cells pronto. I was caught at Camp 1 and had to go back to Camp 2 in the rain. While some ran I just walked at a normal pace. Everyone of us was going to get soaked anyway.

Later I had to go in the rain to dispensary to pick up medicines. I have one new one for hypertension. This is in addition to the diuretic I was already taking. I took the first tab this morning. Perhaps I should alternate with the two morning and one at night. Although it was not suggested it sounds like common sense. I'll ask Mary Ellen what she thinks. She deals with people and their medications all the time.

I think I'll be called out to see one of the doctors July 29, at least that's what is on my report according to the PA. Upon inquiry I was told again that the report of my Tucson primary physician sent to the medical department here in March still is not in my file. The PA flipped through my folder in my presence.

Today looks rainy. It's mostly cloudy. Yesterday's rain was the first of any real consequence that we have had since I've been at La Tuna.

I read more in Dorothy Kazel's biography last night. It gets me back into those days of the Salvadoran civil war. My involvement in Latin American issues began in earnest shortly after her rape and murder. This book's witness is another confirmation for all U.S. citizens who are standing up against the raging tiger of misguided and immoral foreign policy objectives and tactics all these years later. Almost two decades later little or nothing has changed.

The new summary on the Americas, I received yesterday, is testimony as to how long it is taking to bring "objective" evidence to the light of day on human rights abuses. It includes CIA and Contras crack traffic in LA, the assassination of Bishop Gerardi in Guatemala in April, military involvement in Colombian massacres, etc., etc.

I did get a half dozen pieces of mail yesterday. Marvin's letter mentioned that he had changed the address label, removing "Rev" from his church's newsletter so I would get it. I didn't get the July issue. I guess that means it was shredded. It has become clear that I have been a victim of this illegal BOP behavior.

July 26

I had a wonderful visit with Mary Ellen and John yesterday. Joan Brown visited with us for awhile, too. I'm not sure who might come today, but I'm ready if they do. Mary Ellen says Tucson folks plan to participate in a radio call-in show featuring the democratic candidate in our congressional district. They were interested in Randy and me calling in. No can do. It's Monday during a time when I will be at work. It's something they can do just as well.

My op-ed will be published, along with one from Congressman Jim Kolbe, in *The Tucson Citizen,* August 3. We must be "objective" in such things, they say. Being "objective" in the face of atrocity is an abomination. It's a sin against God as well as humanity. Some wondered if I wanted to rewrite my op-ed in the light of the fact it will be published alongside Kolbe's remarks. I said no. It's a gut feeling. Tucsonans can respond with letters to the editor. I'm not going to let Kolbe's article dictate my approach to the subject. We can anticipate what his remarks will be. His will be the Army line. My remarks may not be the best, but they are truthful and humane; which will be more than what we can expect from our opponents whose ultimate value is wielding economic and political power over others. They don't let morals get in the way of their strategic goals. That's why we are in prison.

I discovered that Randy thinks his release is the 22nd. Joan said the women at Pekin believe their release to be on the 24th. We all went into prison on the same day on the same charge with the same sentence. So who's right? This is typical BOP nonsense. I will be disappointed or the others will be happy however this shakes out. I need to talk with Yvonne or Carol at SOA Watch about this discrepancy soon.

I talked to Marvin at length yesterday afternoon late. He sounds so much better. He hopes to send me a copy of his manuscript this week. I told him it had been a good thing that he had not sent it earlier given the shredding of mail here. Mary Ellen had earlier mentioned that sharing the shredding of mail story with the ACLU would be a good thing and she's right. I mentioned this to Marvin.

When Mary Ellen and I embraced as she and John were leaving she was trembling inside. It touched me to the core. I've thought a lot about her trembling since. She seemed to be stifling tears. It must be like I'm dead without being dead as she continues life like it used to be when I was present and a partner in the daily round of things. We really haven't talked about what she's feeling and probably won't until after I'm released. I only held her, kissed and patted her shoulder gently and said, "Soon we will be able to say 'next month.'"

July 27

It would be better if Mr. Green didn't show up for work at all. I resent the fact that I do almost all the work while he lolls around talking to his buddies. He wouldn't know a dirty table if it reached out and bit him in the ass. And he wouldn't take notice if it did.

I called and talked with Carol in the SOA Watch DC office. It was absolutely great to talk with her. I shared my concern that our colleagues might be serving more days than they should. I was given two jail credit days for the days of our arrest and arraignment computed into my 180-day sentence, which give me the release date of September 20. Because it falls on a Sunday I'm due for release on the previous Friday. Carol said she will follow up with an attorney friend of ours. Nevertheless, I went ahead and wrote to Randy today, through Paula, about this inconsistency.

Carol said the media coverage is picking up. Anne Herman was released from Danbury today. Mary McGrory has published another column. I told Carol of the upcoming op-ed in *The Tucson Citizen.*

She said that votes on an amendment to the foreign operations package in both House and Senate could happen as soon as this week or might slip to after the congressional summer recess. A yes vote would deny significant funds to the SOA. Though we would not expect to win this first round in the Senate, she said, if the vote were today we would win the House.

I went down last night to watch a low-pitch softball game between Camp 1 and Camp 2. Our camp won. Their camp won the game before. It was a good diversion. Some men enjoyed playing and some of the rest of us enjoyed watching. It's fun to watch some men struggle to hold onto their tempers in the heat of competition. They all know that if they don't remain under control the privilege of playing ball will be taken away from everyone. It's an effective incentive policed by the inmates themselves. According to the coaches, they recruit "the biggest motherfuckers" to umpire. I agree that some of these umps need glasses and sometimes a brain would help. But, for me, it's all part of the fun.

Some inmates bet on games. The payoff is through the prison commissary. For example, a bet might be a bag of tortilla chips and two Chunky Monkeys.

I have had a very good day today for several reasons. It's been upbeat and for that I'm thankful.

July 28

I've had long conversations with several men who came my way today. Ted was something of a surprise. He borrowed one of three new books that arrived just yesterday afternoon. I received a commentary on *Exodus* by Pixley, on *Ezekiel* by Berrigan, and *Gandhi on Christianity.* He took the Exodus commentary. Ted was raised in the fundamentalist Church of Christ, likes to ride bulls, and was a fairly big time drug dealer in Texas. There's no correlation, of course. He's a good old country boy who's cool, intelligent, and quite pleasant to be around. He's a young man who must keep busy. Although he watches out for his own interests he also is one of the most open and friendly guys here. I often catch him helping someone else out without fanfare. He likes to talk and work. He plays both dominoes and softball. What he can't stand is inactivity.

There's a swallow in the self-service laundry porch nest again this morning. A new brood has been laid. There's a cooling light breeze from the east in a partly cloudy sky tonight.

July 29

It will be August soon. My, how time flies. Today is answer-the-mail day.

I'm also going to thin out my personal library by adding books to the prison library. My locker is getting too full. I'd rather do it than have some rampaging officer do it for me. They go through inmate lockers on a regular basis to make sure we have no "contraband" or too many items of a list of limited articles. We are not supposed to have more than six books. Even in prison my old habits die hard. It's difficult for me to part with books.

I watched a huge thunderstorm moving this way for a long time last night. I don't think we ever got any rain from it. We were getting wind and the smell of rain by the time I went in for bed.

Daylight is getting later and later. I'm on the patio depending on the artificially lit area this early hour. I'm out before the birds start their morning song.

There were many enclosures in my mail yesterday including a generous $25 money order for my commissary account for postage stamps. Prisoners aren't given any money order that arrives but we are suppose to receive a written notification when they are removed from our mail. Another card from T. J. Liggett yesterday. Gary MacEoin is visiting Pilgrim Place at Claremont on his book tour. T. J. said they were talking about me around the dinner table. I received a few copies of the Disciples Peace Fellowship quarterly *NewsNotes* published in June that includes an article on the SOA-related "War in Chiapas," and "Kennon from Prison" that I will insert in some out-going letters. News and opinion articles in this quarterly newsletter and our denominational journal *The Disciple* has generated interest in the issue and letters to me from Disciples around the country.

The "Kennon from Prison" was not, as I thought it would be,

my letter from prison sent to the peace fellowship in April. It was rather a report on my prison transfer in March. It appears they chose not to print my letter. Or, given the revelation of BOP mail shredding last week, perhaps that letter never made it out of here.

I'm having more conversations with fellow inmates around the table and elsewhere these days. I've been around long enough to become comfortable to more and more of my neighbors.

July 30

There's a nice cool breeze this morning. We had thunderstorms in the area last night but, again, not much if any rain here. Today is the first of the Thursday fasts in solidarity with the poor. This is also on my schedule as a letter writing day. I've fallen way behind.

Matt, the wall-builder, is now improving this area next to the Camp 2 south patio. He's a 60's biker doing a long stretch and is Harris' cellie. He's really good at this stone and concrete construction. One only hopes the possibility of these projects continues as long as he is incarcerated. It would be a shame for him to be denied this creative useful occupation. Matt can, like no other man here, survey the beauty and usefulness of his work every day. His new project means I will have to find a different place for journaling at least on some days.

Had my second team meeting yesterday afternoon. It was perfunctory. The unit manager started by asking for an update on the SOA. I told the BOP team about the vote in Congress. I asked about my release. It will be on the hill at the FCI at 8 a.m. Friday, September 18. I asked about the visitor applications that Amy and Marianna submitted in April and again in June and haven't been processed. The counselor says he doesn't have them. "I can't tell you about the mail," the unit manager offered. I bet he can. Obviously they have been shredded. So that's three instances of my mail being tampered with that I specifically know about so far.

I called Mary Ellen and gave her my new release information.

Julie and her boys have been visiting her since Sunday. I talked briefly with all the boys and with Julie. Told her our preliminary plans after my release as I know them.

I also called my Tucson attorney. Mary Ellen insisted he wanted to talk to me. Actually he had very little information for me. Basically Bill wanted to check to see if I am okay and to reassure me that he is there for me if I need him. He said that the government could not take any community property items for the payment of my fine—our business, home, cars, and the like—although that didn't mean they wouldn't try. Inasmuch as the Tucson community raised money specifically to pay the fine for Randy and me then, I think, that's what it should be used for. Many of them see it as a way to participate in this witness. Although I am very sympathetic with the view that the government doesn't deserve to get a dime, we did pledge not to evade the consequences of our actions. Fines are one of those. Therefore we should keep faith with the people who have been so generous. And, with the money available now, there's no reason to be incurring additional interest to the government on top of the fine.

Look. The little swallows are into their morning dance in the air.

July 31

How glorious. This is last day of the month. Yesterday I broke the fast about 1 p.m. with a couple of tortillas. I was a little shaky inside. With this new medicine for high blood pressure I don't know what it does and with the two for diabetes. It's the latter that I shouldn't take on days I'm going to fast. I know this is the case. I routinely took them yesterday morning without thinking. So I didn't make the whole day fasting. But one surely does not want to get sick in here. Next Thursday I'll go without those diabetes meds. They haven't checked my sugar for more than a month. I think it must have been too low yesterday. I ate out of my locker again this evening.

I'm reading *Gandhi on Christianity.* I've already found some challenging ideas. I read *Killing the Dream,* the assassination of MLK Jr. I also read a May 10 issue of *Time* magazine article on new cancer treatments, including information of Marvin's antibody treatment.

Harris announced that he's ready to go with his second book. He plans on expanding on some stories he's already written and add others. He has 12 chapters identified already. It's truly exciting to see his progress and creative output. I am making publication inquiries with two contacts I know for him.

One doesn't have to wait long for things to change around here. About 11:30 a.m. my cellie was notified to pack up his things. He's being moved. Adam was to have his stuff at R&D at 2 p.m. They didn't tell him when he would leave or where he is going. He spent his afternoon getting things together and trying to reach his significant other to tell her not to make the long trip tonight to visit him on the weekend. He says he thinks he might be going to Tucson but he thought that hearing had been postponed. Because I have wondered about his behavior I tried to see if he was being processed like everyone else. He checked in all his stuff to be packed about 3:30. He picked up his mail. He's been out and about ever since which isn't unusual. They usually don't move people on weekends. He is probably here until at least early Monday and maybe Tuesday.

There was a beautiful full and vivid rainbow all the way to the ground on both ends. It framed the Franklin Mountains east of here. A great view was to be had from the patio. It was around in full for almost 45 minutes, and partially even longer as the sun was being obscured by clouds in the west. I've never seen one last so long. It was a rare and spectacular sight. I sat and observed this alluring apparition for many minutes.

Tonight Rich proposed that we put a book together and seek publication. He said he knew a couple of other writers and poets who might contribute as well as some artists. He quickly proposed we spend a couple of hours a week on the project while I'm still here. I told him I'm interested in exploring the possibility. He will be here for several months after my release.

CHAPTER 6

August: Revelations

August 1

I'll be free next month.

Bed check counts at 3, 4, and 5 a.m. I was mostly awake from three on, though I fell back to sleep about 4:30 and awakened for work at five.

I thought about an answer to General Ernst, commander at Fort Benning. I got a letter from him. It is a form letter to the more than 600 who crossed the line last November. It's a puny self-justification for his harsh action against twenty-five peaceful American citizens. The letter was dated June 30, postmarked July 22, sent to my home address and forwarded July 28 from Tucson, received here the afternoon of July 31. It deserves an answer although it's the same ol' same ol'.

It rained last night about 8:30. The BOP calls a special count every time there is a rainstorm. It's a good thing this camp is located where there's a very low average annual rainfall.

I've had an unexpected experience the last couple of days with one of my food service bosses. Yesterday he was trying, again, to "talk some sense into" a young man who has been given the obvious nickname "Doughboy" because of his physical appearance. Robby Wright is very immature and expects the whole world to revolve around him. He has a big mouth, always has to have the last word, and doesn't pull his weight on the job. Wright gives both the officers and his co-workers a fit. Always. He won't listen to anyone.

The boss called him over to the staff table to talk with him to no avail. Then this boss called me over and asked if I had a "good word" for Mr. Wright. He means a Bible quote. Obviously the boss was at the end of his rope.

Advice is not my thing and I have never liked to play the "proof-text game" this boss plays. When he is on duty he invariably asks me for "the good word for the day." This practice always seems a little demeaning to me. Rather than spout something, and noticing about a half dozen other inmates standing nearby overhearing this conversation, I asked, "Does anyone have a Bible word for Mr. Wright?" I never call him "Doughboy" because the nickname is a frontal assault on his self-esteem. One man, not known for his spirituality, immediately said, "As a man thinketh in his heart so is he." I did not have to reply, although I had thought of one, and as the boss and the other inmates continued to talk with Mr. Wright I just slowly moved away and continued my work.

Pretty soon Mr. Wright got up and started to leave. He was immediately surrounded by fellow inmates and verbally bombarded with how they feel about him. Observing from a distance I thought this aggressive encounter might prove helpful to Mr. Wright in the long run. That scene melted away.

The first thing this morning, when I reported for work, the same boss called me to his office off the kitchen.

"What's the good word for today, Kennon," he characteristically asked.

"Well, I thought of one for Mr. Wright," I said.

"Oh? What is that?"

"The tongue is a fire. What a great forest is set ablaze by such a small flame," I replied.

This started a conversation about his seeming failure to "get through" to Mr. Wright. He expressed some sincere concern. And then he asked me what I thought Wright's problem was. While I concurred with some of his diagnosis I told him I thought Mr. Wright wasn't ready to listen and that rather than good advice he needed to discover the answer to his problem within himself and needed to be assisted, if possible, to do that. The boss proceeded to ask about my training and experience as a counselor. He even asked how many years of training I have and where I got my degrees. I've never had such an "among equals" exchange with any of the BOP officers. His problem, and Mr. Wright's problem, remain unresolved but these were unique encounters for me.

August 2

No visitors yesterday. Worked all meals. Read some more of the Gandhi book. It's quite fascinating to me. The big softball game was fun to watch. Joe gave me a "home-cooked" burrito last night. There are small microwave ovens in each camp for inmate use so that foods and beverages purchased at the company store can be heated. The more creative prepare simple meals and snacks from the limited commissary items they can purchase. Often they prefer this option to the food served up at the dining hall. Not everyone has an option.

This morning dawns with flights of swallows performing their ritual in the quadrangle. With all the new ones their numbers have noticeably increased. I think these flights and the seeming playfulness has to do with pairing up. Because of the wetter weather lately there are increased gnats and mosquitoes which the swallows are good at catching. They like to skim over the grass at the right time in the morning just as the insects rise out of the dewy grass and weeds.

I talked to Rich more about the proposed book project. We will get together probably this evening to start working at gathering the materials. The idea is for us to get it pretty much together before I'm released, and then I'll follow up on publication possibilities. I'm not sure I want to do that and I don't want to give him false hopes.

August 3

I was awakened at 1:15 a.m. when a guard entered our cell. He shook Finley and told him to report to the Camp 1 office within fifteen minutes. He's being shipped out this morning. The case manager told Adam Sunday that he was going to Arizona to appear in court. I probably will not see him again. I will never know where he's coming from for sure.

The camp rumor is that our shredding scandal does have personnel from the BOP regional office, FBI, and Postal Inspector's Office investigating, and the case goes even above the unit manager here, and that "heads will roll," with indictments within 30 days. We'll see.

A food service supervisor changed Mr. Green to doing floors only. This means that for two days a week Mr. Roberts and I work alone in dining hall when the other is on their days off. Roberts will have the dining room floor to do only two days a week. I don't do floors. I have done some sweeping but no mopping since my medical restrictions were set. But today I worked overtime doing all the dining hall windows inside and also outside on the entrance wall windows. I worked up a good sweat.

What with conversations with three neighbors following breakfast, I'm getting around to this journaling very late. I'm in my room because the construction project and mowing is now in progress where I usually do my morning writing.

I am alone in the cell for a second time. It's stunning how the situation can change so quickly. What next?

Today my op-ed is scheduled to appear in *The Tucson Citizen.* I have asked for Mary Ellen to see to it that Carol receives a clean reprintable copy at the SOA Watch office in DC.

August 4

I tried to call Mary Ellen this morning at seven. I momentarily got my own voice on the answering machine. And, of course, I can't leave a message because there's no one there to accept my collect call.

Bosses have worked me hard the last two mornings. It can be hard work for a man in my condition. It would have been a snap if I were younger. It's harder on Mr. Robert's days off because Mr. Green is no help and the boss expects the same result.

There's finally a realistic concern expressed by inmates of a complete cover-up of the mail shredding. It is hard to know what to believe and whom. But yesterday a man got back a certified letter return card that he paid postage for, but probably it never left here. The card had a FCI La Tuna date stamp on it. It was to the Warden and signed by Officer Grijalva who some were told was on administrative leave. Grijalva is obviously presently working in the mail room on the hill. They have "fixed" the problem by shifting the same officer to the hill so we will not see him do the same job. Lt. Solis may have no more integrity than any other officer here after all. Or perhaps doing something about this system from the inside is just impossible thanks to the solidarity of the blue line.

I did receive great mail yesterday including another commissary money order from Mary Ellen as requested. It is costing $20 a week just for postage stamps.

An invitation arrived from Anne Barstow, a national board member of Witness for Peace, regarding their 15th anniversary meeting at Los Angeles in early November. They plan to recognize the witness of the SOA 25. We could stay with Marvin and Elaine. Paula has family in the area, too. Perhaps she and Randy and the two of us could drive over together. I'll check with Marvin about preaching at his two churches that Sunday morning. Perhaps that would help him out.

August 5

What a spectacular day. I received Marvin's Mark manuscript yesterday afternoon. I had time to read his afterword before having to report for supper service. It is so powerfully beautiful I wept. Then after supper and commissary I got the manuscript out while a storm was gathering. A strong wind preceded the storm coming from the northwest. As I laid on my bunk reading Marvin's Introduction through Chapter 5, between six and nine o'clock, we had a constant thunderstorm with wind, lightning flashing, thunder banging and rumbling, and driving rain. It was more special effects than Cecil B. DeMille's *Ten Commandments.* What a mysterious backdrop of nature to my reading of Marvin's manuscript. I will never forget it. We have never had any storm like it since I've been here. Sustained thunderstorms one after another. And what a powerful manuscript.

Now it's 5:45 a.m. and as I sit on the patio the sky is clear of clouds as the light has begun peeking over the mountains. A bright Venus sparkles in the eastern sky above those mountains on this moonless morning. There is a very cool light breeze out of the southeast. I love the fresh starting of this day.

I am still enthralled by Marvin's manuscript and will complete reading through it for the first time on this day off for me. It's like no commentary I've ever read. It is not a commentary. It's something else. The Gospel of Mark for the twenty-first century with all its first-century power. It has a quality to it that invites contemplation, meditation, and action. It is spare and direct. I am mightily moved. If last night is any example, so is all Creation.

I did not get through to Mary Ellen yesterday. I'll try again today. I'm interested about whether the op-ed got published as scheduled.

August 6

The op-ed articles were published. They took up most of the front page of the perspective section on Monday. Mary Ellen said, "We made a splash." Now the Tucson SOA Watch is generating letters to the editor to follow up. She has sent me three copies already and will send photocopies for distribution.

I spent most of my day reading Marvin's manuscript. I shared it with Harris and asked for his evaluation. He brought up some good points. I'm so proud of my little brother. He's been researching this book for more than twenty years. He should be feeling pleased at his accomplishment. It is a marvelous contribution to the world.

August 7

The August 3 Perspective page of *The Tucson Citizen* arrived in yesterday's mail. This is a new record time for delivery from Tucson. Two days. It's an eye-catching page layout with photos and quote bars. Kolbe's article is right out of the U.S. Army talking points and nothing new. It all sounds so plausible if one didn't know the truth already. I'm hoping people will wonder why the Army would insist on jailing peaceful SOA protesters if, in truth, it is the noble institution Kolbe says it is. Mary Ellen was right. It is a splash.

I sent one copy on to Carol Richardson, along with *The Citizen's* July 10 editorial column. I'll send another to Marvin. And, I suppose, the third will go to Arizona City.

I received seven books from a Tucson friend with a note. They include *Booknotes,* writers speaking about writing, from the C-SPAN program interviews. I've already started reading it and it's going to be good for me. Another by Maya Angelou, poems by Thomas Merton, *The Cloister Walk,* a blank notebook, and two small books of cartoons from *The New Yorker.*

One interview in *Booknotes* is with Tina Rosenberg who wrote *Children of Cain: Violence and the Violent in Latin America* published in 1991. That's a book I want to read. She attempts to understand and explain why people do evil. Rosenberg lived in El Salvador, Nicaragua, Chile and Peru. "This book is not about the victims. It's the perpetrators. It's about people who commit evil or people who learn to live with evil and why they do it."[17]

I wrote a record 18 letters yesterday. I need to do about that many more over the weekend to catch up.

August 8

Will Mary Ellen be here today? I'm dressed for it. The BOP does not allow food service workers to wear their whites to the visiting room. It's against policy. I guess we have to be properly presentable. Whatever that is it includes no whites. Mary Ellen said she would try to be here. She wanted to come.

Yesterday was fairly uneventful. I am reading *Booknotes* and really enjoying it. I'm taking some notes as I go along since I'm going to pass this book on.

I have misplaced one of the copies of the August 3 piece. I've already sent one to Carol. I probably put it somewhere for safe keeping or it's under something. I don't think I'm losing my mind, but then I'd be the last to know, wouldn't I?

Harris and I have discussed Marvin's manuscript. He's impressed as am I. I'm glad I asked him to read it because he has no baggage he brings to it. He has several suggestions and questions to be considered that will be helpful to Marvin. I asked him to write something down to send on.

August 9

Mary Ellen was able to visit. Bob Allen came for a little while, too.

Last night Rich from next door came over and we had our first sit-down consideration of his book idea using our writings in prison. He has over thirty poems and I have eight. We talked a lot about the focus and nature of such a book. He has some very good ideas but they seem unfocused and disorganized. Rich is going to sit down and write "an introduction" to such a volume, and I am to do the same, and then we will get back together and share them.

Obviously I will need to have more to contribute. He talked of using my prose pieces, "A Letter from Prison," "Enough Is More Than Enough," and perhaps others. He suggested I could include some correspondence and or journal entry excerpts that give a sense of the prison experience of both us.

There are aspects to this experience that we may want to include that neither of us have written about. Perhaps we can create poems, rather than writing about such things in prose, that speak to these realities and our feelings about them. We need to list those for focus.

Rich was eloquent in speaking about the meaning of prison for him and its impact on his life. He suggests we both write about this for the book.

His idea is that I'll see to it that it gets published. This expectation is daunting. He has ten months more to serve than me. He suggested if there is any income from the project it be given to charity. He basically would just like to start getting his work out there and share with the world this something positive that can flow out of a very negative experience.

August 10

Dylan worked his last day yesterday. He has two days off, five days "vacation," then leaves for a halfway house in Arizona a week from today. We have become friends since he transferred from the hill, working together in the dining hall, and sharing common concerns about the impunity of BOP officers. Since he said he wants to be at Arizona City on my first Sunday back I had asked him to sing something. He said he would. I suggested John Lennon's "Imagine" would be great. Dylan said he used to sing that and he'll think about it. We exchanged addresses and phone numbers.

Another day of visiting with Mary Ellen. Although there was nothing earth-shaking about these moments, it's such a pleasure to have time together, despite the greatly circumscribed circumstance. We talked about family and business matters, as is our usual thing to do, and participated in Mass together.

I am still enjoying reading *Booknotes* and finding books reviewed that I want to read when I get out. I'm taking some quotes and notes that relate to what I'm doing and some to Marvin's manuscript.

I have a couple of poem ideas: "Wanted Dead But Alive," "Trembling to the Core." I don't know quite how to go about creating poetry from this other direction; that is, having a theme you are interested in writing about and then finding the best images to convey the thought. Up to this point most of my poetry has started with an image that suggested a poem. Yet, I suppose, it is essentially no different than say my observation of birds. I will simply observe human behavior. Still one needs appropriate expressive images that will carry the freight.

There are a couple of stray mother cats with new litters who have appeared on the compound. Some animal-loving men have been sneaking food from their plates out of the dining hall to feed them. Some also have been fouling the BOP live traps that have been set for them. An official memo was posted at both camps today signed by the acting camp administrator. It threatens, "Any inmate found to be feeding the stray cats, or tampering with the traps, will be subject to disciplinary action."

August 11

There is a prisoner here who is the sole local expert in maintaining the prison's sewage treatment facility for both the FPC and the FCI on the hill. Prison wits say, "He knows all the shit." It becomes very problematic for the BOP to discipline this sewage engineer in any way that would take him off his job because no one else has the expertise to keep it flowing. He knows this and takes advantage of his unique position in small benign but deliberate ways. This dilemma grates the BOP and tickles us.

I wrote to Marvin yesterday to let him know that two of us here have read his manuscript and are impressed and appreciative. It is greatly improved from his first draft. It has come alive. The narrative is powerful. Not only that but reading this work while in prison is a perspective that I didn't realize I would ever have. This vantage point clearly reveals just how vividly true his manuscript is to the text.

August 12

Yesterday was a particularly stimulating day because of two conversations with young men. Almost every man here is young to me. Of course there is old Herb who is pushing eighty and still serving time on a drug-related conspiracy charge. The young ones call him "Pops." His health is bad and he's the only man with a work exemption. Why do they insist on keeping him here?

My first conversation was with a man who was a U.S. Army special forces trainer of SOA trainers. He taught selected Latin American military elites the doctrine and tactics of psychological warfare at Fort Benning. This included torture methods. He had told me he was once at Fort Benning early in my stay here, but yesterday he was very explicit about his involvement with the SOA.

He came to my cell the morning after reading *The Tucson Citizen* op-ed page which had been shared with him by another man I had given it to the night before. He said, "I didn't realize all this stuff." It obviously had got him thinking again about his part in this and other special operations of the U.S. Army he took part in over his years of service.

He went into gory detail about the specific nature of the training he was involved in. He taught Latin American military men how to break down the "enemy" psychologically by experiencing some of the torture techniques themselves. It was a brutal account. For example, being strung bound and upside down to a tree or building or tent support and spun around and around until vomiting and/or passing out. Being buried up to their necks in sand, then having a black hood put over their heads and a draw string pulled and tied under their chins so they couldn't see. With only a small slit for their mouths so they could breathe, these students were buried in rows and then a jeep or other vehicle would be driven up over them. Though they would not be hit by the vehicle they were terrorized. Their trainers threatened to drive over their heads. There were verbal threats as well as the revving of the engine above them while a spare tire would be ominously rolled up against their heads, applying a little pressure each time the engine revved. Vroom. Vroom.

These are just a couple illustrations of what he shared. He said most torture techniques taught by the Army aren't written down anywhere, but are passed on through training like he provided from one class to another. It's not written down because the U.S. Army wants to be able to deny they teach such techniques without the possibility of leaking any written evidence to the contrary. Instructors and students are sworn to secrecy.

It's obvious by his confession that this man is bothered about his involvement in this training. It's one of his many black experiences while in the special forces. He's here on a drug charge and was probably a user. I wonder why? He says, and I believe him, that his service was motivated by patriotism and the desire to be an effective military professional. Now he's bothered by what he did as an obedient soldier. That appears to be the reason why he came to talk with me.

He's not interested in going public because he believes that would only result in getting him in trouble and not make any difference in the covert practices of the U.S. Army.

The other young man came by a little before nine p.m. Ted has had an interest in talking with me in the past. He asks very basic and hard questions about both religion and ethics. It wasn't exactly a conversation. It was mostly Q and A. He asked what I thought about The Book of Revelation. If there is such a thing as a miracle. Do I believe in life after death. The nature of God. If God condemns people to hell, and so forth.

Ted was raised in a very conservative political and religious atmosphere. I always find our encounters interesting because my orientation to life is so very different than his. This probably goes both ways.

August 13

I'm fasting in solidarity today. This morning I have a lab callout (no breakfast). Good timing. A fluke.

We had some rain overnight. I awakened more times than usual last night. Lots of dreaming. But I stayed in bed until 5:30. Wow, what a sleepyhead.

Only about eight letters written and a like number received. Read most of the rest of *Booknotes* and will finish it this morning. Then I'll go exploring another of the books my friend sent.

I've been somewhat surprised by those people I have not heard from while in prison. Why? The reasons why would make an interesting sociological inquiry. Nevertheless, my life is being enriched daily by the blessed exceptions and they are making all the difference.

"You've got nothing coming," is a phrase that is heard a lot around here. It speaks of the inhumanity and hopelessness prisoners experience. I need to find a way to write a poem about this. This prison is run by brutes who are into domination beyond incarceration. This week's posted memo on punishment for feeding kittens is just one more example. Destroying the nests of the barn swallows in the porches, especially while occupied, is another. Destroying the inmates' mail, etc., etc., etc. Systemic brutishness is the order of the day. My guess is that this behavior is not only condoned but encouraged by prison administrators. That's why it's a pattern, not an aberration.

August 15

Five weeks from today Mary Ellen *and* I will be on our way back to Tucson. I will have been out for 24 hours. This is a very pleasant thought indeed.

On Thursday and Friday I read Maya Angelou's new memoir, *Gather Together In My Name.* It starts where *Caged Bird* leaves off and chronicles five or six years in her teens and early twenties. It is an incredibly honest and dramatic story. Her writing style is both so poetic and powerful.

This followed *Booknotes* which proved to be the right book at the right time for me. I've already passed both these along to others. Now I'm into *The Cloister Walk* by Kathleen Norris. I think it will prove as fascinating in its own way as the other two. My friend Mary sent me all of these. Her choices are proving to be especially fortuitous gifts.

I have thought about the images of dryness, aridness, and desert as descriptive of prison experience. I'm trying to jump start some more poems. Last summer at this time I was writing a poem a day.

I have a Kafka-like perception of the way this system and its administrators suck the life fluids out of inmates until all there is left is a shell. Like the attack of a predatory insect dominating others. What is that Kafka book? The title doesn't come to me immediately. I see again that his vision was clear.

Bill Murphy told me of his visit to the hill to see a medical specialist. He said the doctor revealed he had suffered a cervical spinal dislocation (C1-C6) in a job-related accident caused by a La Tuna BOP officer in June. As the specialist tried to explain his injury the BOP director of medical services butted in to say it was only arthritis. The specialist said without the proper physical therapy the condition, and the symptoms, would get progressively worse. The clinical director announced that the BOP has no money for the recommended therapy. The specialist responded, "I'm going to write down my diagnosis and recommendations anyway." Bill is in constant pain and for two months now has been getting progressively worst. So far no treatment and no pain management other than Motrin. It is inhumane negligence.

A young Disciple friend has been living down the hall. He is leaving La Tuna for a halfway house tomorrow. He once told me that the pastor of his home congregation has been a lifesaver for him. She has written to him once a week without fail ever since he has been incarcerated. She probably doesn't realize just how important this outside connection and encouragement has been to him. He has an 18-hour bus ride ahead of him and said, "I'm going to enjoy every minute of it."

There are many men leaving this month and next. The La Tuna FPC population is presently the lowest in memory—157. It was right at 200 when I arrived. Is it a matter of administrators not assigning men to this lower level of security who could very well be here? Randy Serraglio is a good example. Why are they keeping him and others of the SOA 25 in higher security institutions? Pure meanness? It doesn't make any more sense than most other policies and practices of this spiteful Bureau of Prisons.

With fewer and fewer men to accomplish the same work we are all working harder. My job is not a difficult or demanding one but now we have two doing the work four or more used to perform. And, like today and tomorrow, when the other assigned man is having his days off I work alone and vice versa. One good friend here leaves tomorrow.

August 16

I spent last night differently than usual. First of all I went to the softball game. It is entertaining to watch men trying to be boys again. Then I went to the library to scan the Saturday newspaper. Then it was on to the TV room to watch the last quarter and a half of the 49ers/Seahawks preseason game that went down to the last two seconds before it was decided.

I called and talked with Marvin in the afternoon. We talked about his manuscript. He's got my first letter but not my second. He leaves very early Monday morning to drive north to pick up his friend Lee. They are spending several days among the redwoods in Mendocino County north of the Bay Area. It sounds glorious. Cora was with them in Long Beach from Wednesday until Friday when she continued her trip back to Japan.

Earlier in the day I wrote letters and read in *The Cloister Walk.* It's a better book than I ever imagined. The author is a poet who makes the connection between poetry and faith. Her book is so good for me it's hard to write small excerpts from it. I often want whole pages.

I have been excerpting what I want from these books so that I can pass them on to others and eventually leave them here. That's a good discipline for one who has a history of hoarding books.

I am utterly amazed at Mary's selection to send me. I couldn't have done it better myself and probably wouldn't have done it as well. All of these books are very different yet all on target with what I need right now. She even sent a blank one in which I'm writing my notes as I go along.

I have used all the op-ed copies so I'm waiting to send some letters until Tuesday thinking I should receive a new supply from Mary Ellen in Monday's mail.

August 17

Just talked to Mary Ellen. She thinks she and Punch will be coming this weekend.

The powers-that-be called a special count in the middle of Mass yesterday. Two officers showed up at the chapel to shoo us back to our cells. The chaplain was in the middle of his sermon and he told them they'd have to go tell their boss that, "I'm in the middle of the Mass here." That put them back on their heels. They recovered enough to ask for a show of hands for a count of each camp and left. On the plus side it did get the chaplain out of the worst sermon I've heard him preach. After the interruption he just went on to the next thing. Despite the fact that he has been in the BOP for more than 20 years, in some contexts at least, he still recognizes a higher authority.

Mary Ellen said she has talked to the Arizona ACLU regarding the inmates' situation at La Tuna. They asked her to send written information and will do so when she is able.

August 18

We have two restrooms in Camp 2. I prefer to go to the one furthest away because the orderly there puts out soap bars in dishes to wash one's hands and the other doesn't. When the BOP wouldn't give him any deodorant for the urinals this orderly went out and got twigs from nearby creosote bushes and put a twig in each one. He said, "It's better than the smell of urine." Pretty ingenious.

I continued to receive very interesting letters and enclosures. The one I got from Brophy yesterday about his recent trip to Honduras and Guatemala ought to be submitted as an op-ed piece for publication. I will write and tell him so.

The article copies I asked Mary Ellen for a week ago haven't arrived yet. I'm still holding some letters I've written hoping to enclose a copy. Receiving mail is less sure than it ought to be.

I have come out to the laundry porch this morning because it's still cool enough to be pleasant after my morning work. I prefer outside to inside with all its noise of men doing their jobs cleaning the interior of the camp. Orderlies clean all floors, rest rooms, and shower rooms every weekday. I appreciate the resulting cleanliness. But the operation is boisterous.

I had a long conversation with a man late last night on the patio. He will be moving to the hill later this morning to participate in the DAPS program—drug rehab—that will take one year off his sentence when successfully completed. He's a nice person who says he's guilty of doing some not so nice things defrauding institutions he worked for to get money to support his drug habit. We have hit it off well, getting acquainted over lunch, and for the last few weeks as he has been working in the dish room. This is the man who almost died of an allergic reaction when he was prescribed the wrong medication.

August 19

New shoes. Issued yesterday. The right size after five months. While I was counting my blessings another man stopped in front of my cell showing off his shoes. He exclaimed, "Raise a prayer of thanksgiving to God. I got new shoes after two years and four months." Evidently such experience is all too common.

I have become so used to the old too-big shoes that I was somewhat hesitant. The fact that they allowed me to try these new ones on before taking them made me less apprehensive. The worst thing about the old ones is they have no grip left on the soles. I slipped a lot on wet floors and had to be very careful because of my back injury. The dining hall has wet floors after every meal and sometimes at other times. That alone convinced me to go ahead and get them. They issued about fifty pair in all. I heard that they issued them because "they needed the room in the warehouse." I don't know if this is true or not. Inmates are cynical. They are taught to be by this barbaric system. There are 160 men in camp right now. At least a third of us have been needing decent shoes for some time now.

The early morning sky is so beautiful. A crescent moon is over the Franklin Mountains, along with Venus, as first light comes. While the sky was very cloudy at sunset last night almost all clouds are gone now. There is Orion in the northeastern sky. "Our stars," as Mary Ellen and I possessively say. We first claimed them long years ago when we were courting teenagers.

What a serene scene in such a place of punishment. The night sounds of the insects are still with us. And the sounds of the laundry machines drone through the walls and the wheels of the semis along I-10 are heard humming beyond them. One feels almost free in the early coolness and quiet of this day. Now the first man leaves the camp building and walks through the patio without a word.

I'm getting my haircut for the second time at ten. I have a

callout for a teeth cleaning in the dental clinic this afternoon at 12:30. It's not like I requested it.

Norris' book is really getting my creative juices flowing and she gives me courage. Her honesty and perspective are very helpful to my journey just now. I'm about halfway through the book.

The op-ed copies did not arrive in yesterday's mail. It's been eight days since Mary Ellen mailed them. I only hope they are only delayed and not lost or destroyed. So much for the record two day delivery.

August 21

Barbara, a correspondent in New Hampshire, typed up an excerpt around a Martin Niemöller's quote from my letter to her on August 11. The quote was on a postcard she sent to me that stirred the story that I wrote to her in response. She wants to post this excerpt on the SOA Watch website so she typed it up and sent me a copy to check over. She did get it posted and I got a letter last night. Here's the quote and what I wrote her:

> *In Germany they first came for the communists, and I didn't speak up because I wasn't a communist. Then they came for the Jews, and I didn't speak up because I wasn't a Jew. Then they came for trade unionists, and I didn't speak up because I wasn't a trade unionist. Then they came for the Catholics, and I didn't speak up because I was a Protestant. Then they came for me—and by that time no one was left to speak up.*
>
> —Pastor Martin Niemöller[18]

> The Niemöller quote is one I used in November 1989. I was at a national conference of Disciple regional ministers (read bishops) and moderators. I was serving as moderator of the Christian Church (Disciples of Christ) in Arizona in those days and as vice-chair of this national conference. It was right after the massacre of the six Jesuits and two women

in San Salvador. The executive committee prepared a resolution regarding that massacre in condemnation of the act and in support of an investigation. It was very unusual for this particular group to bring forth any resolution on any social matter as those mechanisms are lodged elsewhere in our denomination, but this was the only national group meeting at this time.

When the resolution was brought before the membership of the Conference it was being talked to death. "It's not for us to pass such a resolution," etc. etc. All very safe institutional considerations. The discussion made me angry and it looked as though the institutional bootlickers were going to win again. We would not so much as speak out in protest to such an outrage? I don't remember what I said just before the vote. It wasn't much. Then Niemöller's words came to me and I applied them to that the present situation. The resolution passed overwhelmingly.

When I got back to Tucson I learned a demonstration and civil disobedience (C.D.) action was planned at the Federal Building the next day at 4 p.m. I took my new national resolution to the event to distribute to the local media.

I had not planned to participate in the C.D. action because we had a rule that to participate one had to be present and take part in the planning session and covenanting leading up to it. I had been out of town. I knew from previous experience that I could enter the building and proceed with the C.D.'ers to the office of the IRS where they would demand that our tax money not support death squads in El Salvador, and they would sit-in until arrested. There would be a moment when the local police would say, "If you don't leave, you will be arrested," and I would leave then.

At the demonstration outside organizers hung large poster board name tags with the names of the massacred

> around the necks of eight people. I happened to get Segundo Montes' nameplate placed around my neck.
>
> When the C.D.'ers made their move I went with them. Once inside I noticed that I was the only clergyperson in the group. So when the police made the arrest announcement I couldn't bring myself to leave and was arrested with fifteen others.
>
> When we were processed by the officers they had a series of questions they asked everyone. As they got around to me all the questions were asked but one. "Don't you want to know my name?" I inquired of the officer who interviewed me. "I already know your name," he said. "Segundo Montes."
>
> We were taken to court, found guilty, and served one year supervised probation. It was the only other time I served a sentence from a court. The experiences were, of course, a factor in my participation in School of Americas Watch actions.
>
> I have had a special attachment, it seems, to Fr. Montes ever since. The next spring I was in El Salvador with Pastors for Peace. We went to Morazan and participated in the inauguration ceremony for a new community of repatriated refugees—Ciudad de Segundo Montes.

Copies of my op-ed and an article from *The Citizen* were finally received August 20. Eight days in transit. The pages had been shuffled. Mary Ellen included copies of "sensitive" information about the shredding by mistake and I wonder if this caused the delay. I'll never know. But I think so. The one who the material is about is the very one processing the mail on the hill now. Ouch. I had sent this page out as a part of my journaling, so why would Mary Ellen send copies of *that* page back in? The mail officer got an unexpected eyeful.

August 22

On Friday I took my "extra" books to the chapel library. Others I want to keep for the moment, or plan to take home, I parceled out to friends to store for me so I wouldn't have so many in my locker. We are supposed to have no more than six and the word is out that there will be a huge shakedown of all inmate lockers within the next two weeks. There are always rumors. Sometimes they are even true.

One book was a Bible. Actually I had already given mine to a man early on and he requested another which he gave to me in exchange when it arrived. This was that second copy. I had told Harris to give it to some man who wanted it and I'll just borrow a Bible from the chapel if I need one for the remainder of my time here.

Not two hours after that I overheard Jose asking the counselor how to go about ordering a Bible. They were in the hallway and went into the counselor's office. In a little while I went to Jose's cell and told him I'd overheard him inquiring about a Bible and I had one I'd like to give to him if he wanted it. He said he did. That was just before lunch. After lunch I retrieved the study Bible from the chapel and gave it to Jose. I told him that if he met others who wanted one just like it how they could get one free on request and that the chaplain's assistant had the address. He thanked me.

Later in the day Jose appeared at my cell while I was stretched out reading and asked if I would "sign his Bible." Not knowing exactly what he meant I said "Sure," and got up off my bunk.

He placed the Bible on my table and opened it to the presentation page in the front. He had already put his name and the date on it and handed me a pen to sign my name on the line which indicates "given by." I was very touched. "Thank you," Jose said as he left. "De nada," I replied.

I later heard in a conversation with another man that Jose had told him he had had some spiritual awakening in here. He started going to Protestant services, though he was raised a Catholic. "I don't know what I am," he had said. It is clear he is a seeker.

Still later I took a copy of the op-ed down for him to read. I really have never talked to him as to why I am in here. I do know that he, as well as others, are a little confused as to why a Protestant minister participates in the Catholic Mass rather than Protestant services. I have seldom been asked why. Jose has stopped by my cell on occasion to invite me to Protestant services and I have not gone.

So we have a Catholic attending Protestant services and a Protestant minister attending Catholic Mass. It makes more sense than most things here.

I am presently reading *Writing for Story* by Jon Franklin which I borrowed from Harris. He's read it four times seeking guidance for his own writing and has talked a lot about its helpfulness. I'm into it and I think it's going to be helpful to me, too. I must get a copy when I get out. It's especially for "non-fiction short story," but has applications to fiction and longer works. Franklin includes two of his Pulitzer Prize winning stories and uses them to illustrate his approach to the task of writing with a complication-resolution model.

I had a visit with Sr. Jean yesterday. She filled me in on some of the local news and some of the thinking relative to the events for the day of my release. A group will be meeting August 31 to plan the details.

Jean mentioned the possibility of my speaking at colleges at both Las Cruces and El Paso during the day. It sounds like they are really going to use me, which I welcome. A representative delegation will have an appointment with Congressman Reyes in El Paso soon. They have had to work very hard to get an appointment. This group includes very skilled and experienced community organizers among their number.

I'm waiting for Punch Woods and Mary Ellen to arrive for a visit today.

August 23

Lots of visitors yesterday. A record. Bob, Mary Ellen and Punch, and then Nick. When Bob was here one of the Protestant chaplains sat down with the two of us for several minutes to visit. It is more conversation than I've had with him since I've been here. He said that during the Marcos regime he was in the Philippine Army but left because of human rights abuses that they did with impunity. I believe he was a Catholic chaplain then, but he didn't say that. He came to the U.S., stayed, and married. He's presently an Episcopalian priest of the high tradition. He revealed that he has used me "as an illustration of the cost of discipleship."

I had a wonderful visit with Mary Ellen and all the others. We talked about many issues. Mary Ellen tells me Amy and Marianna are planning to visit next weekend and that all but Randy are being released on September 18. Further she said that Randy doesn't want to be involved in media and community immediately after release but wants to "fly away" with Paula. Surely Randy will get the same release date as the rest of us eventually. Preliminary plans call for a community gathering on Saturday morning. Mary Ellen said Amy and Marianna will talk to me about all this during their weekend visit. It's clear that Randy's prison experience has been more difficult than mine.

Mary Ellen said she had sent the copies of my journal page on purpose. I didn't scold her but this enclosure has been a concern to me. There are some possible personal repercussions she is understandably unaware of. Perhaps there will be no fallout from it.

August 24

I received a forwarded letter from a congregation I served as a student in the 50's. First Christian of Granbury, Texas, invited me to their dedication of a new building and reunion. I wrote back my regrets. The occasion will be on the weekend I am released. I shared some stories and history from our days there as well as a full compliment of articles and fact sheets as to why their former pastor is in prison.

Nona sent an article clipped from *The Arizona Republic* about how my Congressman Jim Kolbe and eighteen of his staff members attended training sessions in war and leadership strategies put on and paid for by the U.S. Army. Kolbe's press spokesman told a reporter that the training gave the congressman's staff insight into how to "neutralize the enemy." He used citizens who went to Kolbe's office to peacefully protest the Mount Graham telescope project as a case in point. The Army emphasized that there was no evidence the Army personnel addressed "partisan issues" in their briefing and that their training was on Army procedures. Yeah, sure. How objective can such Pentagon-sponsored sessions be? I have always had the feeling that my congressman and his staff were hand in glove with the U.S. Army. Now here is confirmation along with an example of how such partisan Pentagon chumminess develops. It's scary. So much for an independent congressional oversight.

Kathleen Norris writes:

> A prophet's task is to reveal the fault lines hidden beneath the comfortable surface of the worlds we invent for ourselves, the national myths as well as the little lies and delusions of control and security that get us through the day.[19]

I haven't read Marvin's manuscript a second time but I intend to do that and give him some additional comments.

I have written to my regional minister to inform him in confidence that I plan to resign my pastorate on or before December 31. The die is cast. I'm leaping out of the nest.

August 26

Yesterday was hell for Bill Murphy from morning until night. A little after 7 a.m. they called him to the Camp 1 office to take him to the hole for refusing to work. Because of his injury he can't. He is in constant pain from a June 16th accident on the job and he is yet to receive any meaningful medical care. He asked another inmate to try to notify his El Paso attorneys. He has not seen them but they have been retained.

When the case manager was called to bring handcuffs to the Camp 1 office, and she learned they were for Murphy, she blew a gasket. The upshot was that he was not taken to the hole.

The officers continued to hassle him throughout the day. He told me he was ready to talk to the press. He says he was convicted of wire fraud relating to changing auto odometer readings, serving 16 months, and now he is at the mercy of this medieval system where mercy is a rare occurrence indeed.

Later in the day Bill was called to the acting camp administrator's office, to the education office, to the Camp 1 office at least twice, and again last night to the Camp 2 office where he was given "a shot" by from one of the most draconian officers at La Tuna on orders of the acting camp administrator for refusing to work. "A shot" is a written black mark on a prisoner's record that can be used to justify strong disciplinary measures of one kind or another including solitary confinement and the loss of early release.

In the afternoon this same officer, whom I'll ironically call Igor, raided Murphy's room locker and was going through his personal and legal papers. He had them spread out on the table when Bill walked in and caught him at it. Igor told Murphy two lies about why he was doing this. Bill called him a liar because he was. He shouted at him and told him to stay out of his stuff. The outburst alerted all the men who were in the building. Bill wisely turned on his heel and left the building to cool off because he was so angry. Igor would have liked nothing better than take him to the hole for assaulting an officer.

Murphy's attorneys have not been able to see him because every time they call his counselor to arrange their visit he's "not available."

When they finally took Murphy to the hill for an X-ray of his neck late last month the technician told him to stay in the room while he left to get a doctor. One of the doctors examined the X-rays and exclaimed, "Oh, my God," or words to that effect. "Man, why didn't you get in here immediately?" Murphy told him he had been trying to ever since the accident on June 16. "This is very serious," the doctor said. And then he wouldn't tell him any more without speaking first to the clinical director. Murphy was given Motrin for pain. That was the extent of it.

It was several weeks later, with the pain increasing, that they took him to the hill for a consult with the specialist. Nothing further has been done in the way of medical service for Murphy despite the specialist's recommendation.

This week the doctor, who first evaluated his X-rays, was ordered by the clinical director to put Murphy back to work. Murphy's symptoms have got progressively worst. Yesterday he was complaining of numbness down his arms and in both hands. He has refused to work.

This morning, as I wrote the first page of these notes about 7:10, Murphy stopped at the patio to talk with me. I got a little information from him. He said he hadn't slept all night. As we were speaking, he was called to the Camp 1 office. There he was handcuffed and, when I saw him, he said they were taking him to the hill. A few minutes before he was called we had seen the acting camp administrator enter Camp 1. I told Bill I was praying for him.

Today I will write to the editor of *The Tucson Citizen* about Murphy and the wider criminal neglect of inmates' health here.

This situation took a lot of my attention yesterday. I did write some letters. Got a book of Howard Thurman writings from Sue. I started reading *Biko* by Donald Woods I borrowed from Rich.

The scorpions and black widow spiders are multiplying. There are brown recluse spiders here too. A few men have got bit. Then there are those big fuzzy tarantulas.

August 27

It's 5:40. I'm ready for breakfast, but have 20 minutes, so I'll journal some. Light is barely appearing at the ridge line of the eastern mountains.

The mail officer had taken all the stuff, including copies of the letters to the editor, out of the envelope Mary Ellen mailed to me and put them in another envelope. Obviously he had gone through everything. I don't know exactly when she sent them but I received them August 26 at a late mail call. Since they moved the mail operation up the hill the delivery of our mail is almost always in the evening rather than the afternoon.

I held up on the *Citizen* letter regarding Bill since they obviously are watching my mail, but I will send it.

Marjorie of Seattle wrote back that she is getting me *God and Caesar at the Rio Grande* and will be sending it. I shamelessly ask her for it when she previously asked if there was a book she could send me. This is the one that Barbara in New England says mentions me in relationship to the sanctuary movement in southern Arizona. I haven't seen a copy.

I just got off the phone with Mary Ellen. The Tucson folks are meeting next week to plan for Randy's and my homecoming. There will be some media work and community celebrating.

August 28

Murphy returned to FPC from two days in solitary confinement. The rumor was going around that he was taken to the hospital. That never happened. Murphy did pass out again as they were taking him in handcuffs to the FCI. He said they have given him four disciplinary "shots," including one from the clinical director for passing out while handcuffed. The good doctor called it malingering.

They are still making it difficult for Murphy's new attorney to get in to see him. One delaying tactic after another using their abundant bureaucratic red tape.

Bill is almost beside himself. An officer caused his injury, they will not treat it, the pain and numbness is increasing, the demands of the BOP administration are increasing, and they will not allow his attorney to see him. He's trapped and feeling it.

Angela Herrman of *The Disciple* magazine called and left word with my counselor for me to call her in Indianapolis. He gave me the number so I could call collect. Mary Ellen had told me to expect her call. I phoned and talked with Angela this morning. She had talked with Mary Ellen for a long time yesterday. Among other things she asked if, after I get out, I would be interested in writing an article for *The Disciple.* I said yes, of course.

Well three weeks from today at this time I will be walking free. I wonder if these weeks will go slower than the rest of the time. I hope not.

August 30

Nick and Louise were my first visitors yesterday and then Amy and Marianna arrived about 9:15. They stayed until closing and will be back this morning for part of the day before returning to Tucson.

It sounds like oodles of Tucsonans are going to the November event at Fort Benning this year. We will have to count them up today as well as we can, or they can send me a total known before my release, so I will have a ballpark figure for the press on September 18. We had seven participate last fall. We know of two to three times that number already. El Paso/Las Cruces is getting up a group, too. It sounds to me like we are going to overwhelm Columbus in numbers this year. And if things go as expected we will have won our first vote in Congress, eliminating about 25% of the SOA operating budget for the year beginning October 1.

I will need to think through what it is that I want to say to the press and how to say it prior to my release so my agenda is set in my mind no matter what the media's agenda. I will need sound bite quotables on both the SOA and my prison experience.

CHAPTER 7

September: Not Enough Time

September 1

I had slowed down on writing letters last week but I've got to pick up again now.

Keith sent an article by Howard Thurman on a distinction between liberty and freedom. Thurman wrote it in 70's and it was reprinted in *The Christian Century* last month. I find it a meaningful distinction that gives me some ideas about how to speak of my experience when I get out. The article is entitled, "A Sense of Option." Thurman's basic thought is that while our liberty can be taken away from us, we are always free to act to influence and change the future.

I got a chuckle out of the title of a recently published article by Richard Boren about Randy and me printed in *The Tucson Weekly:* "After-School Detention." I haven't seen a copy yet.

They put Jim Bob in food service helping me wipe tables starting this morning. He's been working in the library. It is a demotion for him to remind him, once again, of his place. The BOP learned that Jim Bob's son, who has the business in El Paso that was previously his, was hiring men leaving La Tuna for a halfway house there. They said Jim Bob is running a business from prison which is against policy. Well he says he is not. It's likely he may have served as a reference for these men who his son's company hired. Is this "running a business?" This information must have come to the ears of the BOP by way of a snitch.

The other end of this story is that while the BOP insists that men who go to halfway houses find work, or face being returned to prison, they ordered the five or six men who were working at his son's business to quit. Why?

Our population is down to 144. One more man is leaving today for a halfway house. He's serving a year and a day. He just told me that he has been in here on a political charge.

Murphy is "cooling it." So I'm not sending a letter to *The Citizen* after all. They have really raked him over the coals and it doesn't stop. But he doesn't want to stir things up any further at this point, he says, and I certainly understand why. He has been treated with callous cruelty.

Because of the low population I suppose I will continue to be alone in my cell. It's okay by me. This way I can use the cell's table, without having to share, any time I want and turn off the light and go to bed at my own pace.

I'm reading some books on writing and finding my mind turning more and more to my new calling these days. As I read I relate the points to my novel. It's a way to start doing something that will give me a head start when I'm out.

It has been glorious to receive Van Gogh postcards from Marvin throughout my incarceration. They are in my photo album and I get them out to view them as a source of beauty and spirituality from time to time.

My mail is picking up again after the shredding summer lull. Also the time relating to my fellow prisoners has picked up as we have got acquainted and trust has built over the months.

I had asked Marvin to send me the lectionary readings for my first Sunday back at Arizona City. I was staggered by their obvious appropriateness. Especially Psalm 137 and Luke 17:5-10. The Gospel reading seems meant especially for me:

> "Do you thank the slave for doing what was commanded? So you also, when you have done all that you were ordered

> to do, say, 'We are worthless slaves; we have done what we ought to have done!'" (vv. 9-10)[20]

I have no idea yet what I'll say to the congregation, but these verses have already said a lot to me. I have only done what I ought to have done.

September 2

It's 4 a.m. and I've been awake since three. I'm writing by the floodlight that shines through the window into my cell. I've been thinking about how I might be of help to Murphy. While his neck and head pain is a reality, his psychic pain is making his life even more unbearable. He's in a panic. He's convinced that he must get out of here and appears ready to do almost anything to accomplish an exit, even to absolve the BOP of its responsibility for his injury in exchange for an early release. They continue to deny him any care for it. They are all over the landscape with what they are telling him. In addition to the injury itself the prison administration is jerking him around. This is all on top of the difficult task of simply dealing with one's loss of liberty and this barbaric system on a daily basis. His anger because of how he is being treated is eating him up. I haven't seen a more ruthless example of this inhumane system at La Tuna.

I spent last night writing out my editorial notes on Marvin's manuscript to send to him. I plan to spend the day reviewing and re-reading his manuscript so I can complete these comments. I have many letters to write but those must wait until I complete this review that I've put off several weeks now.

The light is so dim here in my cell right now it's hard to keep my writing on the line and I can't turn on the light because of the lights-out policy at this time of day.

September 3

I spent the entire day working on editorial notes for Marvin. I am surprised at the time it's taking, but then I'm doing a thorough job with the piddling stuff like punctuation. And I'm having to do it in long-hand without the aid of a computer or even a typewriter. I am, once again, spiritually stirred by his work.

I am enjoying this process as well as really getting into Marvin's book in some depth. I laugh out loud at his right-on ironic observations. I celebrate his very faithful and bold proclamation of The Gospel of Mark for twenty-first century ears. I will continue this process on this day off. Although I'm feeling a little antsy about putting off letter writing it's a priority for me to complete this work for Marvin.

September 4

Up early again this morning. Awoke before four. Rose about 4:45 for the day. I've spent two days editing Marvin's manuscript and I'm becoming imbued with the good news of Mark. His is a remarkable new benchmark. Unfortunately I go back to work for the BOP this morning.

It's obvious that my last two weeks of incarceration will be busy ones. I got three more new books which I probably won't read before release. The mail is picking up in number and I have not spent much time this week in writing replies. And now Joan writes to see if I will write a new op-ed and a shorter piece that can be used in several newsletters of various groups and communities.

As of this morning I'm 13 days and a wake-up away from release. The guys are aware my time is short and many have mentioned it on occasion this last week. To see others leaving is always a sign of hope. So many still face years to go. Kevin left yesterday for his halfway house after serving 49 months in prison. God bless him and all the other men and women here and elsewhere daily serving time and fielding indignities and inhumanity all in the name of justice.

Mary Ellen and others will be here this Labor Day weekend and that will be a pleasure.

September 8

I have been so busy with tasks to which I have committed myself that I have failed to keep up my journal writing.

Mary Ellen was here to visit all three days of Labor Day weekend. It was great. I told her that the next time she comes she will have to take me home whether she likes it or not. She says Paul plans to come to Arizona in early October to take part in a family reunion just before I return to work in Arizona City. Paul told me in a letter about getting better acquainted with a new employee at work. In sharing about their families he told her his father was in a federal prison. He reported, "It was a real icebreaker."

I wrote to "The Saints in Arizona City" regarding my first Sunday back. I told them I would be getting a copy of the worship bulletin to them when I got out. I think we will have that guitarist-singer friend there to participate. My biggest problem is to narrow down what to include in my first sermon out. Of course, preachers always have this problem, but it's compounded given my experience over these six months. I suggested we might follow the service with a potluck so as to give an opportunity for informal conversation about my experience. I do expect some visitors that morning.

I have been approached by two of my neighbors who asked if I would, upon release, help them and others get legal representation to pursue their grievances against the BOP regarding their medical care and mail destruction issues, either individually or in a class action suit. I told them that I would on one condition. I would have to have a list of the men, their names and numbers, who are willing to take the heat that would surely come if any actions where initiated. Because we know the possibilities of retaliation all men would have to give their permission freely. They think that such a list is possible. They will work on it and get back to me.

September 9

I have completed my review and editing notes on Marvin's manuscript and sent them to him in yesterday's outgoing mail. My review was not only a joy, and several days of work, but a deeply touching spiritual meditation of a sacred story passionately told. It has recovered its power. It reveals the Jesus I know.

Then I started to catch up on my replies to mail. I'm about 60 or 70 pieces behind. I started with family and some other letters that need earlier replies. Two evenings ago Harris said to me: "The Apostle Paul is a piker. He wrote only five letters from prison. When the church reads your letters I can just see the minister saying, 'Now let us turn to Epistle Four Hundred Thirty-eight.'"

I have joked about not having enough time to complete what needs to be done in the time I have left. Hopefully I can get through my mail for the most part. Today I need to figure how many more stamps I'll need to complete the job here inside since my last commissary opportunity is tonight.

An inmate received a letter from Adam Finley's girlfriend in yesterday's mail. It tells a fantastic story about his treatment since he left here. It's hard to believe. He was put on diesel therapy August 3 for a Tucson court appearance on August 14 which was postponed to October 23. He has not been returned to La Tuna.

The phrase "diesel therapy" describes what occurs during the transporting of federal prisoners from place to place. It's a process that usually takes days, weeks, and even months between two points during which the prisoner is held incommunicado and housed temporarily at a variety of jails before arriving at his destination.

Reportedly Adam had an angioplasty during all this back and forth, and is presently incarcerated at Florence, AZ, awaiting his October hearing. We still don't know if this is all true but, as I reminded this fellow inmate, we know of some pretty unbelievable things have been done to men by this rotten system.

September 10

As of last night I have a new cellie. His name is Leo Blanco. He was transferred from one of those corporate prisons in New Mexico.

I wrote 24 or 25 letters yesterday. I received another half dozen or so. I've been using a lot of cards trying to use those up as well. Hallmark has been a blessing.

I talked with Mary Ellen yesterday morning early. She is anxious about the possibility of a change in my release and wants me to call again later this week.

Marvin wrote about his trip and camping in the redwoods with Lee. I must admit I am envious. But he didn't give me any word about the results of a CT scan regarding his cancer. I tried to call Labor Day weekend but missed him. I'm still awaiting word.

I very much like the piece of a poem that was sent to me by a supporter who lives in the Northeast:

> . . . sometimes when our fights begin,
> I think I'll let the dragon win.
> And then I think perhaps I won't,
> Because they're dragons, and I don't.[21]

September 12

What a remarkable day. Five days and a wake-up until release.

Nick visited and outlined local plans.

I found that my new cellie Leo can wear my old shoes. He, too, is having a problem getting a pair that fit him. It is appropriate that these old prison shoes continue their journey with yet another inmate as beat up as they are. As he tried them on I recited aloud the poem I wrote about them.

I have learned for certain Leo is not "the son of Jesus Cruz." He had a conversation in our cell, to which I was privy, with three other men who have been at La Tuna since before I arrived. They chatted with him about their common acquaintances who are at the CCA prison from which he transferred.

Leo has shared with me the story of a former DEA agent who was called to be an expert witness in his case who may, because of his experience, have information regarding SOA and its graduates in Latin America.

Then this evening I had two very different significant conversations. One about issues involving the BOP and inmates that I have written about before and the other an entirely separate personal matter with Harris.

Dorothy Day: Selected Writings has proved to be a life-changing reading for Harris. First he told me he was not interested in reading it so I put it in the camp library. Later he found it on the shelf and got interested in reading it. He is awed by the oneness of Dorothy Day's life beliefs and actions. Her influence, all these years after her death, has been raised in a powerful personal challenge for Harris.

September 13

Today was a very touching emotional day. Surprisingly so. No visitors, which was okay by me. I went to three services. I was invited by Jose to the first so I went. I also went to the weekly Protestant service although I was late due to my work responsibilities. The Catholic Mass was the moving one. It has been my spiritual home here. Again we sang a hymn from the Prophet Isaiah text that is always joyously stirring. The refrain is:

Though the mountains may fall and the hills turn to dust,
yet the love of the LORD will stand
as a shelter for all who will call on his name.
Sing the praise and the glory of God.[22]

I was asked to read the second lesson. I have been reading one of the lessons for many Sundays now. At the end of the Mass the priest had me come forward and blessed me. And the men sang a blessing as they do for all men leaving La Tuna. This occasion really got to me. I had tears in my eyes and a lump in my throat. It brought into focus this entire six-month experience and the reality that all those who blessed me this morning must stay in prison. Even the chaplain.

After this there is no way I'll ever be the same.

September 14

Today it's letter writing. I did four letters yesterday, but spent my time beyond the worship services reading, watching some pro football on TV and going to my last La Tuna League slow pitch softball game at the field.

Prison life is in many respects a living death where men can, and often do, lose everything—property, families, mates, self-respect, and the support of their community. I have thought of writing a poem, "A Living Death," to try to express this reality.

I happened to notice, through the window in his office door, a chalked message in large block letters on the unit manager's blackboard yesterday. It reads: "GOD IS COMING AGAIN! LOOK BUSY!" Har-de-har-har. They don't get it. I much prefer the version that was on my teenage son's irreverent T-shirt years ago. He enjoyed wearing it to church. It read: "Jesus is coming again and is he pissed!"

September 15

I got a good idea for the brief newsletter article I've been asked to write. It came from a letter from a dear friend who has a chronic heart problem. I'll write it later today.

This is my last day at work. The boss said, "We will miss your good humor and wisdom," then promptly gave me extra work to do. I stood for too long feeding bread in and out of the commercial toaster. My legs are still numbly speaking to me.

I have tried to get Mary Ellen twice this morning to no avail. She wrote that she wants me to call.

I have an appointment to get my hair cut this afternoon. Still no callout nor processing that I can see from R&D (Receiving and Departure).

I counted up my stamp purchase from commissary receipts—1,035. It looks like I will have to use almost all, or indeed all of them, before I leave. Despite the efforts of the mail officer some postage stamps slipped through undetected and I used them in addition to those purchased. I counted my mail list and it shows I have heard from about 500 different people over the six months.

Today is Julie's 37th birthday. What a joy she is.

September 16

I did get hold of Mary Ellen later yesterday. I was able to answer her questions. I learned of the latest community plans in Tucson for my homecoming. Despite the fact that Randy will be held until September 22, they are going ahead with a potluck gathering on Sunday evening and a press conference on Monday morning.

The news this morning is that all Camp 2 inmates are moving to Camp 1. Camp 2 will be renovated. This is probably the reason for letting the population drop. The move started after lunch. I moved to B11 with three new cellies. One moved to an upper bunk so I could have the lower. My first night with two on a bunk bed. It wasn't as bad as I thought it might be, at least not for me. No more wake ups than usual. I was tired after all the extra activity and slept soundly.

I teased about how I must be responsible for this move. The BOP decided I didn't have enough experience of chaos while I've been here and were making up for it. Half as many toilets, half as many showers, half as many telephones, and half the space for the entire inmate population. There was the to-be-expected whining. A so-called counselor put it well I thought: "What do you think this is? Holiday Inn?" Hell no. This is a sardine can.

My last day of work, beyond the extra duty, was routine and uneventful. I threw my paper food service cap, a symbol of my status here, in the trash can outside the dining room door as I left.

One inmate said they were going to miss having "the Wal-Mart Greeter" in the dining hall. Meaning me. I have come to assume the unassigned role of kibitzing greeter at the beginning of the food line at the meals I've worked in the last several months.

Mail was very late in its distribution last night. I got yet another a half dozen pieces, including a note from El Paso regarding the final plans for my first day out. Enclosed was a flyer the committee distributed.

I got a third idea regarding an article after release, "Stepping Beyond Fear," but I didn't have time to develop any of these ideas because of the chaos of the move. I will work on a couple of them, that I need on release, later today.

The mattress in B11 is better than the one I had at Camp 2 so I didn't have to lug a mattress during the move. This mattress has only one place where the springs are broken and poking through the ticking to get me. Some towels strategically placed do the trick of body protection.

I've become expert at such improvisations. For example, using the grooves in a small metal screw I found as a screwdriver to tighten the tiny screw that kept coming loose on my eyeglass frame throughout my sentence.

I'm doing my laundry for the last time in prison this morning before breakfast. It's a very cool morning with a strong breeze. I'm wearing my long-sleeved brown shirt. Actually it's the only one I have clean until my laundry is finished.

I received quite a letter from Marvin. I read it twice. A lot in it about his present and past inner journey. It makes me want to see him more urgently at an earlier date, but I guess telephone conversations will have to do because I don't see how I can get there earlier than November as planned.

There is a strong rumor in camp among the inmates that one reason for the Camp 2 renovation is the presence of asbestos in the ceiling, on pipes, and in the floor tile. So, the inmate orderlies have been buffing the asbestos five days a week? How ducky. One inmate, who is assigned to camp maintenance, told me he had personally seen asbestos in the ceiling during maintenance jobs he had to perform over a period of months. Perhaps it's just a rumor.

September 17

My last full day at La Tuna. Only a "wake-up" tomorrow remains. This is also a day off and I'll do my "merry-go-round" this morning. A prison "merry-go-round" is the process of going from office to office to get officers to sign-off on a form in preparation for your departure. I assume that I'll get to pick out my departure clothing at R&D sometime today. I'm a little surprised that they haven't called me in long before now.

Yesterday was about the longest day ever it seemed. Today probably will be no different. I did get caught up on my mail. I got only one piece last night. Maybe some mail today. I'm expecting a book that hasn't arrived yet.

Yesterday at lunch time I was recalled to the dining hall to sign a form allowing for a telephone interview with a reporter from *The El Paso Times.* The acting camp administrator had been by my room earlier to mention this to me.

In the midst of a chance conversation with my case manager I discovered she was expecting me to go out of here by bus. I reminded her that at my last team meeting in July I had waived my right to such transportation and that my wife would be picking me up.

"You haven't signed a waiver form," she said.

"You haven't given me an opportunity to do so," I replied.

So I went to her office about an hour later and executed the form and they will cancel my bus reservation. The case manager said to have Mary Ellen appear at the lobby of the FCI La Tuna, up the hill, with her ID and tell them she's there to pick me up at 7:30 a.m. on Friday. Later in the day I was able to get through to Mary Ellen to give her the latest news. She has had a Channel 9 reporter trying to get hold of her about my release. I still have to write a one-page statement for the Tucson news conference. I have some ideas.

I did a draft of a newsletter article for the Border folks—"America's Heart Problems." I'll let it perk and will finish it up before the day is out.

I also organized my locker contents into things that stay here and things that are going with me. Just a couple articles of clothing (sweats) purchased here, papers, and books are leaving with me. I've been giving all other stuff away to men who can use it. I have a little more of that to do. I have also been giving my address and phone number out to a few men.

There was an excellent and perfectly timed letter to the editor published in *The Times* yesterday morning regarding the SOA and my release by Guillermo Medina of El Paso. I don't know him.

[Later] Here it is already about 7:45 p.m. I'm packed and ready to go. I've come back to the Camp 2 patio. It has been my favorite writing place here in prison. And I hope I don't get chased in by the mosquitoes. Now it's less than eleven hours until I appear with my stuff at R&D tomorrow morning for processing out.

I received a final six letters and cards in tonight's mail.

I was able to complete a short op-ed piece. I changed the title to, "Let Your Hearts Be Troubled." I will hand it to Jean Miller tomorrow. It turned out pretty well. It is as follows:

Let Your Hearts Be Troubled

Rape, torture, assassination, disappearance, massacre in the Americas by the authorities is an ongoing occurrence.

It has become increasingly apparent that the worst

human rights abusers in the Americas have one thing in common. They are graduates of the U.S. Army School of the Americas (SOA) at Fort Benning, Georgia.

In country after country, year after year, their cruel crimes continue.

This is not just *any* military school. It teaches the doctrine and tactics of counterinsurgency to keep people "in line." There is absolutely nothing democratic about it.

Taught mostly by Latin American officers, it is a political school for Latin American military elites. In the twenty-four neighboring nations SOA graduates today "protect" the status quo for powerfully entrenched economic forces.

I write as a prisoner of conscience about to be released after six months in a U.S. federal prison. Twenty-five citizens received this outrageous sentence for an entirely peaceful protest of the atrocious acts committed over the last fifty years and continuing today. This mayhem is all solely funded by our government using our tax dollars.

During my imprisonment I have written more than a thousand letters of reply. Correspondence has been received from almost every one of the United States and several other nations.

Two letters I received stand out in my memory just now.

One was a humbling message of thanks from Guatemalan victims of SOA graduates. Among other cruelties they experienced disappearance, torture, and death of loved ones. Our national policy keeps this human misery machine in place despite its dark history and present maniacal manifestations.

Through previous personal experience I am aware of the magnitude of Guatemalan suffering and losses. And the victims thanked me?

A second letter, recently received, is from an old friend.

He has a history of heart problems and entered the hospital for yet another surgical procedure in mid-September.

His wife wrote that they are still hoping his physical condition will improve so they both can participate in the SOA Watch action at Fort Benning in November. My friend wants to be one of the more than one thousand peacemakers who "cross the line" in non-violent protest, "even if he has to do it in a wheelchair."

> God comes, and his ways are near to us.
> God saves in history.
> Each person's life, each one's history,
> is the meeting place God comes to.
> How satisfying to know one need not go to the desert
> to meet him,
> need not go to some particular spot
> in the world.
> God is in your own heart.
>
> —Archbishop Oscar Romero
> [December 10, 1978][23]

Today was taken up with the "merry-go-round." It ended at R&D where the officer outfitted me with jeans (right size waist, but the legs are 5 inches too long), a yukky green pullover knit shirt, a belt that's barely long enough, and dark blue canvas shoes made in China. What a wardrobe. Now all I need is a straw hat and a hayseed to put in my teeth to complete this sporty ensemble. Usually men are allowed to have clothes sent in. I had decided I wanted to be turned out in all the BOP's best. And since they forgot to even mention this option to me—I learned about it from other inmates—I guess it is a good thing I felt this way because I had no option.

My telephone interview with a reporter of *The El Paso Times* was at nine. The acting camp administrator had me do it in his office as he sat across the desk. I told the reporter up front that the conversation was being monitored. He took the cue and didn't ask any BOP questions. I think it went very well. At least I felt good about my responses. The reporter ended by going over the Friday schedule of events and told me he would be seeing me during the day.

The acting camp administrator is the man who was the unit manager when I entered La Tuna. He's the one who tries to intimidate every new inmate who enters here. He was very interested in my telephone conversation. After I hung up he asked me some questions. I was still on my guard.

One of my food service bosses told me he had read the letter to the editor in the morning paper yesterday. He had told his boss about it. That's this man. I was evasive about some of the administrator's questions. But I quickly learned that all I had to do was pause and he would start giving his own opinion rather than waiting to hear mine. He can't stand silence and quickly filled in all the voids with various BOP myths.

He said something to the effect that despite the system's best efforts most all the men would return to prison. Then he asked about what I think of the BOP.

"It doesn't surprise me that so many men return," I said. "This place isn't at all about rehabilitation. It's only about punishment."

"You're right," the administrator tersely confirmed. Then he counseled me to keep my nose clean.

"I don't want to see you back in here," he said. "Find some other way to make your point."

Over the past six months I've learned some things first-hand about our federal prison system. There are some good people in prison. The system is not interested in better people leaving prison. They'd rather have them back. Prisons are big business. The system is cruel as usual. It is run by crazy makers interested in their own careers. In many cases the criminals are the ones with the badges.

I may have some time to journal in the morning prior to breakfast inasmuch as I'm packed and ready.

September 18

Today is independence day. Let the fireworks commence. I awoke at four. That's pretty usual. There was no problem sleeping last night. I did go to bed a little late by the measure of my six-month routine. About 10 p.m.

Many men made a point of saying goodbye to me last night and to encourage me in our struggle to change government policy. Some others on the patio of Camp 1 late in the evening recalled Will Prior's stay here two years ago as one of the SOA 13. Several men are still here who had known him during his imprisonment. It was the prison sentences of the SOA 13 that spurred me to go to Fort Benning in the first place. Will and I shared in the SOA Watch 40-day fast on the U.S. Capitol steps in 1994. Yesterday afternoon I talked quite a while with a man who knew Will well.

I have only a little bedding to distribute. I gave everything else to the guys. I was surprised at the number of books and the tall stack of paper I'm taking out. Together it weighs quite a bit. There's very little else.

Many of the men had read the Medina letter to the editor of two days ago in *The El Paso Times* from the library copy. They know there will be a demonstration at the La Tuna gate at 8 a.m.

I'm on the south porch of Camp 2 now for the last time. It's not just a little ironic that I am greeted this very early morning by a sliver of moon rising late over the Franklin Mountains. It was a sliver of moon that greeted me to La Tuna my first night here as I remember. It was the inspiration for my first prison poem. Orion is overhead to the south. For some reason the objects in the sky seem clearer this morning. Perhaps it's only because some high magnitudes are visible from this location at this time just before dawn. There is the barest hint of light behind the mountains in the east.

Breakfast is at six and then I report to R&D at 6:45. with my stuff.

September 20

On September 18, after journaling, I went to the dining hall for a breakfast of raisin bran, banana, and coffee. At about 6:30. I returned to my cell, picked up my bag of personal items and went to R&D. The bedspreads had already been picked up off my bunk bed. I had promised them to a particular inmate. I went to make sure he got them. Some items, like these spreads, are items for an inmate's "last will and testament." That is to say one bequests to other inmates such items as are in his control. This practice is honored by the inmates and, generally speaking, not interfered with by the officers. I even gave a partial tube of toothpaste to one of the men after I brushed my teeth. A partial tube of non-generic toothpaste is no small thing on the inside.

The R&D officer was already in his office when I got there. He immediately took me in so I could change into my street clothes—the jeans, pullover shirt and canvas shoes—while he inventoried my personal items. The personal items were placed in a box and taped shut and I took the box with me out to the waiting area.

The men had presented me with a list of those who want to seek legal representation on their grievances against the BOP and who are willing to take the heat. I buried it within the stack of paper I was taking out. Just in case the R&D officer found it as he inventoried and boxed my things, we had arranged for one of the inmates to come by the bench outside the office and surreptitiously hand me a copy to put in my pocket. The grievance list includes ten men who want representation regarding medical issues and eleven men who want the BOP to be held accountable for their practice of shredding their personal and legal mail, certified checks, and money orders.

It wasn't long before the acting camp administrator himself showed up and said he was going to see to it I got processed immediately. The R&D officer took me in an office to thumb print me on four copies of a form. I signed a certain form.

The administrator himself then escorted me to his vehicle and took me to the hill. He lectured me about staying out of prison and personally processed me at the hill including giving me the $86.14 that remained in my commissary account in cash. Then he cut me loose.

It was only 7:15. I took my box of personal belongings and went out on the porch to wait for Mary Ellen, John and Jeannie. As I was waiting an inmate from the camp I know well arrived on the hill to go to work. I told him about my personal processing by the administrator and told him to share that word with others. It seemed clear that the administration wanted me out of there before television crews arrived for the prayer vigil at the main road entrance just off La Tuna property. I can't think of any other reason for this early release. The vigil had been announced in *The El Paso Times,* so both the BOP and the inmates knew about it.

Mary Ellen, John and Jeannie parked in the lower lot and walked up the stairs, across the parking area just in front of the La Tuna FCI main building as I playfully hid behind a pillar waiting until they appeared on the porch. I stepped out from my hiding place and said, "Boo!" We had a simple but joyous reunion.

John went down and brought the car up and we got in and left. We had some time to waste before people gathered at the gate so we drove about a quarter of a mile or so toward Anthony, parked, and I got some items out of my box. The article I had written the day before, "Let Your Hearts Be Troubled," a blessing prayer sent to me earlier in the week by a supporter who lives in Grand Rapids, Michigan, and some other items.

The blessing is simply entitled "A Prayer." It was distributed by the Interfaith Council for Peace and Justice, Ann Arbor, Michigan, but the source is unknown to me. I shared this prayer at the La Tuna vigil and again in El Paso.

> May God bless you with discomfort at easy answers, half-truths, and superficial relationships, so that you will live deep in your heart.

> May God bless you with anger at injustice, oppression, and exploitation of people and the earth so that you will work for justice, equity and peace.
>
> May God bless you with tears to shed for those who suffer so you will reach out your hand to comfort them and change their pain into joy.
>
> And may God bless you with the foolishness to think that you can make a difference in the world, so you will do the things which others say cannot be done.[24]

There were about fifty at the La Tuna vigil. They had bought coffins to the site to remind us of the SOA victims. There were signs. It was wonderful to see old friends and meet new ones. The first one I met was the author of the letter that was published two days before in *The Times*. The *Times* reporter was present. News crews from two television channels were there. Before the vigil started I had on-camera interviews with both, a few words with the newspaper reporter to set up an interview at the International Women's Center in Anthony later, and then the prayer service began, lead by Ruben Garcia. There was a guitarist and singing, prayer, I spoke briefly, recited my poem "Used," thanked everyone, and read the blessing. My friend Bob Allen shared a brief homily. The people were invited to the Center for informal talk, my further remarks, and the showing of the SOA Watch video, *An Insider Speaks Out.*

Soon after arriving at the Center I got with the newspaper reporter for an interview and he stayed for my remarks that were translated for the Spanish-speakers present. I explained what the SOA is because I was advised that many of the Spanish speaking folks there did not know the story. I emphasized SOA involvement today in Southern Mexico. And I spoke of the the daily problems federal inmates face at La Tuna focusing on the mail shredding and criminal neglect of their medical needs.

I was able to informally converse with several people at the Center before and after my presentation. Old Sanctuary Movement buddies Cliff and Dorothy traveled all the way from Silver City in order to be there. Their presence was very special to me. I gave Jean the article I had promised. I also used the outline of this piece as a guide for my remarks at the Center.

From the Center eight of us went together to a restaurant of my choice so I could enjoy an oriental chicken salad my first meal out. There was wonderful conversation around the table and the food was by far the best I'd had in six months. After lunch John and Jeannie headed back to Tucson.

We went to a classroom at UTEP to speak to a small group. I particularly enjoyed an informal conversation I had with two students, one from DePaul University and the other from Earlham College, who are at UTEP for a semester studies related to the border. One wrote out a copy of the blessing which I ended with there too.

Following the UTEP session Mary Ellen and I took off on our own to find a motel for the night and relax for a little while. Then we went to First Christian Church for an evening community potluck supper and program.

I learned at this gathering that earlier that very day the amendment to deny funds to the SOA had failed 201 to 212 in the U. S. House of Representatives. This is a disappointment and is a reminder of what we are up against. There will no doubt be a calling to account of those members of Congress who, after pledging their votes to us, switched sides under the pressure of both the Administration and the Pentagon. No one said this was going to be easy. Persist!

Our program was over before nine. We returned to our motel room after saying our goodbyes.

We arose yesterday "late." Took our time. Had breakfast close by. Starting back to Tucson about ten, stopping in Lordsburg for lunch, we arrived home a little after four.

Welcome banners hung on the carport. Balloons were on the door and a message strung across our living room wall reads, "We Survived the SOA."

I had some personal letters awaiting me, including one from

my friend from La Tuna, Dylan Roberts, now in a halfway house. He wrote me that he still plans to be at Arizona City for my first Sunday back. It got to me. I broke down and had a good cry. His letter brought home that there's a whole other group of sufferers in prison who are on my agenda now. I'm home and they remain in that very inhumane environment with its daily indignities and inaneness.

There were several messages on the answering machine from family, friends, and other prisoners of conscience. I made some calls.

It's true. Randy is not getting out until Tuesday. Nick and Dan (and maybe Bill) are not getting out until Monday. I shared the news of my release and SOA Watch actions in the area with Carol in the SOA Watch DC office. She said some gathering of the SOA 25 is planned just prior to the November action at Fort Benning.

We went out to the Maya Quetzal restaurant on 4th Avenue for dinner last night. There was a warm reunion with Sandra and Wendy. They would not let us pay for our dinner and also brought plantain to our table as a special dessert treat. We have known them ever since they arrived in Tucson during the early Sanctuary Movement days as refugees from Guatemala.

When we returned home there were even more messages.

I had a long phone conversation with Marvin. He said his lymphoma is not entirely gone though it may be only scar tissue from previous radiation treatments that they are seeing. It is very much better. The medicine is probably still working on the bad cells (if any) and he will have another CT scan in November that hopefully will be more definitive. He also invited me to preach at his churches on November 8 when Mary Ellen and I will be California. The gospel lectionary, he said, is Luke's Beatitudes (6:20-26); yet another ironic conjunction of my experience and the scriptural lectionary.

Mary Ellen and I are going to Southside Presbyterian for the 9 o'clock service and then on to Desert Dove Christian for their 10:30 service this morning.

We are going on with plans arranged for a celebration tonight at five at the Hallihans and a press conference at ten tomorrow at Southside Presbyterian. There will be another celebration for Randy on Friday.

I awoke at four, 5 a.m. La Tuna time, and got up to do this journaling before the experiences get too distant.

It's wonderful to be home with Mary Ellen, among my favorite things, free and enjoying the quiet and the old familiar sounds again. Free to tend my garden. Yet today has something of a surreal feel about it.

Looking at it again, I thought, I'll have to take that banner on our wall with me to Georgia in November to share with the other ex-cons: "We Survived the SOA!"

We still have work to do.

EPILOGUE

'Twixt Darkness and Light

A lot has happened since my imprisonment.

That first weekend we did participate in services with the Southside Presbyterian and Desert Dove Christian congregations. It was a most tender time of reentry. Without any input from me, both congregations sang the hymn "Here I Am, Lord." It was as moving an experience to me as it had been in the prison chapel on the second Sunday of my incarceration. I had been there and done that.

We did have a celebration of my liberty at Bill and Rosemary's house with many friends. It was a potluck and I was still savoring the taste of good food just like one does after a long fast. Not only that, food for the soul was in that company for the partaking. I helped myself to a double portion.

In the early morning two days later Mary Ellen and I were driving east on I-10 on our way to Safford Federal Correction Institution about 120 miles away. We were to meet Paula there to greet Randy when he was released. Yes, the BOP kept him four days longer than the rest of us.

It seemed strange sitting in a prison waiting room so soon after my own release. As I slyly eyed the officers, the silly question went through my mind: Do I looked like I belong inside?

Following a leisurely meal together in a Safford restaurant, Randy and Paula headed for a few days of R and R camping in the White Mountains. Mary Ellen and I drove on to Julie's Flagstaff retreat for some of the same tonic.

After several days, the children and grandchildren gathered

for a pleasant family reunion at a Casa Grande motel the day before I returned to my pastoral duties in Arizona City.

The family shared my first service back the next morning. I was pleased that Dylan Roberts, who wiped many a La Tuna table with me, did come with his wife from Phoenix. He played his guitar and sang John Lennon's *Imagine* with feeling. It was good to be back among these saints at Arizona City. I can never thank them enough.

My big sister, Lynn, died of her chronic illness at home less than a month after I was released. Although I never saw her again, I was grateful that I was free to go to her funeral. Marvin and I flew back to Maryland to be with her family and participate in her memorial service. His cancer was in remission. It was a bittersweet reunion with my beloved siblings.

In early November, Mary Ellen and I flew to California to participate in the 15th Anniversary Celebration of Witness for Peace. The SOA 25 had been invited to attend the event. It was so good to touch base with many of my colleagues in the struggle. There is nothing quite like six months in prison to weld folks together.

Now we all had an added concern heightened—U.S. federal prisons and prisoners. Many of us ex-cons have spent considerable energy on prison issues. We have attempted to follow through with concerns, growing out of our experience, only to be thwarted by a very buttoned-down system at every turn. Very few Americans are interested in prisoners. The majority have stereotypical views that support the government's short-sighted vindictive policies. As a result of this mind-set our communities have become even more dangerous while the prison industrial complex grows in power and wealth.

If you haven't already guessed, all ex-convicts must find a way to deal with the two-headed monster of post-prison depression and anger. People deal with this differently. But those who fail to deal constructively with this dragon will be done in themselves.

I did resign from the Arizona City church, effective December 31, and moved into retirement to start a new life that includes my writing interests. I've had a major project on the back burner for years.

Of course, I returned to Fort Benning for the annual SOA Watch vigil and action. I did not "cross the line" that year. Twenty-five hundred did, including our son Paul.

"You don't have to do this again, Dad," he told me, "because I'm crossing in your place."

Thousands were gathered at what is called "the south gate" to Fort Benning. It's the main gate. There's only a welcoming sign there. No gate, no fence, no wall, no guard house or sentries regularly posted. Just an open two lane road inbound, a broad grassy median, and two lanes coming out of this military post. A small white line painted across the asphalt lanes marks where Columbus ends and Fort Benning begins.

As in previous years, commemorating the anniversary of the murders of six Jesuit priests and two women at UCA, a funeral procession marched in silence. Those in the front carried coffins. They were followed by hundreds carrying little white crosses or stars of David bearing the names, countries, and ages of some SOA victims. There were people of every stripe imaginable, from every state of the Union, in this column. I especially recall the ones in wheelchairs. Parents with their small children. Punkers with their colorful hair walking side-by-side with nuns in their traditional habits. I saw one sightless man being escorted by a sighted friend and overheard his friend telling him, "Now, we are crossing the line."

As they crossed drums were banged slowly by native peoples, like the heartbeat of the Earth made audible. Names of victims of this school of assassins were sung over the loud speaker one at a time, from a list of tens of thousands, as a seemingly endless procession of peacemakers walked eight to ten abreast quietly winding their way on the road toward the SOA headquarters. After every name was announced the people who remained at the gate cried out, "Presente." The voice of the voiceless was heard again that day echoing among the tall Georgian pines on that military reservation.

My brother Marvin was there, too. With his cancer history he had promised his family he would avoid arrest. I saw him nearby as others crossed together line after line after line risking arrest and prison. Tears streamed down his face. He so wanted to join that solemn procession.

We have come within a handful of votes in the U.S. Congress of closing down this granddaddy of all international military schools. In 2000, as a result of increasing public pressure the Pentagon proposed a cosmetic bill to change its name. A bipartisan amendment to definitively close the SOA was defeated in the House by a vote of 204-214.

In January 2001, the SOA clone—the Western Hemisphere Institute for Security Cooperation (WHISC)—"opened" in the same place with the same mission. Congressman Joe Moakley of Massachusetts remarked that this cynical deception is "like pouring perfume on a toxic dump."

Nevertheless, each year more and more people of conscience cross that line marching peacefully toward the school of the assassins on Fort Benning. More and more work with their members of Congress to finally close it down. More and more are put on trial by a government unwilling to own up to the bloody results of its policy of providing military muscle to back corporate greed in the Americas.

The mission of this U.S. military school has caused, and continues to cause, great suffering throughout the Americas. So more and more citizens of conscience continue to protest and to be sent to prison in a struggle for our nation's soul.

In the decade of the 90's forty-eight women and men served a total of 30 years in U.S. prisons. Ten more served time in 2000. Twenty-six more in 2001. Prison time is used as a warning to all would-be peacemakers who might consider taking any direct non-violent action against government-sponsored atrocities. Nevertheless, we persist.

Updates on SOA Watch prisoners of conscience are available on-line at <www.soaw.org> and its links to other web sites.

ACKNOWLEDGMENTS

I wish to thank my life partner, Mary Ellen, and our children from my heart. They have always been supportive partners in the struggle for a more humane world and, for good and ill, recipients of life-shaping consequences that flow from my choices.

I am invigorated by all those women and men, past and present, who give more than lip service to conscience; who with their whole being say no to the powers of death and yes to the sources of life.

Also I lift up my thanks for the members of Community Christian Church of Arizona City who proved faithful under fire, and for all peacemakers in every place, whose witness is my inspiration and the hope of the world. My mentors have been many.

My dear brother, Marvin, is a constant source of strength and my good friend. His encouragement and commentary on drafts of this book, along with that of my friends Jerry Gill, Rachel Srubas, and William Walker, spurred me on. Thanks also go to Sterling Vinson, photographer, and Gene Flint, who helped me with computer graphics. In 1960 my father, Raymond K. Kennon, created the watercolor, "Silence," that graces the cover.

A debt of gratitude is owed to my editor, Florence Davis, who has generously shared the wealth of her knowledge and expertise with this neophyte.

NOTES

[1] Excerpt from *Here I Am, Lord*: © 1981 Daniel L. Schutte and New Dawn Music, 5536 NE Hassalo, Portland OR 97213. All rights reserved. Used with permission.

[2] This is a paraphrase of a passage long remembered from Albert Camus' *Resistance, Rebellion, and Death* that I read in the 1960's.

[3] Henri J. M. Nouwen, *The Road to Peace*, p. 94ff, © 1997 Orbis Press, Maryknoll NY. Used with permission.

[4] Carol Richardson, *The Search*, 1998. All rights reserved. Used with permission.

[5] Excerpt from *One Bread, One Body*: © 1978 John B. Foley, S.J. and New Dawn Music, 5536 NE Hassalo, Portland OR 97213. All rights reserved. Used with permission.

[6] Excerpt from *Peace Is Flowing Like a River*: Textual adaptation © 1975, 1979, NALR. Published by OCP Publications, 5536 NE Hassalo, Portland OR 97213. All rights reserved. Used with permission.

[7] Nelson Mandela, *The Long Walk to Freedom: The Autobiography of Nelson Mandela*, p. 122, © 1994 Nelson Mandela, Boston: Little, Brown and Co., Inc.

[8] Mandela, *op.cit.*, p. 624.

[9] Oscar Romero, *The Violence of Love*, p. 4. Compiled and translated by James R. Brockman, S.J., text copyright ©1988 by the Chicago Province of the Society of Jesus; edition published 1998 by The Plough Publishing House, Farmington PA, by arrangement with HarperCollins Publishers, Inc. Used with permission.

[10] Fred Kronen, M.D., *In Search of Peace: An American Doctor in Sandinista Nicaragua*, p. 139, © 1994 by Fred Kronen, M.D., printed by CRUSE Publications, San Jose CA. All rights reserved. Used with permission.

[11] Kronen, *op.cit.*, p. 147. Used with permission.

[12] Kronen, *op.cit.*, p. 203. Used with permission.

[13] A U.S. cargo plane on a *contra* resupply flight was shot down inside Nicaragua in 1986. American Eugene Hasenfus was captured and two other Americans were killed in the crash. The three were subsequently linked to the U.S. Central Intelligence Agency. The plane had been photographed earlier that year at Southern Air Transport in Florida, a company with long-standing ties to the CIA.

[14] Annie Dillard, *Pilgrim at Tinker Creek*, p. 268, © 1974 by Annie Dillard, published by Harper & Row Publishers, Inc., New York.

[15] Author unknown.

[16] *The Nightingale's Song*, ©1995 by Robert Timberg, New York: Simon & Schuster, p. 16. Used with permission. Timberg's note on p. 481 says Barbara Feldon told the tale of the nightingale on March 30, 1987, to a U.S. Labor Department conference on Work and Family.

[17] Brian Lamb, *Booknotes: America's Finest Authors on Reading, Writing, and the Power of Ideas*, p. 299, © 1997 by Brian Lamb, published by Times Books, New York.

[18] This famous quote, and its wording variations, is circa 1945. Pastor Niemöller used words to this effect following World War II during public speaking engagements in both Europe and the United States.

[19] Kathleen Norris, *The Cloister Walk*, p. 34, © 1996 by Kathleen Norris, published by Riverhead Books, The Berkley Publishing Group, Penguin Putnam, Inc., New York. All rights reserved. Used with permission.

[20] All scripture quotations are from the New Revised Standard Version Bible, copyright 1989, Division of Christian Education of the National Council of the Churches of Christ in the United States of America, and are used with permission.

[21] These are the last four lines of A. A. Milne's poem, "Knight-in-Armour," *Now We Are Six*, p. 53, © renewal 1955 by A. A. Milne, republished 1988 by E. P. Dutton, New York.

[22] Excerpt from *Though the Mountains May Fall*: © 1975 by Daniel L. Schutte and New Dawn Music, 5536 NE Hassalo, Portland OR 97213. All rights reserved. Used with permission.

[23] Romero, *op.cit.*, p. 105. Used with permission.

[24] Author unknown.